CHILTON BOOK COMPANY

REPAIR & TUNE-UP GUIDE

DATSUN/NISSAN 1200 · 210 SENTRA 1973-86

All U.S. and Canadian models of DATSUN 1200, 210 ·
NISSAN Sentra

President LAWRENCE A. FORNASIERI
Vice President and General Manager JOHN P. KUSHNERICK
Executive Editor KERRY A. FREEMAN, S.A.E.
Senior Editor RICHARD J. RIVELE, S.A.E.
Editor MARTIN J. GUNTHER

CHILTON BOOK COMPANY
Radnor, Pennsylvania
19089

SAFETY NOTICE

Proper service and repair procedures are vital to the safe, reliable operation of all motor vehicles, as well as the personal safety of those performing repairs. This book outlines procedures for servicing and repairing vehicles using safe, effective methods. The procedures contain many NOTES, CAUTIONS and WARNINGS which should be followed along with standard safety procedures to eliminate the possibility of personal injury or improper service which could damage the vehicle or compromise its safety.

It is important to note that repair procedures and techniques, tools and parts for servicing motor vehicles, as well as the skill and experience of the individual performing the work vary widely. It is not possible to anticipate all of the conceivable ways or conditions under which vehicles may be serviced, or to provide cautions as to all of the possible hazards that may result. Standard and accepted safety precautions and equipment should be used when handling toxic or flammable fluids, and safety goggles or other protection should be used during cutting, grinding, chiseling, prying, or any other process that can cause material removal or projectiles.

Some procedures require the use of tools specially designed for a specific purpose. Before substituting another tool or procedure, you must be completely satisfied that neither your personal safety, nor the performance of the vehicle will be endangered.

Although information in this guide is based on industry sources and is as complete as possible at the time of publication, the possibility exists that the manufacturer made later changes which could not be included here. While striving for total accuracy, Chilton Book Company cannot assume responsibility for any errors, changes, or omissions that may occur in the compilation of this data.

PART NUMBERS

Part numbers listed in this reference are not recommendations by Chilton for any product by brand name. They are references that can be used with interchange manuals and aftermarket supplier catalogs to locate each brand supplier's discrete part number.

SPECIAL TOOLS

Special tools are recommended by the vehicle manufacturer to perform their specific job. Use has been kept to a minimum, but where absolutely necessary, are they referred to in the text by the part number of the tool manufacturer. These tools can be purchased, under the appropriate part number, from Kent-Moore Corporation, 29784 Little Mack, Roseville, Michigan 48066. For Canada, contact Kent-Moore of Canada, Ltd., 2395 Cawthra Mississauga, Ontario, Canada L5A 3P2 or an equivalent tool can be purchased locally from a tool supplier or parts outlet. Before substituting any tool for the one recommended, read the SAFETY NOTICE at the top of this page.

ACKNOWLEDGMENTS

The Chilton Book Company thanks the Nissan Motor Corporation in U.S.A., Gardena, California 90247, and Devon Datsun, Devon, Pennsylvania, for their assistance in the preparation of this book.

Copyright © 1986 by Chilton Book Company
All Rights Reserved
Published in Radnor, Pennsylvania 19089 by Chilton Book Company

Manufactured in the United States of America
1234567890   5432109876

Chilton's Repair & Tune-Up Guide: Datsun/Nissan 1200, 210, Sentra 1973–86
ISBN 0-8019-7679-0 pbk.
Library of Congress Catalog Card No. 85-47969

CONTENTS

Quick Reference Specifications For Your Vehicle

Fill in this chart with the most commonly used specifications for your vehicle. Specifications can be found in Chapters 1 through 3 or on the tune-up decal under the hood of the vehicle.

Tune-Up

Firing Order_____

Spark Plugs:

    Type_____

    Gap (in.)_____

Torque (ft. lbs.)_____

Idle Speed (rpm)_____

Ignition Timing (°)_____

    Vacuum or Electronic Advance (Connected/Disconnected)_____

Valve Clearance (in.)

    Intake_____   Exhaust_____

Capacities

Engine Oil Type (API Rating)_____

    With Filter Change (qts)_____

    Without Filter Change (qts)_____

Cooling System (qts)_____

Manual Transmission (pts)_____

    Type_____

Automatic Transmission (pts)_____

    Type_____

Front Differential (pts)_____

    Type_____

Rear Differential (pts)_____

    Type_____

Transfer Case (pts)_____

    Type_____

FREQUENTLY REPLACED PARTS

Use these spaces to record the part numbers of frequently replaced parts.

PCV VALVE	OIL FILTER	AIR FILTER	FUEL FILTER
Type_____	Type_____	Type_____	Type_____
Part No._____	Part No._____	Part No._____	Part No._____

General Information and Maintenance

HOW TO USE THIS BOOK

This book is divided into ten easy to follow chapters, avoiding mechanic's jargon and highlighting important procedures with illustrations wherever possible. As time goes by, you'll probably find that some chapters such as Chapter 2 (Tune Up) naturally accumulate more dirty fingerprints than others, but everything from engine rebuilding to waxing the car is covered here. Of course, even professional mechanics won't attempt a repair without the proper tools and a thorough knowledge of the work required. This is why operations like rebuilding your transmission or rear axle assembly are not covered here -- they require a range of special tools which are too expensive, and a technical knowledge too extensive to be useful to you, the owner/mechanic.

Before loosening a single nut, read through the entire section you are dealing with and make sure you have the time, tools, and replacement parts necessary to do the job. This will save you much frustration, many hassles, and a walk to the bus stop Monday morning because you needed a part or were without a tool Saturday afternoon. Remember, too, that auto parts stores sometimes have to order certain parts, so it's wise to run through a procedure and make a couple phone calls to be sure a part will be available when you need it.

Each section begins with a brief description of the particular system and the basic theory behind it. When repairs involve a level of technical know-how beyond most owner/mechanics, we tell you how to remove the part and replace it with a new or rebuilt unit. This way you can at least save the cost of labor, and the percentage that is often placed on top of the retail cost of new parts.

There are a few basic mechanic's rules that should be followed:

1. Left side of the car means the driver's side; right side is the passenger's side.

2. Most screws, bolts and nuts are right handed -- they are tightened by turning them clockwise and removed by turning them counterclockwise.

3. Never crawl under a car supported only by a bumper jack -- jack the car up, then support it with jackstands.

4. Never smoke or position an exposed flame near the battery or any part of the fuel system.

5. USE COMMON SENSE DURING ALL OPERATIONS.

TOOLS AND EQUIPMENT

The following list contains the basic tools needed to perform most of the maintenance and repair procedures covered in this book. All nuts, bolts and thread sizes in your Datsun are metric — you'll need a set of metric wrenches and sockets to work on the car. SAE (U.S. size) wrenches will be either too loose or too tight and will ruin nuts and boltheads if used.

1. Metric sockets, including a $^{13}/_{16}$ in. spark plug socket. Various length socket drive extensions are also very useful. One break in this area, from a monetary standpoint, is that metric sockets available in this country will all fit standard U.S. (SAE) ratchet handles and extensions ($^{1}/_{4}$, $^{3}/_{8}$, and $^{1}/_{2}$ in. drive).

2. Set of metric 'combination' (one end open and one end box) wrenches.

3. Wire-type spark plug feeler gauge.

4. Blade-type feeler gauge for ignition and valve settings.

5. Slot and Phillips head screwdrivers in various sizes.

6. Oil filter strap wrench. Necessary for removing oil filters (never use, though, for installing the filters).

FROM TOP: BATTERY TERMINAL TOOL; FEELER GAUGES; OIL SPOUT; FILTER WRENCH

ALLEN WRENCHES

JACKSTAND

BEAM-TYPE TORQUE WRENCH

DWELL/TACHOMETER

VACUUM GAUGE

COMPRESSION GAUGE

TIMING LIGHT

You need only a basic assortment of hand tools and test instruments for most maintenance and repair jobs

Capacities

Year	Model	Engine Crankcase (qts)		Transmission (pts)			Drive Axle (pts)	Gas Tank (gals)	Cooling System (qts)
		With Filter	Without Filter	4-Spd	5-Spd	Automatic (total capacity)			
1973	1200	3.6	2.6	2.5	—	11.8	1.8	10/10.5 (sedan)	5.2
1974	B-210	3.45	—	2.5	—	11.8	1.8	11.5	5.5
1975	B-210	4.2	3.7	2.7	—	11.4	1.89	11.5	6.25 ①
1976–78	B-210	3.8	3.4	2.75	3.6	11.8	1.8	11.5	6.25 ①
1979–82	210	3.5	3.0	②	2.5	11.8	1.8	13.25	5.25
1982–86	Sentra	4.1	3.6	4.8	5.75	13.1	—	13.25	5.0 ③
1984–86	Sentra Diesel	4.4	3.75	4.8	5.75	12.75	—	13.25 ④	7.4

① Automatic transmission: 6 qts.
② A12A 2.5 pts.; A14, A15 2.75 pts.
③ Automatic transmission: 5.6 qts.
④ MPG Model: 10-⅝ gals.

7. Oil can filler spout, for pouring fresh oil from quart cans

8. Pair of slip-lock pliers.

9. Two (at least) sturdy jackstands for working underneath the car -- any other type of support (bricks, wood and especially cinderblocks) is just plain dangerous.

10. Pair of vise-type pliers.

11. Timing light, preferably a DC battery hook up type, and preferably an inductive type for use on cars with electronic ignition.

This is an adequate set of tools, and the more work you do yourself on your car the larger you'll find the set growing — a pair of pliers here, a wrench or two there. It makes more sense to have a comprehensive set of basic tools as listed above, an̶d̶ ̶t̶h̶e̶n̶ to acquire more along the lines as you need them, than to go out and plunk down big money for a professional size set you may never use. In addition to these basic tools, there are several other tolls and gauges you may find useful. These include:

1. A hydraulic floor jack (1 ½ ton is fine for the Datsun). If you are serous about maintaining your own car, then a floor jack is as necessary as a spark plug socket. The greatly increased utility, strength, and safety of a hydraulic floor jack makes it pay for itself many times over through the years.

2. A compression gauge. The screw-in type is slower to use but it eliminates the possibility of a faulty reading due to escaping pressure.

3. A manifold vacuum gauge, very useful in troubleshooting ignition and emissions problems.

4. A drop light, to light up the work area (make sure yours is Underwriters' approved and has a shielded bulb).

5. A volt/ohm meter, used for determining whether or not there is current in a wire. These are handy for use if a wire is broken somewhere; it is especially necessary for working on today's electronics-laden cars.

As a final note, a torque wrench is necessary for all but the most basic work — it should even be use when installing spark plugs. The more common beam-type models are perfectly adequate and are usually less expensive than the more precise "click" type (on which you preset the torque and the wrench clicks when that setting arrives on the fastener you are torquing.)

NOTE: *Datsun special tools referred to in this guide are available through Kent-Moore Corporation, 29784 Little Mack, Roseville, Michigan 48066. For Canada, contact Kent-Moore of Canada, Ltd., 2395 Cawthra Mississauga, Ontario, Canada L5A 3Ps.*

SERVICING YOUR CAR SAFELY

It is virtually impossible to anticipate all of the hazards involved with automotive maintenance and service, but care and common sense will prevent most accidents.

The rules of safety for mechanics range from, 'don't smoke around gasoline,' to, 'use the proper tool for the job.' The trick to avoiding injuries is to develop safe work habits and take every possible precaution.

Always use support stands when working under your car

Do's

• Do keep a fire extinguisher and first aid kit within easy reach.

• Do wear safety glasses or goggles when cutting, drilling, grinding or prying, even if you have 20-20 vision. They should be made of hardened glass that can serve also as safety glasses, or wear safety goggles over your regular glasses.

• Do shield your eyes whenever you work around the battery. Batteries contain sulphuric acid. In case of contact with the eyes or skin, flush the area with water or a mixture of water and baking soda and get medical attention immediately.

• Do use safety stands for any undercar service. Jacks are for raising vehicles; safety stands are for making sure the vehicle stays raised until you want it to come down. Whenever the car is raised, block the wheels remaining on the ground and set the parking brake.

• Do use adequate ventilation when workingh with any chemicals or hazardous materials. Like carbon monoxide, the asbestos dust resulting from brake lining wear can be poisonous in sufficient quantities.

• Do disconnect the negative battery cable when working on the electrical system. The secondary ignition system can contain up to 40,000 volts.

• Do follow the manufacturer's directions whenever working with potentially hazardous materials. Both brake fluid and antifreeze are poisonous if taken internally.

• Do properly maintain your tools. Loose hammerheads, mushroomed punches and hisels, frayed or poorly grounded electrical cords, excessively worn screwdrivers, spread wrenches (open end), cracked sockets, slipping ratchets, or faulty droplight sockets can cause accidents.

• Keep your tools clean; a greasy wrench can slip off a bolthead, ruining the bolt and often ruining your knuckles in the process.

• Do use the proper size and type of tool for the job being done.

• Do when possible, pull on a wrench handle rather than push on it, and adjust your stance to prevent a fall.

• Do be sure that adjustable wrenches are tightly closed on the nut or bolt and pulled so that the face is on the side of the fixed jaw.

• Do select a wrench or socket that fits the nut or bolt. The wrench or socket should sit straight, not cocked.

• Do strike squarely with a hammer; avoid glancing blows.

• Do set the parking brake and block the drive wheels if the work requires the engine running.

Don'ts

• Don't run an engine in a garage or anywhere else without proper ventilation — EVER! Carbon monoxide is poisonous; it takes a long time to leave the human body and you can build up a deadly supply of it in your system by simply breathing in a little every day. You may not realize you are slowly poisoning yourself. Always use power vents, windows, fans or open the garage doors.

• Don't work around moving parts while wearing necktie or other loose clothing. Short sleeves are much safer than long, loose sleeves; hard-toed shoes with neoprene soles protect your toes and give a better grip on slippery surfaces. Jewelry such as watches, fancy belt buckles, beads or body adornment of any kind is not safe working around a car. Long hair should be hidden under a hat or cap.

• Don't use pockets for toolboxes. A fall or bump can drive a screwdriver deep into your body. Even a wiping cloth hanging from the back pocket can wrap around a spinning shaft or fan.

• Don't smoke when working around the battery. When the battery is being charged, it gives off explosive hydrogen gas.

• Don't use gasoline to wash your hands. There are excellent soaps available. Gasoline may contain lead, and lead can enter the body through a cut, accumulating in the body until you are very ill. Gasoline also removes all the natural oils from the skin so that bone dry hands will suck up oil and grease.

• Don't service the air conditioning system unless you are equipped with the necessary tools and training. The refrigerant, R-12, is extremely cold when compressed, and when released into the air will instantly freeze any surface it contacts, including your eyes. Although the refrigerant is normally non-toxic, R-12 becomes a deadly poisonous gas in the presence of an open flame. One good whiff of the vapors from burning refrigerant can be fatal.

• Don't use screwdrivers for anything other

than driving screws! A screwdriver used as a prying tool can snap when you least expect it, causing injuries.

• Don't use a bumper jack (that little scissors or pantograph jack supplied with the car) for anything other than changing a flat! These jacks were only intended for emergency use out on the road; they were NOT designed as a maintenance and repair tool. If you are serious about maintaining your car yourself, invest in a hydraulic floor jack (1 ½ ton for the Datsun).

HISTORY

The first Datsun automobile was built in 1914, a small 10 horsepower car with motorcycle fenders. The original name of the company, D.A.T., was derived from the last initials of the company's three main financial backers. A sports-type two seater was produced in 1918 and called the "son of D.A.T.", which later evolved into Datsun. Throughout the 20's and '30's the Datsun automobile looked like the English Austin after which it was closely patterned, while the company also began to branch out into the truck market. The year 1933 saw the formation of Nissan Motor Company, and was also the first year Datsuns were exported.

Following the end of World War II (in which Nissan produced military vehicles and aircraft engines), the company managed to resume truck and passenger car production. It wasn't until 1960 that the first Datsun was imported into the United States; since then, Datsun has moved up into second place in imported car sales. The company's introduction of the Sentra model (under the Nissan badge) in 1982 moved Nissan into the forefront of the fuel mileage competition for gasoline-engined cars.

This guide covers all Datsun 1200, B210, and 210 coupes, sedans, hatchbacks and station wagons from 1973 to 1982 (the "A Series" models)as well asthe Nissan Sentra.

SERIAL NUMBER IDENTIFICATION

Chassis

The chassis serial number is stamped into the firewall. The model designation, such as B210, precedes the serial number. The chassis number is also located on a dashboard plate which is visible through the windshield.

Vehicle Identification Plate

The vehicle identification plate is attached to the firewall. This plate gives the vehicle model, engine displacement in cubic centimeters (cc), SAE horsepower rating, wheelbase, engine number, and chassis number.

Engine

All 1200, B210, and 210 series engines are classified as A Series engines. Sentra gasoline engines are E-series. The Sentra diesel engines are CD series. The engine number is stamped on the right side top edge of the cylinder block on all A-series models, and on the up-

General vehicle identification locations, all models

A-series engine number location

DIESEL ENGINE

GASOLINE ENGINE

Sentra engine serial number location

per right front corner just below the distributor on the Sentra Gasoline engine. On the diesel, it is on the block face, just behind the fan. This serial number is preceded by the engine model code.

Manual Transmission Number

The manual transmission serial number is stamped on the front upper face of the transmission bell housing (case).

A-series manual transmission number location

Automatic Transmission Number

Automatic transmission serial numbers are found on a plate attached to the right-hand side of the transmission case.

Automatic transmission number location, A-series

Manual Transaxle Number

The Sentra manual transaxle serial number is attached to the clutch withdrawal lever on the upper end of the transaxle.

Sentra manual transaxle number location

Sentra automatic transaxle number location

Automatic Transaxle Number

The Sentra automatic transaxle serial number label is attached to the upper face of the transaxle case.

ROUTINE MAINTENANCE

Air Cleaner

All Datsuns covered in this guide are equipped with a disposable paper cartridge air cleaner element. At every tuneup, or sooner if the car is operated in a dusty or smoggy area, undo the wing nut, remove the housing top, and withdraw the element. Check the element. Replace the filter if it is extremely dirty. Loose dust can sometimes be removed by striking the filter against a hard surface several times or by blowing through it with compressed air. The filter should be replaced every 24,000 miles. Before installing either the original or a replacement filter, wipe out the inside of the air cleaner housing with a clean rag or paper towel. Install the paper air cleaner filter, seat the top cover on the bottom housing, and tighten the wing nut.

NOTE: *Some flat, cartridge, type air cleaner elements have the word "UP" printed on them. Be sure the side with "UP" on it faces up.*

Air cleaner filter element replacement—gasoline engine

Air Induction Valve Filter

This filter is located in the air cleaner of the later model 210 Datsuns and Sentra. Replace it when you replace your air filter element by removing the screws which attache the valve filter case, and remove the filter case. Install

1. Air induction valve filter
2. Air induction valve

Air induction filter

the new filter, paying attention to which direction the valve is facing so that exhaust gases will not flow backwards through the system.

Positive Crankcase Ventilation Valve

This valve feeds crankcase blow-by gases into the intake manifold to be burned with the normal air/fuel mixture. The PCV valve should also be replaced every 24,000 miles. The PCV filter, located inside the air cleaner canister, should be replaced every 24,000 miles or more frequently under dusty or smoggy conditions. Make sure that all PCV connections are tight. Check that the connecting hoses are clear and not clogged. Replace any brittle or broken hoses.

To replace the valve, which is located in the intake manifold directly below the carburetor:

1. Squeeze the hose clamp with pliers and remove the hose.

2. Using a wrench, unscrew the PCV valve and remove the valve.

⇨ FRESH AIR
➡ BLOW-BY GAS

1. Seal type oil level gauge
2. Baffle plate
3. Flame arrester
4. Filter
5. P.C.V. valve
6. Steel net
7. Baffle plate

Typical PCV valve location

FILTER

PCV filter location in top of air cleaner

3. Disconnect the ventilation hoses and flush with solvent.

4. Install the new PCV valve and replace the hoses and clamp (check to make sure they are pliable and free of cracks first).

Fuel Evaporative Emissions System

Check the evaporation control system every 12,000 miles. Check the fuel and vapor lines for proper connections and correct routing as condition. Replace damaged or deteriorated parts as necessary. Remove and check the operation of the check value on pre-1975 models in the following manner.

1. With all the hoses disconnected from the valve, apply air pressure to the fuel tank side of the valve. The air should flow through the valve and exit the crankcase side of the valve. If the valve does not behave in the above manner, replace it.

2. Apply air pressure to the crankcase side valve. Air should not pass to either of the two outlets.

3. When air pressure is applied to the carburetor side of the valve, the air should pass through to exit out the fuel tank and/or the crankcase side of the valve.

NOTE: *On 1975 and later models, the flow guide valve is replaced with a carbon filled canister which stores fuel vapors until the engine is started and the vapors are drawn into the combustion chambers and burned.*

To check the operation of the carbon canister purge control valve, disconnect the rubber

1. Cover
2. Diaphragm
3. Retainer
4. Diaphragm spring

1975 and later carbon canister fuel evaporative emissions system

The carbon canister has a replaceable filter in the bottom

FUEL FILLER CAP WITH VACUUM RELIEF VALVE

FUEL CHECK VALVE

FUEL TANK

CARBON CANISTER

Evaporative emissions schematic

(1) FROM AIR CLEANER

FROM FUEL TANK

(2) TO CRANKCASE

FLAME ARRESTER

VAPOR-LIQUID SEPARATOR

VAPOR VENT LINE

POSITIVE SEALING FILLER CAP (WITH RELIEF VALVE)

FLOW GUIDE VALVE [THE VALVE OPENS WHEN THE PRESSURE IS OVER 0.4 INCH HG.]

POSITIVE CRANKCASE VENTILATION VALVE (P.C.V. VALVE)

FUEL TANK

1973–74 check valve fuel evaporative emissions system

hose between the canister control valve and the T-fitting, at the T-fitting. Apply vacuum to the hose leading to the control valve. The vacuum condition should be maintained indefinitely. If the control valve leaks, remove the top cover of the valve and check for a dislocated or cracked diaphragm. If the diaphragm is damaged, a repair kit containing a new diaphragm, retainer, and spring is available and should be installed. The carbon canister has an air filter in the bottom of the canister. The filter element should be checked once a year or every 12,000 miles; more frequently if the car is operated in dusty areas. Replace the filter by pulling it out of the bottom of the canister and installing a new one.

Heat Control Valve

The heat control valve, or Early Fuel Evaporative System, is a thermostatically operated valve found in the exhaust manifold of 1200,

B210 and early 210 models. It closes when the engine is warming up to direct hot exhaust gases to the intake manifold, in order to preheat the incoming fuel/air mixture. If it sticks shut, the result will be frequent stalling during warmup, especially in cold or damp weather. If it sticks open, the result will be a rough idle after the engine is warm.

The heat control valve should be checked for free operation every six months or 6,000 miles. Simply give the counterweight a twirl (engine cold) to make sure that no binding exists. If the valve sticks, apply a heat control solvent (usually available in spray cans) to the ends of the shaft. This type of solvent is available in most auto parts stores. Sometimes lightly rapping the end of the shaft with a hammer (engine hot) will break it loose. If this fails, the components will have to be removed from the car for repair.

NOTE: *The 1980 and later 210 engines do not use the heat control valve.*

1. Intake manifold
2. Stove gasket
3. Manifold stove
4. Heat shield plate
5. Snap ring
6. Counterweight
7. Key
8. Stopper pin
9. Screw
10. Thermostat spring
11. Heat control valve
12. Control valve shaft
13. Exhaust manifold
14. Cap
15. Bushing
16. Coil spring

EXHAUST GAS FLOWS:

← VALVE CLOSED

←■■ VALVE OPENED

Heat control valve (early fuel evaporative system) A-series engine

Belts

TENSION CHECKING, ADJUSTING, AND REPLACEMENT

Check the belts driving the fan, air pump, air conditioning compressor, and the alternator for cracks, fraying, wear, and tension every 6,000 miles. It is recommended that the belts be replaced every 24 months or 24,000 miles. Belt deflection at the midpoint of the longest span between pulleys should not be more than 7/16 inch with 22 lbs. of pressure applied to the belt.

To adjust the tension on all components except the air conditioning compressor, power steering pump, and some late model air pumps, loosen the pivot and mounting bolts of the component which the belt is driving, then, using a wooden lever, pry the component toward or away from the engine until the proper tension is achieved.

CAUTION: *Never tighten power steering pump, air conditioning compressor, and air pump belts by prying the pump or compressor away from the engine. Damage to the component will result. Also, do not overtighten belts*

Alternator

WATER PUMP PULLEY

COMPRESSOR PULLEY

CRANKSHAFT PULLEY

IDLER PULLEY

Typical belt arrangement

HOW TO SPOT WORN V-BELTS

V-Belts are vital to efficient engine operation—they drive the fan, water pump and other accessories. They require little maintenance (occasional tightening) but they will not last forever. Slipping or failure of the V-belt will lead to overheating. If your V-belt looks like any of these, it should be replaced.

Cracking or weathering

This belt has deep cracks, which cause it to flex. Too much flexing leads to heat build-up and premature failure. These cracks can be caused by using the belt on a pulley that is too small. Notched belts are available for small diameter pulleys.

Softening (grease and oil)

Oil and grease on a belt can cause the belt's rubber compounds to soften and separate from the reinforcing cords that hold the belt together. The belt will first slip, then finally fail altogether.

Glazing

Glazing is caused by a belt that is slipping. A slipping belt can cause a run-down battery, erratic power steering, overheating or poor accessory performance. The more the belt slips, the more glazing will be built up on the surface of the belt. The more the belt is glazed, the more it will slip. If the glazing is light, tighten the belt.

Worn cover

The cover of this belt is worn off and is peeling away. The reinforcing cords will begin to wear and the belt will shortly break. When the belt cover wears in spots or has a rough jagged appearance, check the pulley grooves for roughness.

Separation

This belt is on the verge of breaking and leaving you stranded. The layers of the belt are separating and the reinforcing cords are exposed. It's just a matter of time before it breaks completely.

-- pulley bearings on the various components will wear out unusually fast.

Tighten the component mounting bolts securely. If a new belt is installed, recheck the tension after driving about 1,000 miles.

NOTE: *The replacement of the inner belt on multi-belted engines may require the removal of the outer belts.*

Belt tension adjustments for the factory installed air conditioning compressor and power steering pump are made at the idler pulley. The idler pulley is the smallest of the three pulleys. At the top of the slotted bracket holding the idler pulley there is a bolt which is used to either raise or lower the pulley. To free the bolt for admustment, it is necessary to loosen the lock nut in the face of the idler pulley. After adjusting the belt tension, tighten the lock nut in the face of the idler pulley.

NOTE: *Some 1980 and later California Datsuns come equipped from the factory with special fan belts which, if loose, generate friction heat by slipping and shrink, taking up the slack. If your car is new or has low mileage on it, it may still have this type of belt(s) on it. The optical air conditioning drive belt is adjusted in a similar manner.*

Extra belts, especially alternator drive belts, should be part of your car's emergency equipment particularly if the brunt of your mileage is driven on the highway. Along with the new belts should be any tools (wrenches, wooden prybars, etc.) needed to install the belts while out on the road.

Cooling System

Your Datsun's internal combustion gasoline engine generates power by the controlled explosion of a mixture of gasoline and air in the combustion chamber of each cylinder. The piston of each cylinder is at the top of its upward travel when this explosion occurs. The explosion (ignition) forces the piston downward, turning the crankshaft and creating mechanical energy. But not all of the force of the ignited fuel mixture is expended in forcing the piston downward; some heat is released, from the combustion, from the friction of the piston and piston rings moving up and down against the inside of the cylinder bore, and from the movement of the engine's other internal parts. The job of the cooling system is to effectively remove that heat from the engine before it raises the cyclinder head and block temperatures too greatly.

DRAINING THE COOLING SYSTEM

To drain the cooling system, allow the engine to cool down *before attempting to remove the ra-*diator cap. Wrap a heavy rag or cloth around the cap to avoid burns, and turn it just enough until it hisses. This removes the pressure from the radiator; wait until the hissing stops before removing the cap. After removing the cap, drain the radiator by unscrewing the petcock or drain plug at the bottom of the radiator. See Coolant section under Fluid Level Checks in this chapter for refilling procedures.

Radiator drain petcock location

COOLANT HOSE REPLACEMENT

Remove the radiator cap, unscrew the drain petcock or plug, and drain the radiator into a clean pan if you are going to use the old coolant. Disconnect the hose clamps and remove the hose by either cutting it off or twisting it to break its seal on the radiator and engine coolant inlets. Radiator hoses should always be pliable. Any hose that feels brittle or hard should be replaced, as this condition indicates the hose could split anytime (usually when you are miles from any service facility). When installing the new hose, do not overtighten the hose clamps or you might slice the hose underneath. Refill the radiator, run the engine with the radiator cap on and recheck the coolant level.

NOTE: *As with your extra belts, you should carry extra radiator hoses if you plan to travel long distances, or if your normal mileage is on the highway. Don't forget whatever tools you may need to remove the hose clamps and hoses.*

Air Conditioning

This book contains no repair or maintenance procedures for the air conditioning system. It is recommended that any such repairs be left to the experts, whose personnel are well aware of the hazards and who have the proper equipment.

CAUTION: *The compressed refrigerant (R-12) used in the air conditioning system expands into the atmosphere at a temperature of -21.7°F or lower. This will freeze any sur-*

HOW TO SPOT BAD HOSES

Both the upper and lower radiator hoses are called upon to perform difficult jobs in an inhospitable environment. They are subject to nearly 18 psi at under hood temperatures often over 280°F., and must circulate nearly 7500 gallons of coolant an hour—3 good reasons to have good hoses.

Swollen hose

A good test for any hose is to feel it for soft or spongy spots. Frequently these will appear as swollen areas of the hose. The most likely cause is oil soaking. This hose could burst at any time, when hot or under pressure.

Cracked hose

Cracked hoses can usually be seen but feel the hoses to be sure they have not hardened; a prime cause of cracking. This hose has cracked down to the reinforcing cords and could split at any of the cracks.

Frayed hose end (due to weak clamp)

Weakened clamps frequently are the cause of hose and cooling system failure. The connection between the pipe and hose has deteriorated enough to allow coolant to escape when the engine is hot.

Debris in cooling system

Debris, rust and scale in the cooling system can cause the inside of a hose to weaken. This can usually be felt on the outside of the hose as soft or thinner areas.

face, including your eyes, that it contacts. In addition, R-12 decomposes into a poisonous gas in the presence of flame. Do not open or disconnect any part of the air conditioning system.

SIGHT GLASS CHECK

You can safely make a few simple checks to determine if your air conditioning system needs service. The tests work best if the temperature is warm (about 70°F).

NOTE: *If your vehicle is equipped with an after-mar-ket air conditioner, the following system check may not apply. You should contact the manufacturer of the unit for instructions on systems checks.*

1. Place the automatic transmission in Park or the manual transmission in Neutral. Set the parking brake.

2. Run the engine at a fast idle (about 1,500 rpm) either with the help of a friend, or by temporarily readjusting the idle speed screw.

3. Set the controls for maximum cold with the blower on high.

4. Locate the sight glass in one of the system lines. Usually it is on the left alongside the top of the radiator.

5. If you see bubbles, the system must be recharged. Very likely there is a leak at some point.

6. If there are no bubbles, there is either no refrigerant at all or the system is fully charged. Feel the two hoses going to the belt-driven compressor. If they are both at the same temperature, the system is empty and must be recharged.

7. If one hose (high pressure) is warm and the other (low pressure) is cold, the system may be all right. However, you are probably making these tests because you think there is something wrong, so proceed to the next step.

8. Have an assistant in the car turn the fan control on and off to operate the compressor clutch. Watch the sight glass.

9. If bubbles appear when the clutch is disengaged and disappear when it is engaged, the system is properly charged.

10. If the refrigerant takes more than 45 seconds to bubble when the clutch is disengaged, the system is overcharged. This usually causes poor cooling at low speeds.

CAUTION: *If it is determined that the system has a leak, it should be corrected as soon as possible. Leaks may allow moisture to enter and cause a very expensive rust problem.*

NOTE: *Operate the air conditioner for a few minutes, every two weeks or so, during the cold months. This avoids the possibility of the compressor seals drying out from lack of lu-*

The sight glass is located in the head of the receiver-dryer (arrow)

brication, a major cause of air conditioner system maintenance and repair.

Fluid Level Checks
ENGINE OIL

The best time to check the engine oil is before operating the engine or after it has been sitting for at least 10 minutes in order to gain an accurate reading. This will allow the oil to drain back into the crankcase. To check the engine oil level, make sure that the vehicle is resting on a level surface, remove the oil dipstick, wipe it clean and reinsert the stick all the way down again until the cap seats itself in the tube. Pull the dipstick out again and level it for an accurate reading.

The oil dipstick has two marks on it to indi-

Oil level gauge location—gasoline engine

Oil level gauge location—diesel engine

cate high and low oil level. If the oil is at or below the low level mark on the dipstick, oil should be added as necessary. The oil level should be maintained in the safety margin, neither going above the high level mark or below the low level mark.

TRANSMISSION

Manual Transmission/Transaxle

Check the level of the lubricant in the transmission every 3,000 miles. The lubricant level should be even with the bottom of the filler hole. Hold in on the filler plug when unscrewing it. When you are sure that all of the threads of the plug are free of the transmission case, move the plug away from the case slight-

FILLER PLUG

ⓣ 25–34 N·M
(2.5–3.5 KG-M,
18–25 FT-LB)   FILL TO THIS LEVEL

Transmission oil should be level with the bottom of the filler plug on manual transmissions

ly. If lubricant begins to flow out of the transmission, then you know it is full. If not, add SAE 90W gear oil as necessary. It is recommended that the transmission lubricant be changed every 24,000 miles.

Automatic

Check the level of the automatic transmission fluid every 2,000 miles. There is a dipstick at the right rear of the engine under the hood. It has a scale on each side, one for COLD and the other for HOT. The transmission is considered hot after 15 miles of highway driving.

Park the car on a level surface with the engine running. If the transmission is not hot, shift into Drive, Low, then Neutral or Park. Set the handbrake and block the wheels.

Remove the dipstick, wipe it clean, then reinsert it firmly. Remove the dipstick and check the fluid level on the appropriate scale. The level should be at the Full mark.

If the level is below the Full mark, add Type A or DEXRON® type automatic transmission fluid as necessary, with the engine running, through the dipstick tube. *Do not overfill,* as this may cause the transmission to malfunction and damage itself.

ADD TO "H" LEVEL.
DO NOT OVERFILL.

Remove the automatic transmission dipstick with engine warm and idling in Park

BRAKE AND CLUTCH MASTER CYCLINDER

Both systems use a DOT 3 type brake fluid. The Sentra does not have a hydraulic clutch.

Check the levels of brake fluid in the brake and clutch master cylinder reservoirs every 3,000 miles. The fluid level should be maintained to a level not below the bottom line on

Brake master cylinder, all models similar

Clutch master cylinder, 1200, B210 and 210

the reservoirs and not above the top line. Any sudden decrease in the level in either of the three reservoirs (two for the brakes and one for the clutch) indicates a prbable leak in that particular system and the possibility of a leak should be checked out.

NOTE: *The clutch in your 1200, B210 or 210 model Datsun is operated hydraulically, employing a system much the same as the hydraulic brake system in the car.*

COOLANT

Check the coolant level every time you change the oil. Check for loose connections and signs of deterioration of the coolant hoses. Maintain the coolant level 3 in. below the level of the filler neck when the engine is cold. Add a mixture of 70% to 50% water and 30% to 50% ethylene glycol antifreeze as necessary. See "Draining the Cooling System" in this chapter for radia-

tor cap removal cautions and radiator draining.

Never add cold water to an overheated engine while the engine is not running; this can cause the engine block to crack. Run the engine until it reaches normal operating temperature after filling the radiator to make sure that the thermostat has opened and all air is bled from the system.

REAR AXLE

Check the rear axle lubricant on the 1200, B210 and 210 cars every 6,000 miles. Remove the filler plug in the axle housing. The lubricant should be up to the bottom of the filler hole with the vehicle resting on a level surface. Add SAE 90W gear oil as necessary to bring the lubricant up the proper level.

Checking rear axle oil level, 1200, B210 and 210. Fill to the level of the filler plug hole

STEERING GEAR

Check the level of the lubricant in the steering gear box every 12,000 miles. If the level is low, check for leakage. An oily film is not considered a lea; solid grease must be present. Change the lubricant every 36,000 miles. Use

Check the rubber gasket on the cap when checking the coolant level

When topping up steering gearbox, check these areas for leaks

steering gear lubricant. The lubricant is added and checked through the filler plug hole in the top of the steering gear.

POWER STEERING RESERVOIR

Check the fluid level in the reservoir by observing the dipstick when the fluid is cold. Add fluid as necessary to bring the level into the proper range on the dipstick. DO NOT OVERFILL.

Power steering reservoir check

Windshield Wipers

Intense heat from the sun, snow and ice, road oils and the chemicals used in windshield washer solvent combine to deteriorate the rubber wiper refills. The refills should be replaced about twice a year or whenever the blades begin to streak or chatter.

WIPER REFILL REPLACEMENT

Normally, if the wipers are not cleaning the windshield properly, only the refill has to be replaced. The blade and arm usually require replacement only in the event of damage. It is not necessary (except on new Tridon® refills) to remove the arm of the blade to replace the refill (rubber part), though you may have to position the arm higher on the glass. You can do this by turning the ignition switch on, and operating the wipers. When they are positioned where they are accessible, turn the ignition switch off.

There are several types of refills and your car could have any kind, since aftermarket blades and arms may not use exactly the same type refill as the original equipment.

Most Trico® styles use a release button that is pushed down to allow the refill to slide out of the yoke jaws. The new refill slides in and locks in place. Some Trico® refills are removed by locating where the metal backing strip or the refill is wider. Insert a small screwdriver blade between the frame and metal backing strip. Press down to release the refill from the retaining tab.

The Anco® style is unlocked at one end by squeezing 2 metal tabs, and the refill is slid out of the frame jaws. When the new refill is installed, the tabs will click into place, locking the refill.

The polycarbonate type is held in place by a locking lever that is pushed downward, out of the groove in the arm, to free the refill. When the new refill is installed, it will lock in place automatically.

The Tridon® refill has a plastic backing strip with a notch about an inch from the end. Hold the blade (frame) on a hard surface so that the fram is tightly bowed. Grip the tip of the backing strip and pull up while twisting counterclockwise. The backing strip will snap out of the retaining tab. Do this for the remaining tabs until the refill is free of the arm. The length of these refills is molded into the end and they should be replaced with identical types.

No matter which type of refill you use, be sure that all of the frame claws engage the refill. Before operating the wipers, be sure that no part of the metal frame is contacting the windshield.

Battery

The battery in your Datsun is located in the engine compartment. Keep an eye on the battery electrolyte (fluid) level and its specific gravity. A few minutes occasionally spent monitoring battery condition is worth saving hours of frustration and hassle when your car won't start due to a dead battery. Use only distilled water (available in most supermarkets and hardware stores) to top up the battery, as tap water in many areas contains harmful chemicals and minerals.

Four tools that will make battery maintenance easier are a hydrometer, a squeeze bulb filler (syringe or common turkey baster), a battery terminal brush and a battery clamp puller. All of these tools are inexpensive and widely available at auto parts stores, hardware stores, etc. The specific gravity of the electrolyte should be between 1.27 and 1.20 (often shown by a color on the float of the hydrometer). Keep the top of the battery clean, as a film of dirt can sometimes completely discharge a battery. Clean this surface with a solution of baking soda and water, using an old toothbrush to remove the crystallized electrolyte (the whitish powder which sometimes builds up near the terminal posts). Flush the top of the battery with clear water.

Battery terminal posts and terminal clamps can be cleaned with the battery terminal brush. Unbolt the clamps from the terminals

TRICO

BLADE FRAME LEVER

RUBBER BLADE ELEMENT ASSY.

SQUEEZE SIDES OF RETAINER

LEVER JAWS

LATCH LOCK RELEASE

METAL BACKING IS WIDER

HOLD FRAME FROM TWISTING

METAL BACKING STRIP

RETAINING TABS

METAL BACKING STRIP

FRAME

INSERT SCREWDRIVER BEHIND TAB AND PUSH HANDLE DOWN.

ANCO

LATCH-PIN

YOKE JAWS

RUBBER BLADE ELEMENT ASSY.

YOKE JAWS

POLYCARBONATE

UNLOCKED

LOCKED

TRIDON

PLASTIC BACKING STRIP

NOTCH

FRAME

PULL UP & TWIST

PRESSURE DOWN

RUBBER BLADE

RETAINING TABS

16

16.5

THE LENGTH OF THE 16" AND 16.5" TRIDON BLADES ARE MOLDED IN EACH END. REPLACE ONLY WITH IDENTICAL BLADES OR REFILLS.

FIRM SURFACE

FRAME

Popular styles of wiper refills

OVERFLOW   CORRECT   SHORTAGE

INDICATOR

Make sure the electrolyte in the battery is level with the bottoms of the filler holes

Use the terminal brush to get the insides of the terminal clamps shiny

and remove them using the clamp puller (you can twist them up and off without the puller, but if they're stuck you may twist the terminal off with the clamp). Clean the insides of the clamps with the wire brush, until the insides are shiny. Clean the terminal posts with the female end of the brush unit, turning the brush around on the posts until the posts are shiny. The cleanliness of the posts and clamps is crucial to a good electrical connection. Assemble the battery wire clamps to the terminal posts and lightly coat the clamps with petroleum jelly to help retard corrosion.

CAUTION: *Battery electrolyte is an acid, and should be kept away from the skin, especially the eyes. If it is accidentally splashed, flush the area immediately with cold, clean water. Never smoke or place any open flame near a battery, as it is constantly giving off an explosive gas while charging.*

Tires

Check the air pressure in your tires every few weeks. Make sure that the tires are cool, as you will get a false reading when the tires are heated because air pressure increases with temperature. A decal (usually on a door jamb or inside the glove compartment) tells you the proper tire pressure for the standard equipment tires. Naturally, when you replace tires you will want to get the correct tire pressures for the new ones from the dealer or manufacturer. It pays to buy a tire pressure gauge to keep in the car, since those at service stations are usually inaccurate or broken.

While you are checking the tire pressure, take a look at the tread. The tread should be wearing evenly across the tire. Excessive wear in the center of the tread could indicate overinflation. Excessive wear on the outer edges could indicate underinflation. An irregular wear pattern is usually a sign of incorrect front wheel alignment or wheel balance. A front end that is out of alignment will usually pull the car to one side of a flat road when the steering wheel is released. Incorrect wheel balance will produce vibration in the steering wheel, while unbalanced rear wheels will result in floor or trunk vibration.

Rotating the tires every 6,000 miles or so will

When bands appear as shown, your tire tread is below $1/16$ inch. Tire should be replaced

Tire rotation patterns

result in increased tread life. Use the correct pattern for your tire switching. Most automotive experts agree that radial tires are better all around performers, giving longer wear and better handling. An added benefit which you should consider when purchasing tires is that radials haved less rolling resistance and, when properly inflated, can give up to a 10% increase in fuel economy over a bias-ply tire.

Never mix bias tires and radials, or vice versa, as this can cause serious handling problems. Always replace tires in sets of four or five when switching tire types and never substitute a belted tire for a bias-ply, a radial for a belted tire, etc. An occasional pressure check and periodic rotation can make your tires last much longer than a neglected set, while maintaining the safety margin which was designed into them.

Fuel Filter

REPLACEMENT

Gasoline Engine

The fuel filter on all models is a disposable plastic unit. It's located on the right inner fender. The filter should be replaced at least every 24,000 miles. A dirty filter will starve the engine and cause poor running.

1. Locate fuel filter on right-side of the engine compartment.

2. Disconnect the inlet and outlet hoses from the fuel filter. Make certain that the inlet hose (bottom) doesn't fall below the fuel tank level or the gasoline will drain out.

Typical fuel filter, all models

3. Pry the fuel filter from its clip and replace the assembly.

4. Replace the inlet and outlet lines; secure the hose clamps to prevent leaks.

5. Start the engine and check for leaks.

Diesel Engine

The filter should be replaced at least every 30,000 miles or more often under extremely adverse weather conditions or in areas where ambient temperatures are either extremely low or extremely high. The fuel filter on the diesel engine includes the priming pump and the fuel filter sensor.

1. Remove the fuel filter sensor and drain the fuel in an appropriate container.

2. Unscrew the fuel filter and discard.

3. Install the fuel filter sensor to the new fuel filter.

PRIMING PUMP

BLEEDER SCREW

FUEL FILTER

FUEL FILTER SENSOR

DRAIN COCK

Fuel filter assembly—diesel engine

Loosen the priming pump vent screw by turning counterclockwise with a screwdriver

When installing the fuel filter, hand tighten only

Prime the priming pump and check for an air bubble at the hose end

4. Hand tighten the fuel filter to the priming pump.

5. Bleed the fuel system as outlined in the following proceedure.

Bleeding The Fuel System (Diesel Engine)

NOTE: *Air should be bled out of the fuel system when the injection pump is removed or the fuel system is repaired. This is also required if the fuel tank has been completely emptied.*

1. Loosen the air vent screw or cock.

2. Move the priming pump up and down until no further air bubbles come out of the air vent screw or cock, then tighten the air vent screw or cock.

3. Disconnect the fuel return hose on the pump side, then install a suitable hose on the pump side.

4. Prime the priming pump to make sure that a bubble does not appear at the hose end and connect the return hose.

NOTE: *If the engine does not operate smoothly after it has started, race it two or three times. If the engine does not start, loosen the injection tubes at the nozzle side and crank the engine until fuel overflows from the injection tubes. Tighten the injection tube flare nuts.*

Draining Water From The Fuel System (Diesel Engine)

If the filter warning light illuminates and a chime sounds (on models so equipped) while the engine is running, drain any water that is in the fuel filter.

1. Disconnect the harness connector at the bottom of the fuel filter assembly.

2. Place a container under the fuel filter, then loosen the drain cock 4 or 5 turns to drain the water.

NOTE: *If the water does not drain sufficiently move the priming pump up and down.*

3. After draining the water completely, close the drain cock and reconnect the harness connector.

4. Bleed the air from the fuel system as outlined earlier.

LUBRICATION

Oil and Fuel Recommendations

Your Datsun is designed to operate on regular low lead or lead-free fuel. The octane ratings are listed on the inside of the fuel filler door, but these need only be checked when traveling outside of the United States. Should you find the regular gasoline available, say in Mexico, to be of too low an octane, mix a 50/50 regular

Select the proper oil viscosity for anticipated temperatures between oil changes

leaded-to-unleaded Premium ratio. This will give your car the lead it needs (if designed to run on leaded gas) and also the octane it needs. 1975 California cars and all 1976 and later models will run happily on the unleaded gasoline available in the United States.

Oil must be selected with regard to the anticipated temperatures during the period before the next oil change. Using the chart, select the oil viscosity for the lowest expected temperature and you will be assured of easy cold starting and sufficient engine protection. The oil you pour into your Datsun equipped with a gasoline engine should have the designation SF marked on the top of its container. Or in combination with other categories, for example, SF/CC. In diesel engine equipped cars, use oils with the designations SE/CC, SF/CC, SE/CD, SF/CD or CD.

SYNTHETIC OIL

There are many excellent synthetic and fuel-efficient oils currently available that can provide better gas mileage, longer service life, and in some cases better engine protection. These benefits do not come without a few hitches, however — the main one being the price of synthetic oils, which is three or four times the price per quart of conventional oil.

Synthetic oil is not for every car and every type of driving, so you should consider your engine's condition and your type of driving. Also, check your car's warranty conditions regarding the use of synthetic oils.

Both brand new engines and older, high mileage engines are the wrong candidates for synthetic oil. The synthetic oils are so slippery that they can prevent the proper break-in of

new engines; most manufacturers recommend that you wait until the engine is properly broken in (5,000) until using synthetic oil. Older engines with wear have a different problem with synthetics: they use (consume during operation) more oil as they age. Slippery synthetic oils get past these worn parts easily. If your engine is using conventional oil, it will use synthetics much faster. Also, if your car is leaking oil past old seals you'll have a much greater leak problem with synthetics.

Consider your type of driving. If most of your accumulated mileage is high speed, highway type driving, the more expensive synthetic oils may be of benefit. Extended highway driving gives the engine a chance to warm up, accumulating less acids in the oil and putting less stress on the engine over the long run. Under these conditions, the oil change interval can be extended (as long as your oil filter can last the extended life of the oil) up to the advertised mileage claims of the synthetics. Cars with synthetic oils may show increased fuel economy in highway driving, due to less internal friction. However, many automotive experts agree that 50,000 miles is too long to keep any oil in your engine.

Cars used under harder circumstances, such as stop-and-go, city type driving, short trips, or extended idling, should be serviced more frequently. For the engines in these cars, the much greater cost of synthetic or fuel-efficient oils may not be worth the investment. Internal wear increases much quicker on these cars, causing greater oil consumption and leakage.

NOTE: *The mixing of conventional and synthetic oils is not recommended. If you are using synthetic oil, it might be wise to carry two or three quarts with you no matter where you drive, as not all service stations carry this type of lubricant.*

Oil Changes
CHANGING YOUR ENGINE OIL

The mileage figures given in your owner's manual are the Datsun recommended intervals for oil and filter changes assuming average driving. If your Datsun is being used under dusty, polluted, or off-road conditions, change the oil and filter sooner than specified. The same thing goes for cars driven in stop-and-go traffic or only for short distances.

Always drain the oil after the engine has been running long enough to bring it to operating temperature. Hot oil will flow easier and more contaminants will be removed along with the oil than if it were drained cold. You will need a large capacity drain pan, which you can purchase at any store which sells automotive parts. Another necessity is containers for the used oil. You will find that plastic bottles, such as those used for bleach or fabric softener, make excellent storage jugs. One ecologically desireable solution to the used oil disposal problem is to find a cooperative gas station owner who will allow you to dump your used oil into his tank or take the oil to a reclamation center (often at garages and gas stations).

Datsun recommends changing both the oil and filter during the first oil change and the filter every other oil change thereafter. For the small price of an oil filter, it's cheap insurance to replace the filter at every oil change. One of the larger filter manufacturers points out in its advertisements that not changing the filter leaves one quart of dirty oil in the engine. This claim is true and should be kept in mind when changing your oil.

1. Run the engine until it reaches normal operating temperature.

2. Jack up the front of the car and support it on safety stands if necessary to gain access to the filter.

3. Slide a drain pan of at least 6 quarts capacity under the oil pan.

4. Loosen the drain plug. Turn the plug out by hand. By keeping an inward pressure on the plug as you unscrew it, oil won't escape past the threads and you can remove it without being burned by hot oil. Use a rag to unscrew the plug.

5. Allow the oil to drain completely and then install the drain plug. *Don't overtighten the plug*, or you'll be buying a new pan or a self-tapping replacement plug for buggered threads.

6. Using the oil filter strap wrench, remove the oil filter. As the filter unscrews the final turn, level it as you pull it off the engine block. Keep in mind the filter is still filled with about a quart of dirty, hot oil.

7. Empty the old filter into the drain pan and dispose of the filter.

8. Using a clean rag, wipe off the filter adapter on the engine block. Be sure that the rag doesn't leave any lint which could clog an oil passage.

9. Coat the rubber gasket on the new filter with a wipe of fresh oil. Spin it onto the engine by hand; when the filter begins to snug up against the mounting surface give it another ½–¾ turn. *Do not turn it any more* or you'll ruin the gasket and the filter will leak.

10. Refill the engine with the correct amount of fresh oil. See the Capacities chart.

11. Crank the engine over several times and then start it. If the oil pressure indicator light doesn't go out or the pressure gauge shows

Oil filler, drain and filter locations. All engines similar

Apply a light coat of oil to the rubber gasket on the oil filter before installing it

A strap wrench will make oil filter removal easier. Do not install a filter with a strap wrench

zero, shut the engine down and find out what's wrong.

12. If the oil pressure is OK and there are no leaks, shut the engine off and lower the car.

MANUAL TRANSMISSION/TRANSAXLE

Change the transmission lubricant in your manual transmission every 36,000 miles as follows:

1. Park the car on a level surface and apply the parking brake. Jack up the car and support it on stands.

2. Remove the oil filler plug (the upper one). The Sentra filler plug is on the side of the transaxle.

3. Place a drain pan under the drain plug in the transmission bottom pan. Drain plug for the Sentra transaxle is on the side of the transaxle case, below the filler plug.

4. Slowly remove the drain plug keeping an upward pressure on it until you can quickly pull it out.

5. Allow all of the old gear oil to drain and then replace the plug. Don't overtighten it.

6. Fill the transmission with SAE 90W gear oil. Refill with the quantity shown in the Capacities chart. An oil suction gun or squeeze bulb filler (turkey baster) are handy for this chore and can be sued for the rear axle, too (except on the Sentra, which is front wheel drive).

7. Replace the filler plug and lower the car.

AUTOMATIC TRANSMISSION/TRANSAXLE

The transmission fluid in an automatic transmission should be changed every 24,000 miles of normal driving or every 12,000 miles of driving under abnormal or severe conditions (such as frequent trailer pulling). The fluid should be drained immediately after the vehicle has been driven, but before it has had the chance to cool.. Follow the procedure given below:

1. Drain the automatic transmission fluid from the transmission into a large drain pan, by removing the transmission bottom pan screws, pan, and gasket on the 1200, B210 and 210. On the Sentra transaxle, remove the hexagon drain plug first. When all fluid has drained, remove the pan guard, pan, and gasket.

2. Thoroughly clean the bottom pan and position a new gasket on the pan mating surface. Use petroleum jelly on the gasket to seal it. In-

Sentra automatic transmission drain plug

stall the bottom pan and secure it with the attaching screws, tightening them to 3-5 ft.lb.

3. Pour the correct amount of DEXRON® type automatic transmission fluid, as specified in the Capacities chart, in through the filler pipe. Make sure that the funnel, container, hose, or any other item used to assist in filling the transmission is clean.

4. Start the engine, Do NOT race it. Allow the engine to idle for a few minutes.

5. Place the selector lever in Park and apply the parking brake. With the transmission fluid at operating temperatures, check the fluid level; add fluid to bring the level to the FULL mark on the dip-stick.

REAR AXLE

Change the gear oil in the rear axle every 36,000 miles as follows:

1. With the car on a level surface, jack up the rear and support it with stands.

2. Slide a drain pan under the drain plug,

● : JACK-UP POINT FOR PANTOGRAPH JACK
◉ : JACK-UP POINT FOR GARAGE JACK
▨ : SUPPORTABLE POINT FOR SAFETY STAND

Jacking and towing locations, 210. 1200 and B210 models similar except they use the rear spring shackles as tow hooks. Sentra has single central tow hook on each end.

remove the plug, and allow the oil to drain out.

3. Install the drain plug, but don't overtighten it. Remove the filler plug.

4. Refill the rear axle with SAE 90 gear oil up to the level of the filler plug. A kitchen turkey baster is useful here in adding the oil. Also, some oil brands come in plastic bottles with useful built-in spouts.

Chassis Greasing

Datsun doesn't install lubrication fittings (grease nipples) in lube points on the steering linkage or suspension. You can buy metric threaded fittings to grease these points or use a pointed, rubber end tip on your grease gun. Lubricate all joints equipped with a plug every 24,000 miles. When greasing, keep the grease gun as square with the fitting as possible, or grease will just squeeze out around the fitting instead of inside the fitting. Replace the plugs after lubrication

JUMP STARTING A DEAD BATTERY

The chemical reaction in a battery produces explosive hydrogen gas. This is the safe way to jump start a dead battery, reducing the chances of an accidental spark that could cause an explosion.

Jump Starting Precautions

1. Be sure both batteries are of the same voltage.

2. Be sure both batteries are of the same polarity (have the same grounded terminal).

3. Be sure the vehicles are not touching.

4. Be sure the vent cap holes are not obstructed.

5. Do not smoke or allow sparks around the battery.

6. In cold weather, check for frozen electrolyte in the battery.

7. Do not allow electrolyte on your skin or clothing.

8. Be sure the electrolyte is not frozen.

Jump Starting Procedure

1. Determine voltages of the two batteries; they must be the same.

2. Bring the starting vehicle close (they must not touch) so that they batteries can be reached easily.

3. Turn off all accessories and both engines. Put both cars in Neutral or Park and set the handbrake.

4. Cover the cell caps with a rag; do not cover terminals.

5. If the terminals on the run-down battery are heavily corroded, clean them.

6. Identify the positive and negative posts on both batteries and connect the cables in the order shown.

7. Start the engine of the starting vehicle and run it at fast idle. Try to start the car with the dead battery. Crank it for no more than 10 seconds at a time and let it cool off for 20 seconds in between tries.

8. If it doesn't start in 3 tries, there is something else wrong.

9. Disconnect the cables in the reverse order.

10. Replace the cell covers and dispose of the rags.

PUSHING, TOWING AND JUMP STARTING

All Datsun 1200, B210 , 210 and Sentra models with manual transmissions can be push started, except 1976 and later California cars, as push starting may damage the catalytic converters. All models equipped with automatic transmissions, including Sentra, may NOT be push started.

Before starting, check to make sure that the bumpers of both vehicles are aligned as much as possible. An old tire placed between the bumpers of both vehicles makes a good cushion against damage to either car. Make sure that all electrical components are turned off (headlights, heater, etc.). Turn the ignition switch on, push in the clutch pedal and place the shift lever in third gear. Give the driver of the push vehicle the signal to go; at about 15 mph, signal the driver to fall back, depress the accelerator pedal and release the clutch pedal slowly (check to be certain the ignition switch is on). The engine should start.

You can perform the same procedure as above, but without a push car, if you are within access to a long hill (devoid of traffic, of course). In either situation, it is not advisable to tow-start your Datsun for fear of ramming the towing vehicle when the engine starts.

Both manual and automatic 1200, B210, and 210 Datsuns may be towed for short distances and at speeds no more than 20 mph. NEVER tow a Sentra model with automatic transmission with the front (drive) wheels touching the ground. If the car must be towed a long distance, it should be done with either the drive wheels off the ground or the driveshaft disconnected. Sentra manual transaxle models should be towed with their drive (front) wheels off the ground to avoid transaxle damage. If

JUMP STARTING A DEAD BATTERY

The chemical reaction in a battery produces explosive hydrogen gas. This is the safe way to jump start a dead battery, reducing the chances of an accidental spark that could cause an explosion.

Jump Starting Precautions

1. Be sure both batteries are of the same voltage.
2. Be sure both batteries are of the same polarity (have the same grounded terminal).
3. Be sure the vehicles are not touching.
4. Be sure the vent cap holes are not obstructed.
5. Do not smoke or allow sparks around the battery.
6. In cold weather, check for frozen electrolyte in the battery.
7. Do not allow electrolyte on your skin or clothing.
8. Be sure the electrolyte is not frozen.

Jump Starting Procedure

1. Determine voltages of the two batteries; they must be the same.
2. Bring the starting vehicle close (they must not touch) so that the batteries can be reached easily.
3. Turn off all accessories and both engines. Put both cars in Neutral or Park and set the handbrake.
4. Cover the cell caps with a rag—do not cover terminals.
5. If the terminals on the run-down battery are heavily corroded, clean them.
6. Identify the positive and negative posts on both batteries and connect the cables in the order shown.
7. Start the engine of the starting vehicle and run it at fast idle. Try to start the car with the dead battery. Crank it for no more than 10 seconds at a time and let it cool off for 20 seconds in between tries.
8. If it doesn't start in 3 tries, there is something else wrong.
9. Disconnect the cables in the reverse order.
10. Replace the cell covers and dispose of the rags.

Side terminal batteries occasionally pose a problem when connecting jumper cables. There frequently isn't enough room to clamp the cables without touching sheet metal. Side terminal adaptors are available to alleviate this problem and should be removed after use.

Make certain vehicles do not touch

This hook-up for negative ground cars only

this is not possible, place the transaxle in neutral and make sure the ignition switch is NOT in the LOCK position. Try to restrict towing an automatic transmission car to a distance of less than 20 miles. Any towing of a manual transmission car over 50 miles should be done with the driveshaft disconnected.

Jump starting a dead battery is a procedure that should be known to every car owner (see illustration). Make sure the cars are not touching, the cables are not crossed, and the clamps connected positive-to-positive and negative-to-negative. You should carry a set of good quality jumper cables in your car at all times.

JACKING

NEVER use the bumper jack—the jack supplied with the car—for anything other than changing tires. If you are serious about performing your own maintenance, invest in a 1 ½ ton hydraulic floor jack and (at least) two sturdy jackstands. A hydraulic jack will pay for itself very quickly in safety, time saved and overall utility.

ALWAYS chock the wheels when changing a tire or working beneath the car. This cannot be overemphasized. CLIMBING UNDER A CAR SUPPORTED BY ONLY A JACK IS EXTREMELY DANGEROUS.

HOW TO BUY A USED CAR

Many people believe that a two or three year old, or older, car is a better buy than a new one. This may be true. The new car suffers the heaviest depreciation in the first few years, but is not old enough to present a lot of costly repairs. Whatever the age of the used car you want to buy, this section and a little patience will help you select one that should be safe and dependable.

Shopping Tips

1. First, decide what model you want and how much you want to spend.
2. Check the used car lots and your local newspaper ads. Privately owned cars are usually less expensive, however, you will not get a warranty that, in most cases, comes with a used car purchased from a dealer.
3. Never shop at night. The glare of the lights makes it easy to miss defects in the paint and faults in the body caused by accident or rust repair.
4. Once you've found a car that you're interested in, try to get the name and phone number of the previous owner. Contact that person for details about the car. If he or she refuses information about the car, shop elsewhere. A private seller can tell you about the car and its maintenance history, but there are few laws requiring honesty from private citizens who are selling used vehicles. There are laws forbidding the tampering with or turning back a vehicle's odometer mileage reading. These laws apply to both a private seller as well commercial dealers. The law also requires that the seller, or anyone transferring ownership of a vehicle, must provide the buyer with a signed statement indicating the mileage on the odometer at the time of transfer.

5. Write down the year, model and serial number of the car before you buy it. Then, dial 1–800–424–9393, the toll-free number of the National Highway Traffic Safety Administration, and ask if the car has ever been included on any manufacturer's recall list. If so, make sure the necessary repairs were made.

6. Use the Used Car Checklist in this section, and check all the items on the used car that you are considering. Some items are more important than others. You've already determined how much money you can afford for repairs, and, depending on the price of the car, you should consider doing some of the needed repairs yourself. Beware, however, of trouble in areas involving operation, safety or emissions. Problems in the Used Car Checklist are arranged as follows:

1–8: Two or more problems in this segment indicate a lack of maintenance. You should reconsider your selection.

9–13: Indicates a lack of proper care, however, these can usually be corrected with a tune-up or relatively simple parts replacement.

14–17: Problems in the engine or transmission can be very expensive. Walk away from any car with problems in these areas.

7. If you are satisfied with the apparent condition of the car, take it to an independent diagnostic center or mechanic for a complete checkout. If your state has a state inspection program, have it inspected immediately before purchase, or specify on the invoice that purchase is conditional on the car's passing a state inspection.

8. Road test the car. Refer to the Road Test Checklist in this section. If your original evaluation, and the road test agree, the rest is up to you.

Used Car Checklist

NOTE: *The numbers on the illustration correspond to the numbers in this checklist.*

1. *Mileage:* Average mileage is about 12,000

miles per year. More than average may indicate hard usage. Catalytic converter equipped models may need converter service beyond the 50,000 mile mark.

2. *Paint:* Check around the tailpipe, molding and windows for overspray, indicating that the car has been repainted.

3. *Rust:* Check fenders, doors, rocker panels, window moldings, wheelwells, flooring and in the bed, for signs of rust. Any rust at all will be a problem. There is no way to stop the spread of rust, except to replace the part or panel.

4. *Body Appearance:* Check the moldings, bumpers, grille, vinyl roof, glass, doors, tail gate and body panels for overall condition. Check for misalignment, loose holddown clips, ripples, scratches in the glass, rips or patches in the top. Mismatched paint, welding in the bed, severe misalignment of body panels or ripples may indicate crash work.

5. *Leaks:* Get down under the car and take a good look. There are no "normal" leaks, other than water from the air conditioning condenser drain tube.

6. *Tires:* Check the tire air pressure. A common trick is to pump the tires up hard to make the car roll more easily. Check the tread wear and the spare tire condition. Uneven wear is a sign that the front end is, or was, out of alignment. See the Troubleshooting Chapter for indications of treadwear.

7. *Shock Absorbers:* Check the shocks by forcing downward sharply on each corner of the car. Good shocks will not allow the car to rebound more than twice after you let go.

8. *Interior:* Check the entire interior. You're looking for an interior condition that agrees with the overall condition of the car. Reasonable wear can be expected, but be suspicious of new seatcovers on sagging seats, new pedal pads, and worn armrests. These indicate an attempt to cover up hard usage. Pull back the carpets and/or mats and look for signs of water leaks or flooding. Look for missing hardware, door handles, control knobs, etc. Check lights and signal operations. Make sure that all accessories, such as air conditioner, heater, radio, etc., work. Air conditioning, especially automatic temperature control units, can be very expensive to repair. Check the operation of the windshield wipers.

9. *Belts and Hoses:* Open the hood and check all belts and hoses for wear, cracks, or weak spots. Check around hose connections for stains, indicating leaks.

10. *Battery:* Low electrolyte level, corroded terminals and/or a cracked battery case, indicate a lack of maintenance.

11. *Radiator:* Look for corrosion or rust in the coolant, indicating a lack of maintenance.

12. *Air Filter:* A dirty air filter element indicates a lack of maintenance.

13. *Spark Plug Wires:* Check the wires for cracks, burned spots or wear. Worn wires will have to be replaced.

14. *Oil Level:* If the level is low, chances are that the engine either uses an excessive amount of oil, or leaks. If the oil on the dipstick appears foamy or tan in color, a leakage of coolant into the oil is indicated. Stop here, and go elsewhere for your car. If the oil appears thin or has the smell of gasoline, stop here and go elsewhere for your car.

15. *Automatic Transmission:* Pull the transmission dipstick out when the engine is running in PARK. If the fluid is hot, the dipstick should read FULL. If the fluid is cold, the level will show about one pint low. The fluid itself should be bright red and translucent, with no burned odor. Fluid that is brown or black and has a burned odor is a sign that the transmission needs major repairs.

16. *Exhaust:* Check the color of the exhaust smoke. Blue smoke indicates excessive oil usage, usually due to major internal engine problems. Black smoke can indicate burned valves or carburetor problems. Check the exhaust system for leaks. A leaky system is dangerous and expensive to replace.

17. *Spark Plugs:* Remove one of the spark plugs. An engine in good condition will have spark plugs with a light tan or gray deposit on the electrodes. See the color Tune-Up section for a complete analysis of spark plug condition.

Road Test Check List

1. *Engine Performance:* The car should have good accelerator response, whether cold or warm, with adequate power and smooth acceleration through the gears.

2. *Brakes:* Brakes should provide quick, firm stops, with no squealing, pulling or fade.

3. *Steering:* Sure control with no binding, harshness or looseness, and no shimmy in the wheel should be encountered. Noise or vibration from the steering wheel means trouble.

4. *Clutch:* Clutch action should be quick and smooth with easy engagement of the transmission.

5. *Manual Transmission:* The transmission should shift smoothly and crisply with easy change of gears. No clashing and grinding should be evident. The transmission should not stick in gear, nor should there be any gear whine evident at road speed.

6. *Automatic Transmission:* The transmission should shift rapidly and smoothly, with no noise, hesitation or slipping. The transmission

should not shift back and forth, but should stay in gear until an upshift or downshift is needed.

7. *Differential:* No noise or thumps should be present. No external leakage should be present.

8. *Driveshaft, Universal Joints:* Vibration and noise could mean driveshaft problems. Clicking at low speed or coast conditions means worn U-joints.

9. *Suspension:* Try hitting bumps at different speeds. A car that bounces has weak shock absorbers. Clunks mean worn bushings or ball joints.

10. *Frame:* Wet the tires and drive in a straight line. Tracks should show two straight lines, not four. Four tire tracks indicates a frame bent by collision damage. If the tires can't be wet for this purpose, have a friend drive along behind you and see if the car appears to be traveling in a straight line.

Tune-Up and Performance Maintenance

2

TUNE-UP PROCEDURES

The tune-up is a routine maintenance operation which is essential for the efficient and economical operation, as well as the long life, of your car's engine. The interval between tune-ups is a variable factor which depends upon the way you drive your car, the conditions under which you drive it (weather, road type, etc.) and the type of engine installed in your car. Manufacturer's recommended tune-up intervals should be followed if possible, but it is generally correct to say that no car should be driven more than 12,000 miles between tune-ups, especially in this age of emission controls and fuel shortages. Cars driven extremely hard or under severe weather conditions should be tuned at closer intervals.

The replacement parts involved in a tune-up include spark plugs, air filter, distributor cap, ignition points (if equipped), rotor, and spark plug wires. In addition to these parts and the adjustments involved in properly adapting them to your engine, there are several adjustments of other parts involved in completing the job. Included in these adjustments are carburetor, idle speed and air/fuel mixture, ignition timing, and valve clearance adjustments.

This chapter gives specific procedures on how to tune-up your 1200, B210 or 210 model Nissan, and Nissan Sentra. it is intended to be as complete as possible. Chapter 10, "Troubleshooting," is intended to go hand-in-hand with this chapter; it includes troubleshooting diagnosis for the more experienced owner/mechanic.

Tune up time is also a good time to look around the engine compartment for potential problems, such as fuel and oil leaks, cracking or hard radiator or heater hoses, loose or frayed belts, loose wire connections, etc.

CAUTION: *When working around a running engine, always be certain there is plenty of ventilation. Make sure the transmission is in Neutral (unless otherwise specified) and the parking brake is fully applied. Always keep hands, hair, and clothing away from the fan, hot manifolds and radiator. Remove any jewelry or neckties. When the engine is running, do not grasp the ginition wires, distributor cap or coil wire, as a shock in excess of 20,000 volts may result. Whenever working around the distributor, even if the engine is not running, make sure that the ignition is switched off. Removing or disturbing the distributor cap on an electronic ignition system with the ignition switch "on" can often cause the system to fire.*

For 1973–79 models, Nissan recommends a tune-up, including distributor points (unless equipped with electronic ignition), and spark plugs every 12,000 miles. In 1980 and on later models, Nissan and Nissan have been using a new, more durable spark plug in all models sold in the United States. Nissan recommends that the new plugs be replaced every 30,000 miles or 24 months, whichever comes first. (Of course, the Nissan plugs can be replaced with quality spark plugs from any major manufacturer). Certain Canadian 1980 and later Nissans still use the conventional 12 month, 12,000 mile plugs. Even though the manufacturer suggests such a long life span for the spark plugs on these models, it would be wise to remove, clean, inspect, and regap them every 12,000 miles.

Spark Plugs

A typical spark plug consists of a metal shell surrounding a ceramic insulator. A metal electrode extends downward through the center of the insulator and protrudes a small distance. Located at the end of the plug and attached to the side of the outer metal shell is the side electrode. The side electrode bends in at a 90 de-

When analyzing compression test results, look for uniformity among cylinders, rather than specific pressures.

| Year | Model | Spark Plug | | Distributor | | Ignition Timing (deg) | | Fuel Pump Pressure (psi) | Idle Speed (rpm) | | Valve Clearance | |
		Type	Gap (in.)	Point Dwell (deg)	Point Gap (in.)	MT	AT		MT	AT	In	Ex
1973	1200	BP5-ES	.034	49–55	.020	5B @ 700	5B @ 600	2.6	800	650	0.010 cold / 0.014 hot	0.010 cold / 0.014 hot
1974	B-210	BP5-ES	.033	49–55	.020	5B @ 800	5B @ 650	3.4	800	650	0.014 hot	0.014 hot
1975	B210 (Federal)	BP5-ES	.033	49–55	.020	10B	10B	3.8	700	650	0.014 hot	0.014 hot
	B210 (California)	BP6-ES	.033	Electronic	(1)	10B	10B	3.8	750	650	0.014 hot	0.014 hot
1976	B210 (Federal)	BP5-ES	.033	44–55	.020	10B	10B	3.8	700	650	0.014 hot	0.014 hot
	B210 (California)	BP5-ES	.033	Electronic	(1)	10B	10B	3.8	700	650	0.014 hot	0.014 hot
1977	B210 (Federal)	BP5-ES	.041	49–55	.020	10B	8B	3.8	700	650	0.014 hot	0.014 hot
	B210 (California)	BP5-ES	.041	Electronic	(1)	10B	10B	3.8	700	650	0.014 hot	0.014 hot
1978	B210 (except FU)	BP5-ES	.041	Electronic	(1)	10B	8B (2)	3.9	700	650	0.014 hot	0.014 hot
	B210 (FU model)	BP5-EQ	.047	Electronic	(1)	5B	—	3.9	700	—	0.014 hot	0.014 hot
1979	210	BP5-ES (6)	.041 (7)	Electronic	(1)	10B (3)(5)	8B (3)	3.8	700	650	0.014 hot	0.014 hot
1980	210	BP5-ES	.041	Electronic	(1)	10B (2)	8B	3.8	700	650	0.014 hot	0.014 hot
1981–82	210	BP5-ES11, BPR5-ES11	.041	Electronic	(1)	5B (8)	5B	3.8	700	650	0.014 hot	0.014 hot
1982	Sentra	BPR5ES-11	.041	Electronic	(1)	4A	6A	3.8	750	650	0.011 hot	0.011 hot
1983	Sentra	BPR5ES-11 (9)	.041 (10)	Electronic	(1)	5A (11)	5A	3.8	750	650	0.011 hot	0.011 hot
1984–86	Sentra	BPR5ES-11 (9)	.041 (10)	Electronic	(1)	15B (12)	8B (12)	3.8	800 (13)	650	0.011 hot	0.011 hot

NOTE: Emission control requires a very precise approach to tune-up. Timing and idle speed are peculiar to the engine and its application, rather than to the engine alone. Data for the particular application is on a sticker in the engine compartment on all late models. If the sticker disagrees with this chart, use the sticker figure. The results of any adjustment or modifications should be checked with a CO meter. On many 1980 cars, CO levels are not adjustable.

EFI: electronic fuel injection

NOTE: FU models are Hatchbacks with 5-speed transmissions sold in the U.S.A. except for California

(1) Electronic ignition—reluctor (air) gap: 0.008–0.016 in. (1975–78); 0.012–0.020 in. (1979–84)
(2) A14, A15 engine: 8B
(3) California models: 5B
(4) California: 10B
(5) FU model: 5B
(6) FU model: BP-5EQ
(7) FU model: 0.043–0.051 in.
(8) A12A with M/T, 10B; Canada 10B
(9) Canada: BPR5ES
(10) Canada: .033
(11) M.P.G. Model: 2A
(12) Calif. & Canada: 5A
(13) Calif. & Canada: 750

Diesel Engine Tune-Up Specifications

Year Model	Engine Displacement cu. in. (cc)	Warm Valve Clearance (in.)		Injection Pump Setting (deg)	Injection Nozzle Pressure (psi)		Idle Speed (rpm)	Compression Pressure (psi)
		In	Ex		New	Used		
'83–'85	102 (1680)	0.008–0.012	0.016–0.020	See Text	1,920–2,033	1,778–1,920	750	455 ①
'86	All			See Underhood Specification Sticker				

NOTE: The underhood specification sticker often reflects tune-up specification changes made in production. Sticker figures must be used if they disagree with those in this chart.
① At 200 rpm

gree angle so that its tip is even with, and parallel to, the tip of the center electrode. The distance between these two electrodes (measured in thousandths of an inch) is called the spark plug gap. The spark plug in no way produces a spark but merely provides a gap across which the current can arc. The coil produces anywhere from 20,000 to 40,000 volts, which travels to the distributor where it is distributed through the spark plug wires to the spark plugs. The current passes along the center electrode and jumps the gap to the side electrode, and, in so doing, ignites the air/fuel mixture in the combustion chamber.

Spark plug life and efficiency depend upon the condition of the engine and the temperatures to which the plug is exposed. Combustion chamber temperatures are affected by many factors such as compression ratio of the engine, air/fuel mixtures, exhaust emission equipment, and the type of driving you do. Spark plugs are designed and classified by number according to the heat range at which they will operate most efficiently.

SPARK PLUG HEAT RANGE

Spark Plug heat range is actually quite simple: the amount of heat the plug absorbs is determined by the length of the lower insulator. The longer the insulator (or the farther it extends into the engine), the hotter the plug will operate; the shorter the insulator the coller it will operate. A plug that absorbs little heat and remains too cool will quickly accumulate deposits of oil and carbon since it is not hot enough to burn them off. This leads to plug fouling and consequently to misfiring. A plug that absorbs too much heat will have no deposits, but, due to the excessive heat, the electrodes will burn away quickly and in some instance, preignition may result. Preignition takes place when plug tips get so hot that they glow sufficiently to ignite the fuel/air mixture before the actual spark occurs. This early ignition will usually cause a pinging during low speeds and heavy loads. In severe cases, the heat may become high enough to start the fuel/air mixture burning throughout the combustion chamber rather than just to the front of the plug as in normal operation. At this time, the piston is rising in the cylinder making its compression stroke. The burning mass is compressed and an explosion results, forcing the piston back down in the cylinder while it is still trying to go up. Obviously, something must go, and it does: pistons are often damaged.

The general rule of thumb for choosing the correct heat range when picking a spark plug is: if most of your driving is long distance high

THE SHORTER THE PATH, THE FASTER THE HEAT IS DISSIPATED AND THE COOLER THE PLUG.

THE LONGER THE PATH, THE SLOWER THE HEAT IS DISSIPATED AND THE HOTTER THE PLUG.

HEAVY LOADS, HIGH SPEEDS

SHORT TRIP STOP-AND-GO

SHORT Insulator Tip
Fast Heat Transfer
LOWER Heat Range
COLD PLUG

LONG Insulator Tip
Slow Heat Transfer
HIGHER Heat Range
HOT PLUG

Spark plug heat range

speed travel, use a colder plug; if most of your driving is stop and go, use a hottter plug. Factoryinstalled plugs are, of course compromise plugs, since the factory has no way of knowing what sort of driving you do. It should be noted that most people never have occasion to change their plugs from a factoryrecommended heat range, but if you spend most of your driving on the highway or around town, you may want to try a set of cooler or hotter than normal spark plugs and run them until the next tune up. Then check the condition of the plugs, comparing them to the color photos in the center of this book.

REMOVAL AND INSTALLATION

1. Grasp the spark plug boot and pull it straight out. Don't pull on the wire. If the boot(s) are cracked, replace them.
2. Place the spark plug socket firmly on the plug. Turn the spark plug out of the cylinder head in a counterclockwise direction.
NOTE: *The Nissan cylinder head is aluminum, which is easily stripped. Remove plugs only when the engine is cold.*
Removal should not be difficult, but if it is loosen the plug only slightly and drip penetrating oil onto the threads. Allow the oil time enough to work and then unscrew the plug. Proceeding in this manner will prevent damaging the threads in the cylinder head. Be sure to keep the socket straight to avoid breaking the ceramic insulator.
3. Continue and remove the remaining spark plugs.
4. Inspect the plugs using the "color center" section illustrations and then clean or discard them according to condition.
New spark plugs come pregapped, but always double check the setting. The recommended spark plug gap is listed in the "Tune-UP Specifications" Chart. Use a spark plug

Correct method of removing spark plug wires on left. Pulling the wire instead of the boot on the right is incorrect

SPARK PLUG WRENCH

Keep the plug socket square on the spark plug

SIDE ELECTRODE

GAP

Check the spark plug gap with a wire gauge

wire gauge for checking the gap. The wire should pass through the electrode with just a slight drag. Avoid adjusting the plug gap with a flat-bladed feeler gauge; a false reading could result. Using the electrode bending tool on the end of the gauge, bend the side electrode to adjust the gap. Never attempt to adjust the center electrode. Lightly oil the threads of the replacement plug and install it hand-tight. It is a good practice to use a torque wrench to tighten the spark plugs on any car and especially on the Nissan, since the head is aluminum. Torque the spark plugs to 14–22 ft.lb. Install the ignition wire boots firmly on the spark plugs.

CHECKING AND REPLACING SPARK PLUG CABLES

Visually inspect the spark plug cables for burns, cuts, or any breaks in the insulation. Check the spark plug boots and the rubber nipples on the distributor and coil for the same. Any damaged wiring must be replaced.

If there is no obvious physical damage to the wires, check them for excessive resistance with an ohmmeter:

1. Remove the distributor cap and leave the wires connected to the cap.

2. Connect one lead of the ohmmeter to the corresponding electrode inside the cap and the other lead to the spark plug terminal (remove it from the spark plug for the test).

3. Replace any wire that shows over $50,000\Omega$ (resistance should not run over $35,000\Omega$ and $50,000\Omega$ should be considered the outer limits of acceptability).

Test the coil wire by connecting the ohmmeter between the center contact in the cap, and either of the primary terminals at the coil. If the total resistance of the coil and cable is more than $25,000\Omega$, remove the cable from the coil and check the resistance of the cable alone. If the resistance is higher than $15,000\Omega$, replace the cable.

It should be remembered that wire resistance is a function of length. The longer the cable the greater the resistance. Thus, if your cables are longer than factory originals, their resistance could be greater.

When installing a new set of spark plug cables, replace the calbes one at a time so there will be no mixup. Start by replacing the longest cable first. Install the boot firmly over the spark plug. Route the wire exactly the same as the original. Insert the nipple firmly into the twoer on the distributor cap. Repeat the process for each cable.

Connect an ohmmeter between the spark plug terminal (in boot) and the electrode inside the cap to check spark plug cable resistance

Breaker Points and Condenser

NOTE: *Nissan California B210 models manufactured in 1975–77, and all 1978 and later B210, 210 and Sentra models are equipped with electronic, breakerless ignition* systems. *The 1200 series and the non-California B210 models prior to 1978 have the point type ignition systems. The following section covers maintenance procedures for these points systems.*

INSPECTION OF THE POINTS

1. Disconnect the high tension wire from the top of the distributor and the coil.

2. Remove the distributor cap by prying off the spring clips on the sides of the cap.

3. Remove the rotor from the distributor shaft by poulling it straight up. Examine the condition of the rotor. If it is cracked or the metal tip is excessively worn or burned, it should be replaced. Clean the tip with fine emery paper.

4. Pry open the contacts of the points with a screwdriver and check the condition of the contacts. If they are excessively worn, burned or pitted, they should be replaced.

5. If the points are in good condition, adjust them and replace the rotor and the distributor cap. If the points need to be replaced, follow the replacement procedure given below.

REPLACEMENT OF THE BREAKER POINTS AND CONDENSER

1. Remove the coil high tension wire from the top of the distributor cap. Remove the distributor cap and place it out of the way. Remove the rotor from the distributor shaft by pulling up.

NOTE: *A magnetic screwdriver or one with a holding (locking) mechanism is very handy here and for all ignition work. Most screws used for points and other distributor assemblies are very small, hard to handle, and easily dropped. A locking or magnetic screwdriver makes removal and installation of these screws safer and much easier. A screw dropped into a distributor body usually means having to remove the entire distributor to retrieve the screw.*

2. Remove the condenser from the distributor body. Remove the points assembly attaching screws and then remove the points. A magnetic screwsriver or one with a holding mechanism will come in handy here. After the points are removed, wipe off the cam and apply new cam lubricant. If you don't the points will wear out in a few thousand miles.

3. Slip the new set of points onto the locating dowel and install the screws that hold the assembly onto the plate. Don't tighten them all the way yet, since you'll only have to loosen them to set the point gap.

4. Install the new condenser on single point models and attach the condenser lead to the points.

5. Set the point gap and dwell (see the following sections).

ADJUSTMENT OF THE BREAKER POINTS WITH A FEELER GAUGE

1. If the contact points of the assembly are not parallel, bend the stationary contact so that they make contact across the entire surface of the contacts. Bend only the stationary bracket part of the point assembly; not the movable contact.

2. Turn the engine until the rubbing block of the points is on one of the high points of the distributor cam. You can do this by either turning the ignition switch to the start position and releasing it quickly ("bumping" the engine) or by using a wrench on the bolt which holds the crankshaft pulley to the crankshaft.

3. Place the correct size feeler gauge between the contacts (see the Tune-Up Chart). Make sure that it is parallel with the contact surfaces.

4. Loosen both contact plate attaching screws just enough that the contact plate and points gap can be adjusted with the adjusting screw.

5. While holding the feeler gauge in one hand between the points contacts, insert a screwdriver into the eccentric adjusting screw with the other hand. Turn the adjusting screw to either increase or decrease the gap to the proper setting. When the correct gap is found, there should be a moderate drag on the feeler gauge as you pass it through both contacts.

6. Tighten both contact plate attaching screws while still holding the feeler gauge be-

1. Primary lead terminal
2. Ground lead wire
3. Set screw
4. Adjuster
5. Screw

Adjusting screws and lead connections, points type distributor

Turn eccentric screw to get correct point gap. Feeler gauge should slide between the contacts with a slight drag

tween the contacts. Turn the engine through one complete revolution until the points are at maximum "open" again. Recheck the gap; when you are stisfied with it, make sure both contact plate screws are secure.

7. Replace the rotor and distributor cap, and the high tension wire which connects the top of the distributor and the coil. Make sure that the rotor is firmly seated all the way onto the distributor shaft and that the tab of the rotor is aligned with notch in the shaft. Align the tab in the base of the distributor cap with the notch in the distributor body. Make sure that the cap is firmly seated on the distributor and that the retainer clips are in place. Make sure that the end of the high tension wire is firmly placed in the top of the distributor and the coil.

Dwell Angle

The dwell angle or cam angle is the number of degrees that the distributor cam rotates while the points are closed. There is an inverse relationship between dwell angle and point gap. Increasing the point gap will decrease the dwell angle and vice versa. Checking the dwell angle with a meter is a far more accurate method of measuring point opening than the feeler gauge method.

After setting the point gap to specification with a feeler gauge as described above, check the dwell angle with a meter. Attach the dwell meter according to the manufacturer's instruction sheet. The negative lead is grounded and the positive lead is connected to the primary wire terminal which runs from the coil to the distributor. Start the engine, let it idle and reach operating temperature, and observe the dwell on the meter. The reading should fall within the allowable range (see Tune Up spec chart). If it does not, the gap will have to be reset or the breaker points will have to be replaced.

ADJUSTMENT OF THE BREAKER POINTS WITH A DWELL METER

1. Adjust the points with a feeler gauge as previously described.
2. Connect the dwell meter to the ignition circuit as according to the manufacturer's instructions. One lead of the meter is connected to a ground and the other lead is connected to the distributor post on the coil. An adapter is usually provided for this purpose.
3. If the dwell meter has a set line on it, adjust the meter to zero the indicator.
4. Start the engine.
NOTE: *Be careful when working on any vehicle while the engine is running. Make sure that the transmission is in Neutral and that the parking brake is applied. Keep hands, clothing, tools and the wires of the test instruments clear of the rotating fan blades.*
5. Observe the reading on the dwell meter. If the reading is within the specified range, turn off the engine and remove the dwell meter.
NOTE: *If the meter does not have a scale for 4 cylinder engines, multiply the 8 cylinder reading by two.*
6. If the reading is above the specified range, the breaker point gap is too small. If the reading is below the specified range, the gap is too large. In either case, the engine must be stopped and the gap adjusted in the manner previously covered.
After making the adjustment, start the engine and check the reading on the dwell meter. When the correct reading is obtained, disconnect the dwell meter.
7. Check the adjustment of the ignition timing.

Nissan Electronic Ignition

In 1975, in order to comply with California's tougher emissions laws, Nissan introduced electronic ignition systems for all models sold in that state. Since that time, the Nissan and Nissan electronic ignition system has undergone a metamorphosis from a standard transistorized circuit (1975–1978) to an Integrated Circuit system (IC), 1979 and later. Some Canadian 210's with the A12A engine continue to use the points type ignition system.

The electronic ignition system differs from the conventional breaker points system in form only; its function is exactly the same: to supply a spark to the spark plugs at precisely the right moment to ignite the compressed gas in the cylinders and create mechanical movement.

Located in the distributor, in addition to the

normal rotor cap, is a spoked rotor (reluctor) which fits on the distributor shaft where the breaker points cam is found on nonelectronic ignitions. The rotor (reluctor) revolves with

the top rotor cap and, as it passes a pickup coil inside the distributor body, breaks a high flux phase which occurs while the space between the reluctor spokes passes the pickup coil. This

1. Cap	7. Breaker plate	13. Vacuum control assembly
2. Rotor	8. Cam assembly	14. Terminal assembly
3. Condenser	9. Governor spring	15. Clamp
4. Ground wire	10. Governor weight	16. Retaining plate
5. Lead wire	11. Thrust washer	17. Gear set
6. Breaker points	12. Shaft assembly	

Exploded view of points type distributor

IC (electronic) ignition distributor, 1979 and later A-series. Sentra unit similar

1979–80 IC ignition system. 1980 210 shown

allows current to flow to the pickup coil. Primary ignition current is then cut off by the electronic ignition unit, allowing the magnetic field in the ignition coil to collapse, creating the spark which the distributor passes on to the spark plug.

The 1979 and later IC ignition system uses a ring-type pickup coil which surrounds the reluctor instead of the single post type pickup coil on earlier models.

Because no points or condenser are used, and because dwell is determined by the electronic unit, no adjustments are necessary. Ignition timing is checked in the usual way, but unless the distributor is distrubed it is not likely to ever change very much.

Service consists of inspection of the distributor cap, rotor, and ignition wires, replacing when necessary. These parts can be expected to last at least 40,000 miles. In addition, the reluctor air gap should be checked periodically.

ELECTRONIC IGNITION MAINTENANCE

1. The distributor cap is held on by two clips. Release them with a screwdriver and lift the cap straight up and off, with the wires attached. Inspect the cap for cracks, carbon tracks, or a worn center contact. Replace it if necessary, transferring the wires one at a time from the old cap to the new.

2. Pull the ignition rotor (not the spoked reluctor) straight up to remove. Replace it if its contacts are worn, burned, or pitted. Do not file the contacts. To replace, press it firmly onto the shaft. It only goes on one way, so be sure it is fully seated.

3. Before replacing the ignition rotor, check the reluctor air gap. Use a non-magnetic feeler gauge. Rotate the engine until a reluctor spoke is aligned with the pick-up coil (either bump the engine around with the starter, or turn it with a wrench on the crankshaft pulley bolt). The gap should measure 0.008–0.016 in. through 1978, or 0.012–0.020 in. for 1979 and later. Adjustment, if necessary, is made by loosening the pickup coil closer to or farther from the reluctor. On 1979 and later models, center the pickup coil (ring) around the reluctor. Tighten the screws and recheck the gap.

4. Inspect the wires for cracks or brittleness. Replace them one at a time to prevent crosswiring, carefully pressing the replacement wires into place. The cores of electronic wires are more susceptible to breakage than those of standard wires, so treat them gently.

TROUBLESHOOTING

1975–78

The main differences between the 1975–77 and 1978 systems are: (1) the 1975–77 system uses an external ballast resistor located next to the ignition coil, and (2) the earlier system uses a wiring harness with individual eyelet connectors to the electronic unit, while the later system uses a multiple plug connector. You will need an accurate voltmeter and ohmmeter for these tests, which must be performed in the order given.

1. Check all connections for corrosion, looseness, breaks, etc., and correct if necessary. Clean and gap the spark plugs.

2. Disconnect harness (connector or plug) from the electronic unit. Turn the ignition switch On. Set the voltmeter to the DC 50v range. Connect the positive (+) voltmeter lead to the back/white wire terminal, and the negative (–) lead to the black wire terminal. Battery voltage should be obtained. If not, check the black/white and black wires for continuity; check the battery terminals for corrosion; check the battery state of charge.

3. Next, connect the voltmeter + lead to the blue wire and the – lead to the black wire. Battery voltage should be obtained. If not, check the blue wire for continuity; check the ignition coil terminals for corrosion or looseness; check the coil for continuity. On 1975–77 models, leaving the ballast resistor-to-coil wires attached. On 1978 models, disconnect the ignition coil wires. Connect the leads of an ohmmeter to the ballast resistor outside terminals (at each end) for 1975–77, and to the two coil terminals for 1978. With the ohmmeter set in the X1 range, the 1975–78 B210 should show a reading of approximately 0Ω. The maximum allowable limit for the 0Ω models is 1.8Ω. If a reading higher than the limit is received, replace the ignition coil assembly.

4. Disconnect the harness from the electronic control unit. Connect an ohmmeter to the red and green wire terminals. Resistance should be 720Ω. If far more or far less, replace the distributor pick-up coil.

5. Disconnect the anti-diesling solenoid connector (see Chapter 4). Connect a voltmeter to the red and green terminals of the electronic control harness. When the starter is cranked, the needle should deflect slightly. If not, replace the distributor pick-up coil.

6. Reconnect the ignition coil and the electronic control unit. Leave the anti-dieseling solenoid wire disconnected. Unplug the high tension lead (coil to distributor) from the distributor and hold it $1/8$–$1/2$ in. from the cylinder head with a pair of insulated pliers and a heavy

glove. When the engine is cranked, a spark should be observed. If not, check the lead, and replace if necessary. If still no spark, replace the electronic control unit.

7. Reconnect all wires.

1976–77: connect the voltmeter + lead to the blue electronic control harness connector and the – lead to the black wire. The harness should be attached to the control unit.

1978: connect the voltmeter + lead to the – terminal of the ignition coil and the – lead to ground.

As soon as the ignition switch is turned On, the meter should indicate battery voltage. If not, replace the electronic control unit.

1979 and Later

1. Make a check of the power supply circuit. Turn the ignition OFF. Disconnect the connector from the top of the IC unit. Turn the ignition ON. Measure the voltage at each terminal of the connector in turn by touching the probe of the positive lead of the voltmeter to one of the terminals, and touching the probe of the negative lead of the voltmeter to a ground, such as the engine. In each case, battery voltage should be indicated. If not, check all wiring, the ignition switch, and all connectors for breaks, corrosion, discontinuity, etc., and repair as necessary.

2. Check the primary windings of the ignition coil. Turn the ignition OFF. Disconnect the harness connector from the negative coil terminal. Use an ohmmeter to measure the resistance between the positive and negative coil terminals. If resistance is 0.84–1.02Ω (1.04–1.27Ω on the Sentra the coil is OK. Replace it if far from this range.)

If the power supply, circuits, wiring, and coil are in good shape, check the IC unit and pick-up coil, as follows:

3. Turn the ignition OFF. Remove the distributor cap and ignition rotor. Use an ohmmeter to measure the resistance between the two terminals of the pick-up coil, where they attach to the IC unit. Measure the resistance by reversing the polarity of the probes. If approximately 400Ω are indicated, the pick-up coil is OK, but the IC unit is bad and must be replaced. If other than 400Ω are measured, go to the next Step.

4. Be certain the two pin connector to the IC unit is secure. Turn the ignition ON.

Measure the voltage at the ignition coil negative terminal. Turn the ignition OFF.

CAUTION: *Remove the tester probe from the coil negative terminal before switching the ignition OFF, to prevent burning out the tester.*

If zero voltage is indicated, the IC unit is bad

Checking air gap, electronic ignition distributors

and must be replaced. If battery voltage is indicated, proceed.

5. Remove the IC unit from the distributor:

a. Disconnect the battery ground (negative) cable.

b. Remove the distributor cap and ignition rotor.

c. Disconnect the harness connector at the top of the IC unit.

d. Remove the two screws securing the IC unit to the distributor.

e. Disconnect the two pick-up coil wires from the IC unit.

CAUTION: *Pull the connectors free with a pair of needlenosed pliers. Do not pull on the wires to detach the connectors.*

f. Remove the IC unit.

6. Measure the resistance between the terminals of the pick-up coil. It should be approximately 400Ω. If so, the pick-up coil is OK, and the IC unit is bad. If not approximately 400Ω, the pick-up coil is bad and must be replaced.

7. With a new pick-up coil installed, install the IC unit. Check for a spark at one of the spark plugs (see Chapter 10). If a good spark is obtained, the IC unit is OK. If not, replace the IC unit.

Ignition Timing

Ignition timing is an important part of the tune-up. It is always adjusted after the points are gapped (dwell angle changed), since altering the dwell affects the timing. Three basic types of timing lights are available, the neon, the DC, and the AC powered. Of the three, the inductive DC light is the most frequently used by professional tuners. The bright flash put out by the DC light makes the timing marks stand out on even the brightest of days. Another advantage of the DC light is that you don't need to be near an electrical outlet. Neon lights are available for a few dollars, but their weak flash makes it necessary to use them in a fairly dark work area. One neon light lead is attached to the spark plug and the other to the plug wire. The DC light attaches to the spark plug and the wire with an adapter and two clips attached to the battery posts for power. The AC unit is similar, except that the power cable is plugged into a hous outlet.

CAUTION: *When performing this or any other operation with the engine running, be very careful of the alternator belt and pulleys. Make sure that your timing light wires don't interfere with the belt.*

Ignition timing is the measurement, in degrees of crankshaft rotation, of the point at which the spark plugs fire in each of the cylinders. It is measured in degrees before or after Top Dead Center (TDC) of the compression stroke. Ignition timing is adjusted by turning the distributor body in the engine.

Ideally, the air/fuel mixture in the cylinder will be ignited by the spark plug just as the piston passes TDC of the compression stroke. If this happens, the piston will be beginning its downward motion of the power stroke just as the compressed and ignited air'fuel mixture starts to expand. The expansion of the air/fuel mixture then forces the piston down on the power stroke and turns the crankshaft.

Because it takes a fraction of a second for the spark plug to ignite the mixture in the cylinder, the spark plug must fire a little before the piston reaches TDC. Otherwise, the mixture will not be completely ignited as the piston passes TDC and the full power of the explosion will not be used by the engine.

The timing measurement is given in degrees of crankshaft rotation before the piston reaches TDC (BTDC). If the setting for the ignition timing is 5° BTDC (5B), the spark plug must fire 5° before each piston reaches TDC. This only holds true, however, when the engine is at idle speed.

As the engine speed increases, the pistons go faster. The spark plugs have to ignite the fuel even sooner if it is to be completely ignited when the piston reaches TDC. To do this, the distributor has a means to advance the timing of the spark as the engine speed increases. This is accomplished by centrifugal weights within the distributor and a vacuum diaphragm, mounted on the side of the distributor. It is necessary to disconnect the vacuum line from the diaphragm when the ignition timing is being set.

If the ignition is set too far advanced (BTDC), the ignition and expansion of the fuel in the cylinder will occur too soon and tend to force the piston down while it is still travelling up. This causes engine ping. If the ignition spark is set too far retarded, after TDC (ATDC), the piston will have already passed TDC and started on its way down when the fuel is ignited. This will cause the piston to be forced down for only a postion of its travel, resulting in poor engine performance and lack of power.

The timing is best checked with a timing light. This device is connected in series with the No. 1 spark plug. The current which first the spark plug also causes the timing light to flash.

The timing marks are located at the front crankshaft pulley and consist of a notch on the crankshaft pulley and a scale of degrees of crankshaft rotation attached to the front cover.

When the engine is running, the timing light is aimed at the marks on the flywheel pulley and the pointer.

IGNITION TIMING ADJUSTMENT

NOTE: *Nissan does not give ignition timing adjustments for 1980 and later California Nissans and Nissans. The procedure has been discontinued.*

1. Set the dwell to the proper specification.
2. Locate the timing marks on the crankshaft pulley and the front of the engine.
3. Clean off the timing marks so that you can see them (the numbers correspond to degrees before and after Top Dead Center).
4. Use chalk or white paint to color the mark on the crankshaft pulley and the mark on the scale which will indicate the correct timing when aligned with the notch on the crankshaft pulley.
5. Attach a tachometer to the engine (some dwell meters have a tachometer built in).
6. Attach a timing light to the engine, according to the manufacturer's instructions.
7. Leave the vacuum line connected to the distributor vacuum diaphragm on all models except 1979 210 wagons equipped with the A15 engine and automatic transmission, and all 1980 and later 210's and Sentra. Plug disconnected vacuum hoses with golf tees. On Canadian 210 models and Sentra, disconnect the air induction hose from the air cleaner, cap or plug the air pipe.
8. Check to make sure that all of the wires clear the fan and then start the engine. Allow the engine to reach normal operating temperature.
9. Adjust the idle to the correct rpm setting.
10. Aim the timing light at the timing marks. If the marks that you put on the pulley and the engine are aligned when the light flashes, the timing is correct. Turn off the engine and remove the tachometer and the timing light. If the marks are not in alignment, proceed with the following steps:
11. Turn off the engine.
12. Loosen the distributor lockbolt just

Checking ignition timing with timing light. Timing marks shown at left

enough so that the distributor can be turned with a little effort.

13. Start the engine. Keep the wires of the timing light clear of the fan.

14. With the timing light aimed at the pulley and the marks on the engine, turn the distributor in the direction of rotor rotation to retard the spark, and in the opposite direction of rotor rotation to advance the spark.

15. Align the marks on the pulley and the engine with the flashes of the timing light.

16. Tighten the distributor holddown bolt when proper timing is found.

Sentra (E-series) distributor timing adjustment showing adjusting locknut

Valve Lash

Valve adjustment determines how far the valves enter the cylinder and how long they stay open and closed.

If the valve clearance is too large, part of the lift of the camshaft will be used in removing the excessive clearance. Consequently, the valve will not be opening as far as it should. This condition has two effects: the valve train components will emit a tapping sound as they take up the excessive clearance and the engine

will peform poorly because the valves don't open fully and allow the proper amount of gases to flow into and out of the engine.

If the valve clearance is too small, the intake valves and the exhaust valves will open too far and they will not fully seat on the cylinder head when they close. When a valve seats itself on the cylinder head, it does two things: it seals the combustion chamber so that none of the gasses in the cylinder escape and it cools itself by transferring some of the heat it absorbs from the combustion in the cylinder to the cylinder head and to the engine's cooling system. If the valve clearance is too small, the engine will run poorly because of the gases escaping from the combustion chamber. The valves will also become overheated and will warp, since they cannot transfer heat unless they are touching the valve seat in the cylinder head.

NOTE: *While all valve adjustments must be made as accurately as possible, it is better to have the valve adjustment slightly loose than slightly tight, as a burned valve may result from overly tight adjustments.*

This holds true for valve adjustments on most engines.

VALVE ADJUSTMENT

All Except Sentra

1. Run the engine until it reaches normal operating temperature. Oil temperature, not water temperature, is critical to valve adjustment. With this in mind, make sure the engine is fully warmed up since this is the only way to make sure the parts have reached their full expansion. Generally speaking, this takes around fifteen minutes. After the engine has reached normal operating temperature, shut it off.

2. Purchase a new valve cover gasket before removing the valve cover. The new silicone

Adjusting A-series valve clearances

gasket sealers, available in tubes, are just as good or better if you can't find a gasket. Remove valve cover.

3. Note the location of any hoses or wires which may interfere with valve cover removal, disconnect them and move them aside. Then, remove the bolts which hold the valve cover in place.

4. After the valve cover has been removed, the next step is to get the number one piston at TDC on the compression stroke. There are at least two ways to do it; you can bump the engine over with the starter or turn it over by using a wrench on the front pulley attaching bolt. The easiest way to find TDC is to turn the engine over slowly with a wrench (after first removing no. 1 plug) until the piston is at the top of its stroke and the TDC timing mark on the crankshaft pulley is in alignment with the timing mark pointer. Make sure transmission is in Neutral and battery ground cable is disconnected. At this point, the valves for No. 1 cylinder should be checked.

NOTE: *Make sure both valves are closed with the valve springs up as high as they will go. An easy way to find the compression stroke is to remove the distributor cap and see toward which spark plug lead the rotor is pointing. If the rotor points to number one spark plug lead, number one cylinder is on its compression stroke. When the rotor points to number two spark plug lead, number two cylinder is on its compression stroke, etc.*

5. With no. 1 piston at TDC of the compression stroke, check the clearance on valves Nos. 1, 2, 3, and 5 (counting from the front to the rear).

6. To adjust the clearance, loosen the locknut with a wrench and turn the adjuster with a screwdriver while holding the locknut. The correct size feeler gauge should pass with a slight drag between the rocker arm and the valve stem.

7. Turn the crankshaft one full revolution to position the no. 4 piston at TDC of the compres-

sion stroke. Adjust valves nos. 4, 6, 7, and 8 in the same manner as the first four.

8. Replace the valve cover.

Sentra Gasoline Engine

1. Start engine and run it until normal operating temperature has been reached (usually after about fifteen minutes). Turn off the engine.

2. Remove air cleaner securing bolts, disconnect air cleaner hoses and remove air cleaner.

3. Remove the valve rocker cover.

4. Rotate the crankshaft pulley until TDC of the compression stroke of No. 1 cylinder is found (see valve adjustment procedure for the 1200/B210 series for more details on finding TDC).

5. With the No. 1 piston at Top Dead Center on its compression stroke, adjust valve clearance of valves 1, 2, 3 and 6 (see valve arrangement diagram). Adjust the valve by loosening the rocker adjusting screw locknut, inserting the proper feeler gauge between the rocker and the end of the valve stem, and turning the adjusting screw until the specified clearance (0.011 in.) is obtained. After adjustment, tighten the locknut and recheck the clearance (the feeler gauge should drag slightly but should not be tight).

6. Set the No. 4 cylinder at TDC of its compression stroke and adjust valve clearance of valves 4, 5, 7 and 8.

7. Replace the rocker cover, using a new gasket. Replace the air cleaner assembly.

Sentra gasoline engine valve arrangement

Sentra Diesel Engine

1. Run the engine to normal operating temperature.

2. Shut off the engine and remove the valve cover.

3. Turn the crankshaft until #1 piston is at TDC of the compression stroke.

4. The folloiwng valves may now be adjusted:

#1 intake and exhaust
#2 intake

Valve adjusting shim

Inserting shim magnet

Special tool for adjusting valves

Adjusting the Sentra valves. There should be a slight drag on the feeler gauge

#3 exhaust

5. Measure the clearance between the cam lobe and the lifter. Valve clearance should be adjusted one valve at a time. Adjustment is made by removing or adding shims in the lift-

er. Lifters are removed or added, not at TDC, nut ¼ turn PAST TDC, in the normal direction of the rotation. A special tool, Nissan #KV11102600 is used. The tool should be inserted from the injector nozzle side of the head. The lifter has a cutout portion to aid in removing the shim. Turn the lifter so that this cutout is on the nozzle side. The shim should be stamped with their size, in millimeters. If, when you measure the clearance, you find that an adjustment is needed, remove the shim, note what size it is and determine what size you need to correct the gap.

Intake: 0.008–0.012 in.
Exhaust: 0.016–0.020 in.

6. Turn the crankshaft until #4 piston is at TDC compression. The following valves may now be adjusted:

#2 exhaust
#3 intake
#4 intake and exhaust

Carburetor

IDLE SPEED AND MIXTURE ADJUSTMENT

Gasoline Engine

NOTE: *1980 and later model Nissans require a CO Meter to adjust their mixture ratios, therefore no procedures concerning this adjustment are give. Also, many model Nissans have a plug over their mixture control screw. It is suggested that on these models mixture adjustment be left to a qualified technician.*

1. Start the engine and allow it to run until it reaches normal operating temperature.

2. Allow the engine idle speed to stabilize by running the engine at idle for at least two minutes.

3. If you have not done so already, check and adjust the ignition timing to the proper setting.

4. Shut off the engine and connect a tachometer.

5. Disconnect and plug the air hose between the three way connector and the check valve, if equipped. On 1980 and later models, disconnect the air induction hose to the air cleaner and plug the pipe. With the transmission in Neutral, check the idle speed on the tachometer. If the reading is correct, continue on to Step 6 for 1973–79 Nissans. For 1980 and later, and certain California models, proceed to step 10 below if the idle is correct. If the idle is not correct, for all 1200, B210 and 210 models, turn the idle speed adjusting screw clockwise with a screwdriver to increase idle speed or counterclockwise to decrease it, until the prop-

er idle speed is achieved. On Sentra, turn the throttle adjusting screw.

6. With the automatic transmission in Drive (wheels blocked and parking brake on) or the manual transmission in Neutral, turn the mixture screw out until the engine rpm starts to drop due to an overly rich mixture (transmission placed in Drive in order to put a load on the engine for this procedure).

CAUTION: *While making the idle adjustments on automatic transmission cars (transmission in "Drive"), DO NOT race the engine, or even raise the rpm above those engine speeds recommended. The parking brake and wheel chocks cannot be expected to hold the car in this situation, and injury and/or damage will most certainly occur. Before racing the engine, place the transmission in Neutral, make sure the parking brake is firmly applied and the wheels chocked.*

7. Turn the adjusting screw until just before the rpm starts to drop due to an overly lean mixture. Turn the mixture screw in until the idle speed drops 60–70 rpm with manual transmission, or 15–25 rpm with automatic transmission (in Drive) for 1975–76 B210; 35–45 rpm with manual transmission or 10–20 rpm with automatic for 1977–78 B210, 1979 210. If the mixture limiter cap will not allow this adjustment, remove it, make the adjustment, and re-install it. Go on to step 10 for all 1975–79 models.

A-series mixture screw. Note limiter tab

8. On 1973–74 models, turn the mixture screw back out to the point midway between the two extreme positions where the engine began losing rpm to achieve the fastest and smoothest idle.

9. Adjust the curb idle speed to the proper specification, on 1973–74 models, with tidle speed adjusting screw.

10. Install the air hose. If the engine speed increases, reduce it with the idle speed screw until a smooth idle as listed in the Tune-Up specifications chart is achieved.

Diesel Engine

NOTE: *A special tachometer compatible with diesel engines will be required for this procedure. A normal tachometer will not work.*

1. Make sure all electrical accessories are turned off.

THROTTLE ADJUSTING SCREW

Throttle adjusting screw, Sentra carburetor

1. Throttle adjusting screw
2. Idle adjusting screw
3. Idle limiter cap
4. Stopper

Carburetor adjusting screws, A-series engines

Loosen the idle screw locknut while holding the control lever—diesel engine

Idle speed adjusting screw—diesel engines

CD17 idle speed adjustment

2. The automatic transmission (if so equipped) should be in "D" with the parking brake on and the wheels blocked.

3. Start the engine and run it until it reaches the normal operating temperature.

4. Attach the diesel tachometer's pickup to the No. 1 injection tube.

NOTE: *In order to obtain a more accurate reading of the idle speed, you may wish to remove all the clamps on the No. 1 injection tube.*

5. Run the enigne at about 2,000 rpm for two minutes under no-load conditions.

6. Slow the engine down to idle speed for about 1 min. and then check the idle.

7. If the engine is not idling at the proper speed, turn it off and disconnect the accelerator wire from the injection pump control lever.

NOTE: *It is not necessary to disconnect the accelerator wire on the CD17.*

8. Move the control lever to the full acceleration side, and then loosen the idle screw lock nut while still holding the control lever.

9. Start the engine again and turn the adjusting screw until the proper idle is obtained. Stop the engine.

10. Tighten the idle adjusting screw locknut while still holding the control level to the full acceleration side and then connect the accelerator wire.

ENGINE ELECTRICAL

Distributor

REMOVAL

All models

1. Unfasten the retaining clips and lift the distributor cap straight up. It will be easier to install the distributor if the wiring is not disconnected from the cap. If the wires must be removed from the cap, mark their positions to aid in installation.

2. Disconnect the distributor wiring harness.

3. Disconnect the vacuum lines.

4. Note the position of the rotor in relation to the base. Scribe or paint a mark on the base of the distributor and on the engine block (on the end of the head on Sentra) so the marks can be lined up for reinstallation. Align the marks with the direction the metal tip of the rotor is pointing.

5. Remove the bolt(s) which holds the distributor to the engine.

6. Lift the distributor assembly from the engine on the A-series engines. On Sentra, pull the distributor straight out from the end of the head.

Disconnecting distributor wiring harness, all models

INSTALLATION

1. Lightly oil the distributor shaft and insert the shaft and assembly into the engine. Line up the mark on the distributor and the one on the engine with the metal tip of the rotor. Make sure that the vacuum advance diaphragm is pointed in the same direction as it was pointed originally. This will be done automatically if the marks on the engine and the distributor are lined up with the rotor.

2. Install the distributor holddown bolt and clamp. Leave the screw loose enough so that you can move the distributor with heavy hand pressure.

3. Connect the primary wire to the coil. Install the distributor cap on the distributor housing. Secure the distributor cap with the spring clips.

4. Install the spark plug wires if removed. Make sure that the wires are pressed all the way into the top of the distributor cap and firmly onto the spark plug.

5. Adjust the point dwell and set the ignition timing (see Chapter 2 "Tune-Up").

NOTE: *If the crankshaft has been turned or the engine disturbed in any manner (i.e., disassembled and rebuilt) while the distributor was removed, or if the marks were not drawn, it will be necessary to initially time the engine. Follow the procedure given below.*

INSTALLATION -- ENGINE DISTURBED

1. It is necessary to place the No. 1 cylinder in the firing position to correctly install the distributor. To locate this position, the ignition timing marks on the crankshaft front pulley are used.

2. Remove the No. 1 cylinder spark plug. Turn the crankshaft until the piston in the no. 1 cylinder is moving up on the compression stroke. This can be determined by placing your

thumb over the spark plug hole and feeling the air being forced out of the cylinder. Stop turning the crankshaft when the timing marks that are used to time the engine on the front pulley are aligned.

3. Oil the distributor housing lightly where the distributor bears on its mounting flange. Oil the distributor drive gear on A-series engines.

4. Install the distributor so that the rotor, which is mounted on the shaft, points toward the No. 1 spark plug terminal tower position when the cap is installed. Of course, you won't be able to see the direction in which the rotor is pointing if the cap is on the distributor, so lay the cap on the top of the distributor. Make a mark on the side of the distributor housing just below the No. 1 spark plug terminal. Make sure that the rotor points toward that mark when you install the distributor.

5. When the distributor shaft has reached the bottom of the hole, move the rotor back and forth slightly until the driving gear on the end of the shaft enters the slots cut in the end of the oil pump shaft and the distributor assembly slides down into place.

6. When the distributor is correctly installed, the breaker points (if equipped) should be in such a position that they are just ready to break contact with each other. On electronic ignition distributors, the reluctor tooth will be very close to approaching the stator pole. This is accomplished by rotating the distributor body after it has been installed in the engine. Once again, line up the marks that you made before the distributor was removed from the engine.

7. Install the distributor holddown bolt.

8. Install the spark plug into the No. 1 spark plug hole and continue from Step 3 of the preceding distributor installation procedure.

FIRING ORDER

To avoid confusion, replace the spark plug wires one at a time.

A-series engines

E-series (Sentra) engines

Alternator

ALTERNATOR PRECAUTIONS

To prevent damage to the alternator and regulator, the following precautionary measures must be taken when working with the the electrical system.

1. Never reverse battery connections; make sure positive is attached to positive, and negative to negative.

2. Booster batteries for starting must be connected properly. Make sure that the positive cable of the booster battery is connected to the positive terminal of the battery that is getting the boost. This applies to both negative and ground cables.

3. Disconnect the battery cables before using a fast charger; the charger has a tendency to force current through the diodes in the opposite direction for which they are designed. This burns out the diodes.

4. Never use a fast charger as a booster for starting the vehicle.

5. Never disconnect the voltage regulator while the engine is running.

6. Do not ground the alternator output terminal.

7. Do not operate the alternator on an open circuit with the field energized.

8. Do not attempt to polarize an alternator.

REMOVAL AND INSTALLATION

1. Disconnect the negative battery terminal.

2. Disconnect the two lead wires and connector from the alternator.

3. Loosen the drive belt adjusting bolt and remove the belt.

4. Unscrew the alternator attaching bolts and remove the alternator from the vehicle.

5. Install the alternator in the reverse order of removal.

Regulator

REMOVAL AND INSTALLATION

NOTE: *1978 and later models are equipped with integral regulator alternators. Since the regulator is part of the alternator, no adjust-*

1. Pulley assembly
2. Front cover
3. Front bearing
4. Rotor
5. Rear bearing
6. Stator
7. Rear cover
8. Brush assembly
9. Diode set plate assembly
10. Diode cover
11. Through-bolt

Exploded view of 1200 and B210 alternator

1. Pulley assembly
2. Front cover
3. Front bearing
4. Rotor
5. Rear bearing
6. Stator
7. Diode (Set plate) assembly
8. Brush assembly
9. IC voltage regulator
10. Rear cover
11. Through bolt

210 and Sentra-type integral regulator alternator

1. Feeler gauge   3. Phillips screwdriver
2. Screw   4. Upper contact

Adjusting voltage regulator point gap

1. Wrench   3. Adjusting screw
2. Phillips screwdriver   4. Locknut

Adjusting the regulated voltage, voltage regulator models

ments are possible or necessary on these models.

1. Disconnect the negative battery terminal.

2. Disconnect the electrical lead connector of the regulator.

3. Remove the two mounting screws and remove the regulator from the vehicle.

4. Install the regulator in the reverse order of removal.

ADJUSTMENT

1. Adjust the voltage regulator core gap by loosening the screw which is used to secure the contact set on the yoke, and move the contact up or down as necessary. Retighten the screw. The gap should be 0.024–0.039 in.

2. Adjust the point gap of the voltage regulator coil by loosening the screw used to secure the upper contact and move the upper contact up or down. The gap for 1973–76 1200 and B210 models is 0.012–0.016 in. The point gap for all other models with separate regulators is 0.014–0.018 in.

3. The core gap and point gap on the 0.032–0.039 in. and the point gap adjusted to 0.016–0.024 in.

4. The regulated voltage is adjusted by loosening the locknut and turning the adjusting screw clockwise to increase, or counterclockwise to decrease, the regulated voltage. The voltage should be between 14.3–15.3 volts at 68°F.

Starter

Datsun began using a gear reduction starter in 1978 and later Canadian models. The differ-

Alternator and Regulator Specifications

Model	Year	Alternator Identification Number	Rated Output @ 5000 RPM	Output @ 2500 RPM (not less than)	Brush Length	Brush Spring Tension (oz)	Regulated Voltage
1200	1973	LT135-138	35	14	0.571	8.80–12.32	14.3–15.3
B210	1973–74	LT135-13B	35	14	0.571	8.99–12.17	14.3–15.3
		LT150-05 ③	50	28	0.571	8.99–12.17	14.3–15.3
B210	1975–76	LT150-19	50	37.5	0.295	9.0–12.2	14.3–15.3
B210	1977	LT150-26	50	37.5	0.295	9.0–12.2	14.3–15.3
B210	1978	LT150-36 ①	50	40	0.295	9.0–12.2	14.3–15.3
210	1979–80	LR150-36 ①	50	40	0.295	8.99–12.17	14.4–15.0
210	1981–82	LR150-99 ②①	50	40	0.28	8.99–12.17	14.4–15.0
Sentra Gasoline	1982–86	LR150-125B ①	50	42	0.28	8.99–12.17	14.4–15.0
Sentra Diesel	1984–86	LR150-402	50	42	0.28	6.35–12.70	14.4–15.0
		LR160-401	60	50	0.28	6.35–12.70	14.4–15.0

① Uses integral voltage regulator
② LR150-99B in 1982
③ Optional

Note the wire locations before removing the starter

Lift brush spring with a wire hook and remove brush on non-reduction starters

ences between the gear reduction and conventional starters are: the gear reduction starter has a set of ratio reduction gears while the conventional starter does not; the brushes on the gear reduction starter are located on a plate behind the starter drive housing, while the conventional starter's brushes are located in its rear cover. The extra gears on the gear reduction starter make the starter pinion gear turn at about half the speed of the starter, giving the starter twice the turning power of a conventional starter. There is no difference in removal and installation procedures between the two.

REMOVAL AND INSTALLATION

1. Disconnect the negative battery cable from the battery.
2. Disconnect the starter wiring at the starter, taking note of the positions for correct reinstallation.
3. Remove the bolts attaching the starter to the engine and remove the starter from the vehicle.
4. Install the starter in the reverse order of removal.

BRUSH REPLACEMENT

Non-Reduction Gear Type

1. With the starter out of the vehicle, remove the bolts holding the solenoid to the top of the starter and remove the solenoid.
2. To remove the brushes, remove the two thru-bolts, and the two rear cover attaching screws and remove the rear cover.
3. Disconnect the electrical leads, lift up the brush spring with a wire hook and remove the brushes.

4. Install the brushes in the reverse order of removal.

Reduction Gear Type

1. Remove the starter. Remove the solenoid.
2. Remove the through bolts and the rear cover. The rear cover can be pried off with a screwdriver, but be careful not to damage the O-ring.
3. Remove the starter housing, armature, and brush holder from the center housing. They can be removed as an assembly.
4. Remove the positive side brush from its holder. The positive brush is insulated from the brush holder, and its lead wire is connected to the field coil.
5. Carefully lift the negative brush from the commutator and remove it from the holder.
6. Installation is the reverse.

PINION STOPPER
PINION STOPPER CLIP

Pinion stopper removal

STARTER DRIVE REPLACEMENT

Non-Reduction Gear Type

1. With the starter motor removed from the vehicle, remove the solenoid from the starter.
2. Remove the two thru-bolts and separate the gear case from the yoke housing.

18. Center bracket
19. Pinion assembly
20. Dust cover
21. Pinion stopper
22. Stopper clip
23. Gear case
24. Gear case metal

1. Magnetic switch assembly
2. Dust cover
   (Adjusting washer)
3. Torsion spring
4. Shift lever
5. Dust cover
6. Thrust washer
7. E-ring
8. Rear cover metal
9. Through bolt
10. Rear cover
11. Brush holder
12. Brush (−)
13. Brush spring
14. Brush (+)
15. Yoke
16. Field coil
17. Armature

Exploded view of non-reduction gear starter

1. End housing
2. Dust cover
3. Lever
4. Dust cover
5. Pin
6. Solenoid
7. Center bracket
8. Armature
9. Thrust washer
10. Bushing
11. Stop washer
12. Stop clip
13. Pinion retainer
14. Pinion
15. Overrunning clutch
16. Field coil
17. Yoke
18. Brush cover
19. Brush
20. Rear cover
21. Through-bolt

Exploded view of 1200 and B210 starter

1. Magnetic switch assembly
2. Dust cover (Adjusting washer)
3. Torsion spring
4. Shift lever
5. Through bolt
6. Rear cover
7. O-ring
8. Yoke
9. Field coil
10. Brush
11. Armature
12. Center bearing
13. Brush spring
14. Brush holder
15. Dust cover
16. Center housing
17. Reduction gear
18. Pinion gear
19. Packing
20. Gear case

Gear reduction starter

3. Remove the pinion stopper clip and the pinion stopper.

4. Slide the starter drive off the armature shaft.

5. Install the starter drive and reassemble the starter in the reverse order of removal.

Reduction Gear Type

1. Remove the starter.
2. Remove the solenoid and the shift lever.

3. Remove the bolts securing the center housing to the front cover and separate the parts.

4. Remove the gears and starter drive.

5. Installation is the reverse.

Battery

Refer to Chapter One for details on battery maintenance.

Battery and Starter Specifications

All cars use 12 volt, negative ground electrical systems

		Battery Amp Hour Capacity	Starter							Brush Spring Tension (oz)	Min Brush Length (in)
			Lock Test			No Load Test					
Year	Model		Amps	Volts	Torque (ft. lbs.)	Amps	Volts	RPM			
1973	1200	45	420	6.3	6.5 MT	60	12	7,000		56	0.26
					7.2 AT	60	12	6,000		29	0.37
1974–78	B210	60	420	6.3	6.5	60	12	7,000		49–64	0.47
			—	—	—	60	12	6,000 ①		29	0.37
			—	—	—	100 RG	12	4,300 RG		56–70	0.43
1979–82	210	60	—	—	—	60	11.5	7,000		50–64	0.47
						100 RG	11	3,900		56–70	0.43
1982–86	Sentra Gasoline	60/70 ②	—	—	—	60	11.5	7,000		50–64	0.43
1984–86	Sentra Diesel	70/80	—	—	—	<100	11.5	>3,900		56–70	0.43

MT: Manual Transmission
AT: Automatic Transmission
RG: Reducation gear type starter (Canada)

① 1974 Automatic Transmission models only
—: Not recommended
② 1982–83: 30A U.S.A. MPG model; 65A Canada

REMOVAL AND INSTALLATION

1. Disconnect the negative (ground) cable from the terminal, and then the positive cable. Special pullers are available to remove the cable clamps, if they seem stuck.

NOTE: *To avoid sparks, always disconnect the ground cable first, and connect it last.*

2. Remove the battery holddown clamp.

3. Remove the battery, being careful not to spill the acid.

NOTE: *Spilled acid can be neutralized with a baking soda/water solution. If you somehow get acid into your eyes, flush it out with lots of water and get to a doctor.*

4. Clean the battery posts thoroughly before reinstalling, or when installing a new battery.

5. Clean the cable clamps, using a wire brush, both inside and out.

6. Install the battery and the holddown clamp or strap. Connect the positive, and the negative cable (see "Note" above). Do not hammer the cables onto the terminal posts. The complete terminals should be coated lightly (externally) – with petroleum jelly or grease to help prevent corrosion. There are also felt washers impregnated with an anti-corrosion substance which are slipped over the battery posts before installing the cables; these are available in most auto parts stores.

CAUTION: *Make absolutely sure that the battery is connected properly (positive to positive, negative to negative) before you turn the ignition key. Reversed polarity can burn out your alternator and regulator in a matter of seconds.*

ENGINE MECHANICAL

Design

The "A Series" engines used in the 1200, B210 and 210 models covered in this book are all members of the same "family". The A12, A12A, A13, A14 and A15 series of engines are all water cooled, inline, overhead valve, four cylinder powerplants. All of these engines utilize a cast iron block and an aluminum cylinder head. Camshafts in these engines are placed high in the block, allowing for short pushrods, which in turn means low valve train reciprocating weight and higher engine speeds. The A12 through A15's also have in common a five main bearing crankshaft. The engines differ mainly in displacement, which becomes greater as the number after the "A" prefix becomes greater (A12's are 1200 cubic centimeters, A13's 1300 and so on).

The "E series" engines used in the Nissan Sentra depart significantly in engine design from the "A series engines. The Sentra E15 and E16 engine utilizes a single overhead camshaft and "hemi"combustion chambers. Distributor drive on the "E" series engines also departs from its Datsun cousins, and follows proven European practice of driving the distributor directly off of the overhead cam.

In 1984, an all new overhead cam, 4-cylinder diesel was introduced. This lightweight diesel displaces 1680cc and is designated the CD17.

Engines are referred to by model designation codes throughout this book. Use the "General Engine Specifications" table in this chapter for the identification of engines by model and displacement.

Engine Overhaul Tips

Most engine overhaul procedures are fairly standard. In addition to specific parts replacement procedures and complete specifications for your individual engine, this chapter also is a guide to accept rebuilding procedures. Examples of standard rebuilding practice are shown and should be used along with specific details concerning your particular engine.

Competent and accurate machine shop services will ensure maximum performance, reliability and engine life.

In most instances it is more profitable for the do-it-yourself mechanic to remove, clean and inspect the component, buy the necessary parts and deliver these to a shop for actual machine work.

On the other hand, much of the rebuilding work (crankshaft, block, bearings, piston rods, and other components) is well within the scope of the do-it-yourself mechanic.

TOOLS

The tools required for an engine overhaul or parts replacement will depend on the depth of your involvement. With a few exceptions, they will be the tools found in a mechanic's tool kit (see Chapter 1). More in-depth work will require any or all of the following:

• a dial indicator (reading in thousandths) mounted on a universal base
  • micrometers and telescope gauges
  • jaw and screw-type pullers
  • scraper
  • valve spring compressor
  • ring groove cleaner
  • piston ring expander and compressor
  • ridge reamer
  • cylinder hone or glaze breaker
  • Plastigage®
  • engine stand

Use of most of these tools is illustrated in this chapter. Many can be rented for a one-time use from a local parts jobber or tool supply house specializing in automotive work.

Occasionally, the use of special tools is called for. See the information on Special Tools and Safety Notice in the front of this book before substituting another tool.

INSPECTION TECHNIQUES

Procedures and specifications are given in this chapter for inspecting, cleaning and assessing the wear limits of most major components. Other procedures such as Magnaflux® and Zyglo® can be used to locate material flaws and stress cracks. Magnaflux® is a magnetic process applicable only to ferrous materials. The Zyglo® process coats the material with a fluorescent dye penetrant and can be used on any material Check for suspected surface cracks can be more readily made using spot check dye. The dye is sprayed onto the suspected area, wiped off and the area sprayed with a developer. Cracks will show up brightly.

OVERHAUL TIPS

Aluminum has become extremely popular for use in engines, due to its low weight. Observe the following precautions when handling aluminum parts:
  • Never hot tank aluminum parts (the caustic hot tank solution will eat the aluminum.
  • Remove all aluminum parts (identification tag, etc.) from engine parts prior to the tanking.
  • Always coat threads lightly with engine oil or anti-seize compounds before installation, to prevent seizure.
  • Never over-torque bolts or spark plugs especially in aluminum threads.

Stripped threads in any component can be repaired using any of several commercial repair kits (Heli-Coil®, Microdot®, Keenserts®, etc.).

When assembling the engine, any parts that will be frictional contact must be prelubed to provide lubrication at initial start-up. Any product specifically formulated for this purpose can be used, but engine oil is not recommended as a prelube.

When semi-permanent (locked, but removable) installation of bolts or nuts is desired, threads should be cleaned and coated with Loctite® or other similar, commercial non-hardening sealant.

REPAIRING DAMAGED THREADS

Several methods of repairing damaged threads are available. Heli-Coil® (shown here), Keenserts® and Microdot® are among the most widely used. All involve basically the same principle—drilling out stripped threads, tapping the hole and installing a prewound insert—making welding, plugging and oversize fasteners unnecessary.

Two types of thread repair inserts are usually supplied—a standard type for most Inch Coarse, Inch Fine, Metric Course and Metric Fine thread sizes and a spark lug type to fit most spark plug port sizes. Consult the individual manufacturer's catalog to determine exact applications. Typical thread repair kits will contain a selection of prewound threaded inserts, a tap (corresponding to the outside diameter threads of the insert) and an installation tool. Spark plug inserts usually differ because they require a tap equipped with pilot threads and a combined reamer/tap section. Most manufacturers also supply blister-packed thread repair inserts separately in addition to a master kit containing a variety of taps and inserts plus installation tools.

Before effecting a repair to a threaded hole, remove any snapped, broken or damaged bolts or studs. Penetrating oil can be used to free frozen threads; the offending item can be removed with locking pliers or with a screw or stud extractor. After the hole is clear, the thread can be repaired, as follows:

BOLT OR SCREW

THREADED INSERT

DAMAGED THREADS

Damaged bolt holes can be repaired with thread repair inserts

Standard thread repair insert (left) and spark plug thread insert (right)

Drill out the damaged threads with specified drill. Drill completely through the hole or to the bottom of a blind hole

With the tap supplied, tap the hole to receive the thread insert. Keep the tap well oiled and back it out frequently to avoid clogging the threads

Screw the threaded insert onto the installation tool until the tang engages the slot. Screw the insert into the tapped hole until it is ¼–½ turn below the top surface. After installation break off the tang with a hammer and punch

Checking Engine Compression

A noticeable lack of engine power, excessive oil consumption and/or poor fuel mileage measured over an extended period are all indicators of internal engine war. Worn piston rings, scored or worn cylinder bores, blown head gaskets, sticking or burnt valves and worn valve seats are all possible culprits here. A check of each cylinder's compression will help you locate the problems.

As mentioned in the Tools and Equipment section of Chapter 1, a screw-in type compression gauge is more accurate that the type you simply hold against the spark plug hole, although it takes slightly longer to use. It's worth it to obtain a more accurate reading. Follow the procedures below for gasoline and diesel engined trucks.

Gasoline Engines

1. Warm up the engine to normal operating temperature.

2. Remove all spark plugs.

3. Disconnect the high tension lead from the ignition coil.

The screw-in type compression gauge is more accurate

4. On fully open the throttle either by operating the carburetor throttle linkage by hand or by having an assistant floor the accelerator pedal.

5. Screw the compression gauge into the no.1 spark plug hole until the fitting is snug. NOTE: *Be careful not to crossthread the plug hole. On aluminum cylinder heads use extra care, as the threads in these heads are easily ruined.*

6. Ask an assistant to depress the accelerator pedal fully on both carbureted and fuel injected trucks. Then, while you read the compression gauge, ask the assistant to crank the engine two or three times in short bursts using the ignition switch.

7. Read the compression gauge at the end of each series of cranks, and record the highest of

Standard Torque Specifications and Fastener Markings

In the absence of specific torques, the following chart can be used as a guide to the maximum safe torque of a particular size/grade of fastener.

- There is no torque difference for fine or coarse threads.
- Torque values are based on clean, dry threads. Reduce the value by 10% if threads are oiled prior to assembly.
- The torque required for aluminum components or fasteners is considerably less.

U.S. Bolts

SAE Grade Number	1 or 2			5			6 or 7		
Number of lines always 2 less than the grade number.									
	Maximum Torque			Maximum Torque			Maximum Torque		
Bolt Size (Inches)—(Thread)	Ft./Lbs.	Kgm	Nm	Ft./Lbs.	Kgm	Nm	Ft./Lbs.	Kgm	Nm
1/4 — 20	5	0.7	6.8	8	1.1	10.8	10	1.4	13.5
— 28	6	0.8	8.1	10	1.4	13.6			
5/16 — 18	11	1.5	14.9	17	2.3	23.0	19	2.6	25.8
— 24	13	1.8	17.6	19	2.6	25.7			
3/8 — 16	18	2.5	24.4	31	4.3	42.0	34	4.7	46.0
— 24	20	2.75	27.1	35	4.8	47.5			
7/16 — 14	28	3.8	37.0	49	6.8	66.4	55	7.6	74.5
— 20	30	4.2	40.7	55	7.6	74.5			
1/2 — 13	39	5.4	52.8	75	10.4	101.7	85	11.75	115.2
— 20	41	5.7	55.6	85	11.7	115.2			
9/16 — 12	51	7.0	69.2	110	15.2	149.1	120	16.6	162.7
— 18	55	7.6	74.5	120	16.6	162.7			
5/8 — 11	83	11.5	112.5	150	20.7	203.3	167	23.0	226.5
— 18	95	13.1	128.8	170	23.5	230.5			
3/4 — 10	105	14.5	142.3	270	37.3	366.0	280	38.7	379.6
— 16	115	15.9	155.9	295	40.8	400.0			
7/8 — 9	160	22.1	216.9	395	54.6	535.5	440	60.9	596.5
— 14	175	24.2	237.2	435	60.1	589.7			
1 — 8	236	32.5	318.6	590	81.6	799.9	660	91.3	894.8
— 14	250	34.6	338.9	660	91.3	849.8			

Metric Bolts

Relative Strength Marking	4.6, 4.8			8.8		
Bolt Markings						
	Maximum Torque			Maximum Torque		
Bolt Size Thread Size x Pitch (mm)	Ft./Lbs.	Kgm	Nm	Ft./Lbs.	Kgm	Nm
6 x 1.0	2–3	.2–.4	3–4	3–6	.4–.8	5–8
8 x 1.25	6–8	.8–1	8–12	9–14	1.2–1.9	13–19
10 x 1.25	12–17	1.5–2.3	16–23	20–29	2.7–4.0	27–39
12 x 1.25	21–32	2.9–4.4	29–43	35–53	4.8–7.3	47–72
14 x 1.5	35–52	4.8–7.1	48–70	57–85	7.8–11.7	77–110
16 x 1.5	51–77	7.0–10.6	67–100	90–120	12.4–16.5	130–160
18 x 1.5	74–110	10.2–15.1	100–150	130–170	17.9–23.4	180–230
20 x 1.5	110–140	15.1–19.3	150–190	190–240	26.2–46.9	160–320
22 x 1.5	150–190	22.0–26.2	200–260	250–320	34.5–44.1	340–430
24 x 1.5	190–240	26.2–46.9	260–320	310–410	42.7–56.5	420–550

these readings. Repeat this procedure for each of the engine's cylinders. Compare the highest reading of each cylinder to the compression pressure specification in the Tune-Up Specifications chart in Chapter 2. The specs in this chart are maximum values.

A cylinder's compression pressure is usually acceptable if it is not less than 80% of maximum. The difference between each cylinder should be no more than 12–14 pounds.

8. If a cylinder is unusually low, pour a tablespoon of clean engine oil into the cylinder through the spark plug hole and repeat the compression test. If the compression comes up after adding the oil, it appears that the cylinder's piston rings or bore are damaged or worn. If the pressure remains low, the valves may not be seating properly (a valve job is needed), or the head gasket may be blown near that cylinder. If compression in any two adjacent cylinders is low, and if the addition of oil doesn't help the compression, there is leakage past the head gasket. Oil and coolant water in the combustion chamber can result from this problem. There may be evidence of water droplets on the engine dipstick when a head gasket has blown.

Diesel Engines

Checking cylinder compression on diesel engines is basically the same procedure as on gasoline engines except for the following:

1. A special compression gauge adaptor suitable for diesel engines (because these engines have much greater compression pressures) must be used.

2. Remove the injector tubes and remove the injectors from each cylinder.

NOTE: *Don't forget to remove the washer underneath each injector; otherwise, it may get lost when the engine is cranked.*

Diesel engines require a special compression gauge adaptor

Engine I.D. Table

Vehicle	Number of Cylinders	Displacement cu. in. (cc)	Type	Engine Model Code
1200	4	71.5 (1171)	OHV	A12
B210	4	78.59 (1288)	OHV	A13
	4	85.24 (1397)	OHV	A14
210	4	75.5 (1237)	OHV	A12A
	4	85.3 (1397)	OHV	A14
	4	90.8 (1488)	OHV	A15
Sentra	4	90.8 (1488)	OHC	E15
	4	97.6 (1597)	OHC	E16
	4	102.5 (1680)	OHC	CD17

NOTE: OHV is Overhead Valve
OHC is Overhead Cam

3. When fitting the compression gauge adaptor to the cylinder head, make sure the bleeder of the gauge (if equipped) is closed.

4. When reinstalling the injector assemblies, install new washers underneath each injector.

Torque Specifications
All readings in ft. lbs.

Engine Model	Cylinder Head Bolts	Main Bearing Bolts	Rod Bearing Bolts	Crankshaft Pulley Bolt	Flywheel to Crankshaft Bolts	Manifolds Intake	Manifolds Exhaust
A12	40–43	36–43	23–28	108–116	47–54	7–10	7–10
A13	51–54	36–43	23–27	108–145	54–61	7–10	7–10
A12A, A14, A15	51–54	36–43	23–27	108–145	58–65 ①	11–14	11–14
E15	51–54 ②	36–43	23–27	83–108	58–65	12–15	12–15
E16	51–54	36–43	23–27	83–108	58–65	12–15	12–15
CD17	72–80	33–40	23–27	90–98	72–80	13–16	13–16

① 1975–77 A14: 54–61 ft. lbs.
② Second (final) torquing. First torque to 29–33 ft. lbs.

General Engine Specifications

Year	Model	Type (model)	Engine Displacement Cu In. (cc)	Fuel System Type	Horsepower (SAE) @ rpm	Torque @ rpm (ft. lbs.)	Bore x Stroke (in.)	Compression Ratio	Normal Oil Pressure (psi)
1973	1200 Sedan 1200 Coupe	OHV 4 (A12)	71.5 (1171)	2 bbl	69 @ 6000	70 @ 4000	2.87 x 2.76	8.5:1	54–60
1974	B210 Sedan, Coupe	OHV 4 (A13)	78.6 (1288)	2 bbl	75 @ 6000	77 @ 3600	2.87 x 3.03	8.5:1	43–50
1975	B210 Sedan, Coupe	OHV 4 (A14)	85.24 (1397)	2 bbl	78 @ 6000	75 @ 4000	3.09 x 3.03	8.5:1	43–50
1976–78	B210	OHV 4 (A14)	85.2 (1397)	2 bbl	80 @ 6000	83 @ 3600	2.99 x 3.03	8.5:1	43–50
1979–82	210, 210 MPG	OHV 4 (A12A)	75.5 (1237)	2 bbl	58 @ 5600	67 @ 3600	2.95 x 2.75	8.5:1	43–50
		OHV 4 (A14)	85.3 (1397)	2 bbl	65 @ 5600	75 @ 3600	2.99 x 3.03	8.5:1 ①	43–50
		OHV 4 (A15)	90.8 (1488)	2 bbl	67 @ 5200	80 @ 3200	2.99 x 3.23	8.9:1	43–50
1982–83	Sentra	OHC 4 (E15)	90.8 (1488)	2 bbl	67 @ 5200	85 @ 3200	2.99 x 3.23	9.0:1	43–50
1983–86	Sentra	OHC 4 (E16)	97.45 (1597)	2 bbl	69 @ 5200	92 @ 3200	2.99 x 3.465	9.4:1	43–57
		OHC 4 (CD17)	102.5 (1680)	Diesel	55 @ 4800	104 @ 2800	3.15 x 3.29	22.2:1	43–57

NOTE: Specifications given are for United States except California
① 8.9:1 on 1981–82

Crankshaft and Connecting Rod Specifications

Engine Model	Crankshaft					Connecting Rod Bearings	
	Main Brg Journal Dia	Main Brg Oil Clearance	Shaft End-Play	Thrust on No.	Journal Dia	Oil Clearance	Side Clearance
A12 (1200)	1.9671–1.9668	0.001–0.002	0.002–0.006	3	1.7701–1.7706	0.001–0.002	0.007–0.012
A13	1.966–1.967	0.0008–0.002	0.002–0.006	3	1.7701–1.7706	0.0008–0.002	0.008–0.012
A14 (1975–78)	1.966–1.967	0.008–0.002	0.002–0.006	3	1.7701–1.7706	0.0008–0.002	0.008–0.012
A12A, A14, A15 (1979–1982)	1.9663–1.9671	0.001–0.0035	0.002–0.0059	3	1.7701–1.7706	0.0012–0.0031	0.004–0.008
E15	1.9663–1.9671	0.0012–0.0030	0.002–0.0071	3	1.5730–1.5738	0.0012–0.0024	0.004–0.014
E16	1.9663–1.9671	0.0012–0.0030 ①	0.0020–0.0071	3	1.5370–1.5378	0.0012–0.0024	0.0040–0.0146
CD17	2.0847–2.0852	0.0015–0.0026	0.0020–0.0071	3	1.7701–1.7706	0.0009–0.0026	0.0115–0.0125

① #2, 3, 4: 0.0012–0.0036

Piston and Ring Specifications

All measurements in inches

| Engine Model | Piston-to-Bore Clearance | Ring Gap | | | Ring Side Clearance | | |
		Top Compression	Bottom Compression	Oil Control	Top Compression	Bottom Compression	Oil Control
A12 1973	0.001–0.002	0.008–0.014	0.008–0.014	0.012–0.035	0.002–0.003	0.002–0.003	0.002–0.003
A13	0.001–0.002	0.008–0.014	0.008–0.014	0.012–0.035	0.002–0.003	0.002–0.003	—
A14 1975–78	0.0009–0.002	0.008–0.014	0.008–0.014	0.012–0.035	0.002–0.003	0.001–0.002	Combined ring
A12A, A14, A15 1979–82	0.0010–0.0018	0.008–0.014	0.008–0.014	0.012–0.035	0.002–0.003	0.001–0.002	Combined ring
E15	0.0009–0.0017	0.0079–0.0138	0.0059–0.0118	0.0118–0.0354	0.0016–0.0029	0.0012–0.0025	0.0020–0.0057
E16	0.0009–0.0017	0.0079–0.0138	0.0059–0.0118	0.0118–0.0354	0.0016–0.0029	0.0012–0.0025	0.0020–0.0057
CD17	0.0020–0.0028	0.0079–0.0138	0.0079–0.0138	0.0118–0.0177	0.0008–0.0024	0.0016–0.0031	0.0012–0.0028

Valve Specifications

Model	Seat Angle (deg)	Spring Test Pressure lbs @ in.	Free Length (in.)	Stem-to-Guide Clearance (in.)		Stem Diameter (in.)	
				Intake	Exhaust	Intake	Exhaust
A12, A13, A14 (1973–78)	45°	52.7 @ 1.52	1.83	0.0006– 0.0018	0.0016– 0.0028	0.3138– 0.3144	0.3128– 0.3134
A12A, A14 A15 (1979–82)	45°30′	52.7 @ 1.19	1.83	0.0006– 0.0018	0.0016– 0.0028	0.3138– 0.3144	0.3128– 0.3134
E15	45°	51.66 @ 1.543	1.83	0.0008– 0.0020	0.0018– 0.0030	0.2744– 0.2750	0.2734– 0.2740
E16	45°	51.66 @ 1.543	1.83	0.0008– 0.0020	0.0018– 0.0030	0.2744– 0.2750	0.2734– 0.2740
CD17	45°30′	①	②	0.0008– 0.0020	0.0016– 0.0028	0.2742– 0.2748	0.2734– 0.2740

① Inner: 19.2 @ 1.417
   Outer: 33.7 @ 1.555
② Inner: 1.7008
   Outer: 1.8268

Engine

REMOVAL AND INSTALLATION

All A-series Models

NOTE: *The engine and transmission are removed together and then separated when out of the car.*

1. Mark the location of the hinges on the bottom of the hood with a scribe or grease pencil for later installation. Unbolt and remove the hood.

2. Disconnect the battery cables.

3. Drain the coolant from the radiator, and drain the automatic transmission fluid.

CAUTION: *When draining the coolant, keep in mind that cats and dogs are attracted by the ethylene glycol antifreeze, and are quite likely to drink any that is left in an uncovered container or in puddles on the ground. This will prove fatal in sufficient quantity. Always drain the coolant into a sealable container. Coolant should be reused unless it is contaminated or several years old.*

4. Remove the radiator and radiator shroud

Removing the A-series engine. All engines removed in a similar manner, except Sentra which is removed sideways

after disconnecting the automatic transmission coolant tubes (if equipped).

5. Remove the air cleaner.
6. Remove the fan and pulley.
7. Disconnect:
   a. Water temperature gauge wire.
   b. Oil pressure sending unit wire.
   c. Ignition distributor primary wire.
   d. Starter motor connections.
   e. Fuel hose.
   f. Alternator leads.
   g. Heater hoses.
   h. Throttle and choke connections.
   i. Engine ground cable.
   j. Thermal transmitter wire.
   k. Wire to fuel cut-off solenoid.
   l. Vacuum cut solenoid wire.

NOTE: *A good rule of thumb when disconnecting the rather complex engine wiring of today's cars is to put a piece of masking tape on the wire and on the connection you removed the wire from, then mark both pieces of tape 1,2,3, etc. When replacing wiring, simply match the pieces of tape.*

CAUTION: *On models with air conditioning, it is necessary to remove the compressor and the condenser from their mounts. DO NOT ATTEMPT TO UNFASTEN ANY OF THE AIR CONDITIONER HOSES. See chapter one for additional warnings.*

8. Disconnect the power brake booster hose from the engine.

Gearshift lever removal: 1200, B210. 210 similar

COMPRESSOR

Secure A/C compressor to the inside of the fender or frame when removing engine on all models

9. Remove the clutch operating cylinder and return spring.

10. Disconnect the speedometer cable from the transmission. Disconnect the backup light switch and any other wiring or attachments to the transmission.

11. Disconnect the column shift linkage. Remove the floorshift lever. On 1200 and B210 models, remove the boot, withdraw the lock pin, and remove the lever from inside the car.

12. Detach the exhaust pipe from the exhaust manifold. Remove the front section of the exhaust manifold.

13. Mark the relationship of the driveshaft flanges with a centerpunch or scribe and remove the driveshaft. The marks are matched up later during installation; the driveshaft must be installed in the same relationship as it was removed.

14. Place a jack under the transmission. Remove the rear crossmember, keeping the jack underneath just enough for support. On 1200 and B210 models, remove the rear engine mounting nuts. Remove the front engine mount bolts from all models.

15. Attach a strong (heavy chain or heavy rope in good condition) lifting sling to the lifting eyelets on the engine. Run the sling through both eyelets, and then through a suitable pulley or other lifting device.

NOTE: *Make sure that whatever will be supporting the engine as you pull it out of the car will be able to support the weight of both engine and transmission. Many children's swing sets are not sturdy enough for this and are not recommended. Engine lifting tripods are available at any equipment rental shops, and are designed for this work.*

16. Drape a heavy cloth across the grille of the car. This will protect and cushion the grille, crossmember and engine from any damage. Slowly lift the engine up and out of the car. It is helpful to have at least two people working on this job, especially to help the transmission clear its tunnel and engine compartment. When the engine is out of the car, do not rest the weight of the entire unit on the oil pan.

17. Installation is the reverse of removal. If the buffer rod length has not been altered, it should still be correct.

E Series and Diesel Engines

NOTE: *The engine and transaxle must be removed as a unit. Since the Sentra is a front wheel drive car, this is a fairly involved procedure. It is very important to label and mark all cables, hoses and vacuum lines during this procedure. Masking tape works well here. Marking both the disconnected hose,*

1. Rocker cover	5. Piston	9. Camshaft
2. Cylinder head	6. Oil pan	10. Timing chain
3. Cylinder block	7. Flywheel	11. Front cover
4. Crankshaft	8. Valve parts	12. Water pump

A series engine components

etc., and where it was attached will help to avoid the "where did that go?" later.
CAUTION: *Be sure the car is on a flat, solid surface with the wheels chocked before beginning. Do not remove the engine until the exhaust system has cooled off completely; you will avoid burns and fuel line fires this way. Also, when unbolting the air conditioner compressor and idler pulley mount, DO NOT disconnect any A/C fittings or hoses.*

Sentra transaxle linkage attaching points

Sentra rear engine mount

Sentra left side engine mount

Removing Sentra halfshaft. Use care not to damage the grease seal

1. Scribe or draw a line around the hood mounting brackets on the underside of the hood, to facilitate installation later. Remove the hood.

2. Remove battery and battery support bracket.

3. Remove air cleaner and related hoses. Plug the air horn of the carburetor with a clean rag to keep dirt out.

4. Drain engine coolant and remove radiator with the radiator cooling fan.

CAUTION: *When draining the coolant, keep in mind that cats and dogs are attracted by the ethylene glycol antifreeze, and are quite likely to drink any that is left in an uncovered container or in puddles on the ground. This will prove fatal in sufficient quantity. Always drain the coolant into a sealable container. Coolant should be reused unless it is contaminated or several years old.*

5. remove the power steering pump, if equipped.

6. Unbolt the air conditioner compressor and idler pulley bracket from the cylinder block, observing the "Caution" above. Remove the compressor drive belt and hold the compressor unit upright, attached to the car with a wire or rope.

7. Disconnect the exhaust header pipe from the exhaust manifold.

8. Disconnect the manual transaxle control rod link support rod from the transaxle.

9. Disconnect the automatic transaxle control linkage from the transaxle.

10. Remove the lower ball joint. Do not reuse the nuts once they have been removed. Replace them with new nuts.

11. Drain the transaxle gear oil or fluid.

12. Disconnect the right and left halfshafts from the transaxle.

NOTE: *When drawing out the halfshafts, it is necessary to loosen the strut head bolts. Be careful not to damage the grease seal on the transaxle side.*

13. Disconnect the clutch cable.

14. Remove the speedometer cable with the pinion from the transaxle. Plug the hole from which the pinion gear was removed with a clean rag to keep out dirt.

15. Disconnect the accelerator cable.

16. Disconnect any vacuum and air hoses between the engine and vehicle body. Disconnect all cables, wires and harness connectors.

17. Disconnect the fuel hoses from the fuel pump.

18. Attach a suitable sling to the lifting eyelets on the engine.

19. Unbolt the engine mounts, and lift the engine up and away from the car. The Transaxle can now be separated from the engine.

VACUUM TUBE

CARBURETOR

V.V.T. VALVE

E.G.R. VALVE

12–15 FT. LBS.

INTAKE MANIFOLD

OIL FILTER

WATER PUMP

2.7–3.7 FT. LBS.

FUEL PUMP

OIL PUMP

6.7–8.7 FT. LBS.

6.7–8.7 FT. LBS.

83–108 FT. LBS.

2.7–3.7 FT. LBS.

E series outer engine components

INSTALLATION

1. Install engine with transaxle attached, in the reverse order of removal, and following these checks.

a. When installing, make sure that the brake lines, brake master cylinder, etc., do not interfere with the engine and transaxle.

b. Make sure that the A/C compressor and power steering pump (if equipped) are securely out of the way when lowering the engine.

2. Tighten the engine mount bolts, making sure there is some clearance in the rubber insulator.

Rocker Shaft

REMOVAL AND INSTALLATION

A12, A12A, A13, A14, A15 Engines

1. Remove the rocker cover.

2. Loosen the rocker adjusting bolts and

20–25 FT. LBS.

23–31 FT. LBS.

POWER STEERING PUMP

POWER STEERING
BRACKET

OIL LEVEL GAUGE

DISTRIBUTOR

20–25 FT. LBS.

2.7–3.7 FT. LBS.

20–25 FT. LBS.

SPARK PLUG
11–14 FT. LBS.

THERMOSTAT HOUSING

EXHAUST MANIFOLD

12–15 FT. LBS.

29–43 FT. LBS.

29–43 FT. LBS.

E.G.R. TUBE

E.A.I. TUBE

29–43 FT. LBS.

E series outer engine components

EXHAUST MANIFOLD
SIDE

Make sure cutout on Sentra rocker shaft faces exhaust manifold

push the adjusting screws away from the pushrods.

3. Unbolt and remove the rocker shaft assembly.

4. To install, reverse the above. Tighten the rocker shaft bolts to 14–18 ft.lb. in a circular sequence. Adjust the valves.

NOTE: *Both the intake and the exhaust valve springs are the uneven pitch type. That is, the springs have narrow coils at the bottom and wide coils at the top. The narrow coils (paint-*

E series internal engine components

ed white) *must be the side making contact on the cylinder head surface.*

E Series Engines

1. Remove the rocker cover.
2. Loosen each rocker adjusting locknut and screw slightly.

3. Unbolt the rocker shaft assembly and remove from the head.

4. Reverse the procedure for installation, torquing the rocker shaft bolts to 12–15 ft.lb. Adjust the valves.

NOTE: *Make sure that the oil holes in the ends of the rocker shaft face downward when*

E series internal engine components

the rocker shaft is installed. Also, be sure that the cutout in the center retainer of the rocker shaft faces toward the exhaust manifold side when installed.

Thermostat

REMOVAL AND INSTALLATION

All Engines

1. Drain the engine coolant into a clean container so that the coolant remaining in the engine block is below the thermostat housing. Save the drained coolant for use again, if it is still a fresh mixture.

CAUTION: *When draining the coolant, keep in mind that cats and dogs are attracted by the ethylene glycol antifreeze, and are quite likely to drink any that is left in an uncovered* container or in puddles on the ground. This will prove fatal in sufficient quantity. Always drain the coolant into a sealable container. Coolant should be reused unless it is contaminated or several years old.

1980 A-series thermostat: place jiggle valve toward top

0.7–2.2 FT. LBS.

ROCKER COVER

68–75 FT. LBS.

ROCKER COVER GASKET

2.7–3.7 FT. LBS.

CAM
BRACKET

COLLAR
GROMMET

REAR OIL
SEAL

REAR CAMSHAFT PULLEY

REAR BACK COVER

13–16 FT. LBS.

4.6–6.1 FT. LBS.

LIFTER PLATE

VALVE LIFTER

CAMSHAFT

VALVE COTTER

FRONT OIL SEAL

SPRING RETAINER

COLLAR

VALVE STEM SEAL

GROMMET

VALVE SPRING

FRONT BACK COVER

SPRING SEAT

VALVE

SWIRL CHAMBER
(COMBUSTION CHAMBER)

SPRING

FRONT TENSIONER

27–33 FT. LBS.

FRONT CAMSHAFT PULLEY

68–75 FT. LBS.

VALVE SEAT

CD-17 (Diesel) cylinder head assembly

2. Disconnect the upper radiator hose at the water outlet.

3. Loosen the two securing nuts and remove the water outlet, gasket, and the thermostat from the thermostat housing.

4. Install the thermostat in the reverse order of removal, using a new gasket with sealer and with the thermostat spring toward the inside of the engine.

Intake Manifold

REMOVAL AND INSTALLATION

1. Remove the air cleaner assembly together with all of the attending hoses.

2. Disconnect the throttle linkage and fuel and vacuum lines from the carburetor.

3. The carburetor can be removed from the

TO HEATER
UNIT

UP

AIR VENT HOLE

THERMOSTAT
HOUSING

THERMOSTAT

GASKET
ALWAYS REPLACE

WATER OUTLET

E-series thermostat and housing

CD-17 (Diesel) outer engine components

1. Thermostat 2. Air check valve 3. Water outlet
A-series thermostat removal

manifold at this point or can be removed as an assembly with the intake manifold.

4. Disconnect the intake and exhaust manifold on the A series engines unless you are removing both. Loosen the intake manifold attaching nuts, working from the two ends toward the center, and then remove them.

5. Remove the intake manifold from the engine.

6. Install the intake manifold in the reverse order of removal.

CD-17 (Diesel) internal engine components

CD-17 (Diesel) thermostat assembly

A-series engine intake manifold

A-series engine exhaust manifold

Removing the A-series intake and exhaust manifolds as a unit

Exhaust Manifold

REMOVAL AND INSTALLATION

1. Remove the air cleaner assembly, if necessary for access. Remove the heat shield, if present.

2. Disconnect the exhaust pipe from the exhaust manifold. Disconnect the intake manifold from the exhaust manifold (A-series engines only) unless you are removing both.

3. Remove all temperature sensors, air induction pipes and other attachments from the manifold. Disconnect the EAI and EGR tubes from their fittings on the E series manifolds.

4. Loosen and remove the exhaust manifold attaching nuts and remove the manifold from the engine.

5. Install the exhaust manifold in the reverse order of removal.

Radiator

REMOVAL AND INSTALLATION

NOTE: *On some models it may be necessary to remove the front grille.*

RUBBER MOUNTING BRACKET (A/T MODEL ONLY)

RADIATOR FILLER CAP

RADIATOR

FAN

RUBBER MOUNTING BRACKET (A/T MODEL ONLY)

FAN

FAN MOTOR

WATER TEMPERATURE SWITCH
Ⓣ 29 - 49 N·m (3.0 - 5.0 kg-m, 22 - 36 ft-lb)

Sentra radiator and fan assembly, others similar

1. Drain the engine coolant into a clean container.

CAUTION: *When draining the coolant, keep in mind that cats and dogs are attracted by the ethylene glycol antifreeze, and are quite likely to drink any that is left in an uncovered container or in puddles on the ground. This will prove fatal in sufficient quantity. Always drain the coolant into a sealable container. Coolant should be reused unless it is contaminated or several years old.*

2. Disconnect the upper and lower radiator hoses and the expansion tank hose.

3. Disconnect the automatic transmission oil cooler lines after draining the transmission. Cap the lines to keep dirt out of them.

4. If the fan has a shroud, unbolt the shroud and move it back, hanging it over the fan.

5. Remove the radiator mounting bolts and the radiator.

6. Installation is the reverse of removal. Fill the automatic transmission to the proper level. Fill the cooling system.

Water Pump
REMOVAL AND INSTALLATION
All Engines, exc. Diesel

1. Drain the engine coolant into a clean container.

CAUTION: *When draining the coolant, keep in mind that cats and dogs are attracted by the ethylene glycol antifreeze, and are quite likely to drink any that is left in an uncovered container or in puddles on the ground. This will prove fatal in sufficient quantity. Always drain the coolant into a sealable container. Coolant should be reused unless it is contaminated or several years old.*

A-series engine water pump removal

2. On the A-series, loosen the four bolts retaining the fan shroud t the radiator and remove the shroud.

3. Loosen the belt, then remove the ran and pulley from the water pump hub.

4. Remove the bolts retaining the pump and remove the pump together with the gasket from the front cover.

5. Remove all traces of gasket material and install the water pump in the reverse order with a new gasket and sealer. Tighten the bolts uniformly.

CD 17 Diesel

1. Disconnect the negative battery cable. Drain the cooling system.

CAUTION: *When draining the coolant, keep in mind that cats and dogs are attracted by the ethylene glycol antifreeze, and are quite likely to drink any that is left in an uncovered container or in puddles on the ground. This will prove fatal in sufficient quantity. Always drain the coolant into a sealable container. Coolant should be reused unless it is contaminated or several years old.*

2. Remove the alternator and A/C compressor drive belts, if equipped.

3. Remove the front crankshaft pulley after

PULLEY

2.7–3.7 FT. LBS.

GASKET ALWAYS REPLACE

WATER PUMP

WATER PUMP BOLT 6.5–10.1FT. LBS.

E series water pump

12–14 FT. LBS.

30.5 (1.201)

12–15 FT. LBS.

30 (1.18)

20.5 (0.807)

30.5 (1.201)

20.5 (0.807)

12–14 FT. LBS.

⊙ BOLT LENGTH MM (IN)

CD-17 (Diesel) water pump

first setting the No. 1 cylinder at TDC on the compression stroke.

4. Remove the front engine covers.

5. Remove the timing belt.

6. Loosen the mounting bolts and remove the water pump.

7. Installation is the reverse of removal. Clean all gasket surfaces before reassembly.

NOTE: *The water pump cannot be disassembled and must be replaced as a unit. Inspect the timing belt for wear or damage and replace if necessary.*

Cylinder Head

REMOVAL AND INSTALLATION

A Series Overhead Valve Engines

NOTE: *To prevent distortion or warping of the cylinder head, allow the engine to cool completely before removing the head bolts. Also, do not pry the head off of the block. If the head seems stuck, tap lightly around the lower perimeter of the head with a rubber mallet to loosen head from the block.*

1. Drain the coolant.

CAUTION: *When draining the coolant, keep in mind that cats and dogs are attracted by the ethylene glycol antifreeze, and are quite likely to drink any that is left in an uncovered container or in puddles on the ground. This will prove fatal in sufficient quantity. Always drain the coolant into a sealable container. Coolant should be reused unless it is contaminated or several years old.*

2. Disconnect the battery ground cable.

3. Remove the upper radiator hose. Remove the water outlet elbow and the thermostat.

4. Remove the air cleaner, carburetor, rocker arm cover, and both manifolds.

5. Remove the spark plugs.

6. Disconnect the temperature gauge connection.

7. Remove the head bolts and remove the head and rocker arm assembly together. Rap the head with a mallet to loosen it from the block. Remove the head and discard the gasket.

8. Remove the pushrods one by one, marking them with the tape to keep them in order.

A-series cylinder head bolt loosening sequence

A-series cylinder head torque tightening sequence

9. Make sure that head and block surfaces are clean. Check the cylinder head surface with a straightedge and a feeler gauge for flatness. If the head is warped more than 0.004 in., it must be trued. If this is not done, there will probably be a leak. The block surface should also be checked in the same way. If the block is warped more than 0.004 in., it must be trued (machined flat).

10. Install a new head gasket. Most gaskets have a TOP marking. Make sure that the proper head gasket is used on the A12 so that no water passages are blocked off.

11. Install the head. Install the pushrods in their original locations. Install the rocker arm assembly. Loosen the rocker arm adjusting screws to prevent bending the pushrods when tightening the head bolts. Tighten the head bolts finger tight. One of the head bolts is smaller in diameter than the others. This bolt should be inserted in hole number one, center in the illustration.

CAUTION: *The above mentioned bolt is thinner than the others because it acts as the oil passageway for the rocker components. It must be inserted in the correct hole or the valve train will seize up after a few hundred miles.*

12. Refer to the Torque Specifications chart for the correct head bolt torque. Tighten the bolts to one third of the specified torque in the order shown in the head bolt tightening sequence illustration. Torque the rocker arm mounting bolts to 15–18 ft.lb.

13. Tighten the bolts to two thirds of the specified torque in sequence.

14. Adjust the valve to the cold setting.

15. Reassemble the engine. Intake and exhaust manifold bolt torque for 1200 A12 engines is 7–10 ft.lb., for all others 11–14 ft.lb. Fill the cooling system. Start the engine and run it until normal temperature is reached. Remove the rocker arm cover. Torque the bolts in sequence once more. Check the valve clearance.

16. Retorque the head bolts after 600 miles of driving. Check the valve clearance after torquing, as this may disturb the setting.

E series Overhead Cam Engines

NOTE: *Make sure engine is cold before removing head: An aluminum head is prone to warpage if removed while warm.*

1. Crank the engine until the No. 1 piston is at Top Dead Center on its compression stroke and disconnect the negative battery cable. Drain the cooling system and remove the air cleaner assembly.

CAUTION: *When draining the coolant, keep*

Head loosening sequence, Sentra gasoline

Sentra gasoline head torquing sequence

Disconnect EGR (upper) and EAI tubes on Sentra

in mind that cats and dogs are attracted by the ethelyne glycol antifreeze, and are quite likely to drink any that is left in an uncovered container or in puddles on the ground. This will prove fatal in sufficient quantity. Always drain the coolant into a sealable container. Coolant should be reused unless it is contaminated or several years old.

2. Remove the alternator.

3. Number all spark plug wires as to their respective cylinders and remove the distributor, with all wires attached.

4. Remove the EAI pipes bracket and EGR tube at the right (EGR valve) side. Disconnect the same pipes on the front (exhaust manifold) side from the manifold.

5. Remove the exhaust manifold cover and the exhaust manifold, taking note that the center manifold nut has a different diameter than the other nuts.

6. Remove the A/C compressor bracket and the power steering pump bracket (if equipped).

7. Label and disconnect the carburetor throttle linkage, fuel line, and all vacuum and electrical connections.

8. Remove the intake manifold with carburetor.

9. Remove the water pump drive belt and pulley. Remove the crankshaft pulley.

10. Remove the rocker (valve) cover.

11. Remove the upper and lower dust cover on the camshaft timing belt shroud.

12. With the shroud removed, the cam sprocket, crankshaft sprocket, jackshaft sprocket, tensioner pulley, and toothed rubber timing belt are in front of you.

13. Mark the relationship of the camshaft sprocket to the timing belt and the crankshaft sprocket to the timing belt with paint or a grease pencil. This will make setting everything up during reassembly much easier if the engine is disturbed during assembly.

14. Remove the belt tensioner pulley.

15. Mark an arrow on the timing belt showing direction of engine rotation, as the belt wears a certain way and should be replaced the way it was removed. Slide the belt off the sprockets.

16. Carefully remove the cylinder head from the block, pulling the head up evenly from both ends. If the head seems stuck, DO NOT pry it off. Tap lightly around the lower perimeter of the head with a rubber mallet to help break the joint. Label all head bolts with tape or magic marker, as they must go back in their original positions.

17. Thoroughly clean both the cylinder block and head mating surfaces. Avoid scratching either.

18. Turn the crankshaft and set No. 1 cylinder at TDC on its compression stroke. This causes the crankshaft timing sprocket mark to be aligned with the cylinder block cover mark.

19. Align the camshaft sprocket mark with the cylinder head cover mark. This causes the valves for No. 1 cylinder to position at TDC on the compression stroke.

20. Place a new gasket on the cylinder block.

21. Install the cylinder head on the block and tighten the bolts in two stages: first to 29–33 ft.lb. on all bolts, then go around again and torque them all up to 51–54 ft.lb. After the engine has been warmed up, check all bolts and re-torque if necessary.

22. Reassemble in the reverse order of disassmbly, making sure all timing marks are in proper alignment.

CD 17 Diesel

1. Drain the coolant and disconnect the battery.

CAUTION: *When draining the coolant, keep in mind that cats and dogs are attracted by the ethylene glycol antifreeze, and are quite likely to drink any that is left in an uncovered container or in puddles on the ground. This will prove fatal in sufficient quantity. Always*

CD17 head torque sequence. Reverse the sequence for installation

drain the coolant into a sealable container. Coolant should be reused unless it is contaminated or several years old.

2. Disconnect the exhaust pipe.

3. Set the No. 1 cylinder at TDC on the compression stroke. Tag and disconnect all hoses and electrical connections.

4. Remove the valve timing belt on the camshaft pulley side of the engine.

5. Remove the injection pump timing belt.

6. Loosen the injection pump pulley and remove it with a suitable puller.

7. Remove the rear engine cover.

8. Tag and removal the fuel injection lines from the injectors.

9. Remove the camshaft (valve) cover and loosen the cylinder head bolts in the reverse of the torque sequence given in this section.

10. Remove the cylinder head, with the manifolds still attached. If the head will not budge, tap around the head-to-block mating surface with a rubber mallet. The manifolds can be removed on a bench.

11. Reverse the above removal procedure for installation. Head gaskets are selected by measuring the piston projection. See "Piston and Connecting Rod" for an application chart. Torque the head bolts.

CLEANING AND INSPECTION

Using a wire brush, clean the carbon from the cylinder head, then check it for cracks and flaws.

Make sure that the cylinder head and the block surfaces are clean. Check the cylinder

Check the cylinder head for warpage

head surface for flatness, using a straightedge and a feeler gauge. If the cylinder head and/or the block are warped more than 0.004 in., it must be trued by a machine shop; if this is not done, there will probably be a compression or water leak.

Valves and Springs

VALVE ADJUSTMENT

NOTE: *For valve adjustment procedures refer to Valve Lash in Chapter 2.*

REMOVAL AND INSTALLATION

1. Refer to the Cylinder Head, Removal and Installation procedures in this section and remove the cylinder head.
2. Loosen and back off the rocker arm adjusting screws, then remove the rocker arm assembly.

NOTE: *After removing the rocker arm assembly (E-series), remove the spring retainers and the rocker arms from the shaft(s) (be sure to keep the parts in order), then reinstall the rocker arm shaft.*

3. Using the spring compression tool No. ST12070000 (A-series), No. KV101072S0 (E-series), No. KV101092S0 (CD-series) compress the valve springs. Remove the valve keeper, then relieve the spring pressure. Remove the springs, the valve seals and the valves.
4. To install, use new oil seals and reverse the removal procedures. On the CD-series engines use tool No. KV10107900 and drive in the valve seal until it contacts the guide and set the valve lifter plate so that the mark faces the valve lifter side. Tighten the rocker shaft bolts to 14–18 ft.lb. on the A-series engines; 13–15 ft.lb. on E-series engines, in a circular sequence. Adjust the valves. (See the procedure in Chapter 2).

NOTE: *On most engines, the intake/exhaust valve springs are the uneven pitch type. That is, the springs have narrow coils at the bottom and wide coils at the top. The narrow coils (painted white) must be the side making contact on the cylinder head surface.*

INSPECTION

Before the valves can be properly inspected, the stem, the lower end of the stem, the entire valve face and head must be cleaned. An old valve works well for chipping carbon from the valve head, a wire brush, a gasket scraper or a putty knife can be used for cleaning the valve face and/or the area between the face and the lower stem. DO NOT scratch the valve face during cleaning. Clean the entire stem with a rag soaked in thinners to remove all of the varnish and gum.

Thorough inspection of the valves requires the use of a micrometer and a dial indicator. If these instruments are not available, the parts should be taken to a reputable machine shop for inspection. Refer to the Valve Specifications chart, for the valve stem and stem-to-guide specifications.

Using a dial indicator, measure the inside diameter of the valve guides at their bottom, midpoint and top positions, at 90° apart. Subtract the valve stem measurement; if the clearance exceeds that listed in the specifications chart under Stem-to-Guide Clearance, replace the valve(s).

Check the top of each valve for pitting and unusual wear due to improper rocker adjustment, etc. The stem tip can be ground flat if it is worn but no more that 0.020 in. can be removed; if this limit must be exceeded to make the tip flat and square, then the valve must be replaced. If the valve stem tips are ground, make sure that the valve is fixed securely into the jig, so that the tip contacts the grinding wheel squarely at exactly 90°.

REFACING

Valve refacing should only be handled by a reputable machine shop, as the experience and equipment needed to do the job are beyond that of the average owner/mechanic. During the course of a normal valve job, refacing is necessary when simply lapping the valves into their seats will not correct the seat and face wear. When the valves are reground (resurfaced), the valve seats must also be recut, again requiring special equipment and experience.

CHECK SPRINGS

1. Place the valve spring on a flat, clean surface, next to a square.
2. Measure the height of the spring and rotate it against the edge of the square to measure the distortion (out-of-roundness). If the spring height between springs varies or the distortion exceeds more than $\frac{1}{16}$ in., replace the spring(s). The valve spring squareness should not exceed: 0.087 in. (outer-gasoline engine), 0.083 in. (outer-diesel engine) or 0.075 in. (inner).
3. A valve spring tester is needed to test the spring pressure. Compare the tested pressure with the pressures listed in the Valve Specifications chart in this section.

Valve Seats

INSPECTION

Check the valve seat inserts for evidence of pitting or excessive wear at the valve contact surface. Because the cylinder head must be machined to accept the new seat inserts, consult an engine specialist or machinist about this work.

REMOVAL AND INSTALLATION

CAUTION: *To prevent damaging the other cylinder head components, completely disassemble the head.*

1. The old valve seat can be removed by machining it from the head or by heating the head in an 302–320°F (150–160°C) oil bath, then driving it from the head with a punch.

NOTE: *When removing the valve insert, be careful not to damage the cylinder head surface.*

2. Select a valve insert replacement and check the outside diameter, then ream the cylinder head recess at room temperature.

3. Heat the cylinder head to 302–320°F (150–160°C) in an oil bath, then press in the new valve seat, until it seats in the recess.

CUTTING THE SEATS

1. Allow the cylinder head to cool to room temperature. Using a valve seating tool kit, cut a new valve contact surface on the valve seat.

NOTE: *When repairing the valve seat, make sure that the valve and the guide are in good condition; if wear is evident, replace the valve and/or the guide, then correct the valve seat.*

2. To complete the operation, use valve grinding compound and lap the valve to the seat.

3. To install the removed components, reverse the removal procedures.

Valve Guides

REMOVAL AND INSTALLATION

1. Using a 2-ton press or a hammer and a suitable driving tool, drive the old valve guide from the cylinder head, in the rocker cover to combustion chamber direction.

NOTE: *Heating the cylinder head to 302–320°F (150–200°C) will facilitate the operation.*

2. Using the Valve Guide Reamer tool KV11081000 (A series) or ST11081000 (E series) engines, ream the valve guide hole.

3. Using a new valve guide, press it into the cylinder head and ream the guide hole with the proper size reamer.

4. Using a valve seating tool kit, cut a new valve contact on the valve seat.

5. To install the removed components, reverse the removal procedures.

KNURLING

Valve guides which are not excessively worn or distorted may in some cases, be knurled rather than reamed. Knurling is a process in which metal inside the valve guide bores is displaced and raised (forming a very fine cross-hatch pattern), thereby reducing clearance. Knurling also provides for excellent oil control. The possibility of knurling rather than reaming the guides should be discussed with a machinist.

Oil Pan

REMOVAL AND INSTALLATION

All Engines

To remove the oil pan it will be necessary to unbolt the motor mounts and jack the engine to gain clearance. Drain the oil, remove the attaching screws, and remove the oil pan and gasket. Install the oil pan in the reverse order with a new gasket, tightening the screws to 4–7 ft.lb. (3–4 ft.lb. E series).

Oil Pump

The oil pump is mounted externally on the engine, this eliminates the need to remove the oil pan in order to remove the oil pump. The oil pump is actually part of the oil filter mounting bracket.

Removing A-series engine oil pump

OUTER ROTOR

Exploded view of A-series engine oil pump

REMOVAL AND INSTALLATION

1973 and Later All A Series Models

1. Drain the engine oil and remove oil filter.

2. Remove the front stabilizer bar if it is in the way of removing the oil pump (if equipped).

3. Remove the splash shield.

4. Remove the oil pump body with the drive spindle assembly.

5. Install the oil pump in the reverse order of removal, after removing any traces of the old gasket and installing a new gasket.

6. Make sure the pump mounting bolts are tight. Install the oil filter to the oil pump. Check the oil level mark on the dipstick and add oil if necessary. Start the engine and check for leaks.

E Series Engines

1. Loosen the alternator lower bolts.

2. Remove the alternator belt and adjusting bar bolt. Move the alternator aside so there is ample room to work.

3. Disconnect the oil pressure gauge harness.

4. If necessary, remove the oil filter from the engine to give proper access to the oil pump bolts.

5. Unbolt the oil pump from the engine block and remove.

6. If the oil pump gasket is worn, replace it. Install the oil pump, making sure all bolts are tight. You may have to turn the pump body slightly when inserting the pump drive gear into the block, in order to properly engage the drive gear with its drive gear on the engine jackshaft.

Removing oil pressure gauge harness from oil pump, E-series

CD 17 Diesel

1. Remove the valve timing belt.

2. Drain the oil and remove the oil pan.

3. The oil pump is bolted to the front of the engine block, at the front of the crankshaft. Loosen the mounting bolts and remove the oil pump assembly.

NOTE: *Remove the crankshaft key to avoid damage to the oil seal on the pump.*

4. Remove the oil pump rear cover and check gear clearance using a feeler gauge. Body-to-outer gear clearance should be 0.0043–0.0079 in.; outer gear-to-crescent clearance should be 0.0083–0.0126 in.

5. Replace the oil seal in the pump by carefully prying it out. Coat the new seal liberally with clean engine oil before installation.

6. Installation is the reverse of removal. Apply sealer to the four corners of the oil pan and use a new oil pump gasket. Torque the oil pump bolts to 9–12 ft.lb.

Timing Chain Cover

REMOVAL AND INSTALLATION

A12, A12A, A13, A14, A15 Overhead Valve Engines

1. Remove the radiator. Loosen the alternator adjustment and remove the belt. Loosen the air pump adjustment and remove the belt on engines with the air pump system.

CAUTION: *When draining the coolant, keep in mind that cats and dogs are attracted by the ethylene glycol antifreeze, and are quite likely to drink any that is left in an uncovered container or in puddles on the ground. This will prove fatal in sufficient quantity. Always drain the coolant into a sealable container. Coolant should be reused unless it is contaminated or several years old.*

2. Remove the fan and water pump.

3. Bend back the locktab from the crankshaft pulley nut. Remove the nut by affixing a

Removing the A-series engine timing cover

When removing the A-series engine timing cover it is necessary to loosen or remove the oil pan

heavy wrench and rapping the wrench with a hammer. The nut must be unscrewed in the opposite direction of normal engine rotation. Pull off the pulley.

4. It is recommended that the oil pan be removed or loosened before the front cover is removed.

5. Unbolt and remove the timing chain cover.

6. Replace the crankshaft oil seal in the cover. Most models use a felt seal.

7. Reverse the procedure to install, using new gaskets. Apply sealant to both sides of the timing cover gasket. Front cover bolt torque is 4 ft.lb., water pump bolt torque is 7–10 ft.lb., and oil pan bolt torque is 4 ft.lb.

Timing Belt Cover
REMOVAL AND INSTALLATION
E series Overhead Cam Engines

1. Loosen the air conditioner belt and remove.

2. Loosen the alternator adjusting bolt, and remove the alternator belt. Unbolt the alternator mounting bracket and remove the alternator.

3. Remove the power steering belt (if equipped) by loosening the steering pump adjusting bolt.

4. Remove the water pump pulley.

5. Remove the crankshaft pulley.

6. Loosen and remove the eight bolts securing the timing cover and remove the cover.

7. Installation is the reverse of removal. Adjust all accessory drive belts and tighten the mounting bolts. Torque the crank pulley bolt to 83–108 ft.lb.; the water pump pulley bolt to 2.7–3.7 ft.lb.; and the belt cover bolts to 2.7–3.7 ft.lb.

Upper and lower dust retaining bolts

CD 17 Engine

1. Disconnect the negative battery cable. Drain the cooling system and then remove the

Carefully pry out the front oil seal

radiator together with the upper and lower radiator hoses.

CAUTION: *When draining the coolant, keep in mind that cats and dogs are attracted by the ethylene glycol antifreeze, and are quite likely to drink any that is left in an uncovered container or in puddles on the ground. This will prove fatal in sufficient quantity. Always drain the coolant into a sealable container. Coolant should be reused unless it is contaminated or several years old.*

2. Remove the fan, fan coupling and fan pulley. Using a gear puller, remove the crankshaft damper pulley.

3. Remove the power steering pump, bracket and idler pulley.

4. Remove the front belt cover. Remove the valve timing belt (see "Timing Belt and Camshaft" removal in this chapter).

5. Remove the front oil seal by taping the end of a thin prybar or old screwdriver, and carefully pry the old seal out from around the end of the crankshaft. Do not scratch the shaft with the prybar.

6. Coat a new seal with clean engine oil. Slide it onto the cranksahft end and back into place in the front of the block. Use a small drift to evenly drive the seal back until it seats in position.

7. Installation is the reverse of removal. Follow the "Timing Belt and Camshaft" removal and installation procedure when installing the timing belt.

Timing Chain and Camshaft
REMOVAL AND INSTALLATION
A12, A12A, A13, A14, A15 Overhead Valve Engines

NOTE: *It is recommended that this operation be done with the engine removed from the vehicle.*

1. Remove the timing chain cover.
2. Unbolt and remove the chain tensioner.

A-series engine camshaft locating plate correctly installed

A-series engine timing mark alignment

3. Remove the camshaft sprocket retaining bolt.

4. Pull off the camshaft sprocket, easing off the crankshaft sprocket at the same time. Remove both sprockets and chain as an assembly. Be careful not to lose the shim and oil slinger from behind the crankshaft sprocket.

5. Remove the distributor, distributor drive spindle, pushrods, and valve lifters. Number all parts with tape.

NOTE: *The lifter cannot be removed until the camshaft has been removed.*

Remove the oil pump and pump driveshaft.

6. Unbolt and remove the camshaft locating plate.

7. Remove the camshaft carefully. This will be easier if the block is inverted to prevent the lifters from falling down.

8. The camshaft bearings can be pressed out and replaced. They are available in undersizes, should it be necessary to regrind the camshaft journals.

9. Reinstall the camshaft. If the locating plate has an oil hole, it should be to the right of the engine. The locating plate is marked with the word LOWER and an arrow. Locating plate bolt torque is 3–4 ft.lb. Be careful to en-

gage the drive pin in the rear end of the camshaft with the slot in the oil pump driveshaft.

10. Camshaft endplay can be measured after temporarily replacing the camshaft sprocket and securing bolt. The standard endplay specifications for the A12 engine are 0.001–0.003 in. with a service limit (largest allowable endplay limit) of 0.004 in. The A12A, A13, A14 and A15 engines have standard endplay specifications of 0.004–0.002 in. with a service limit of 0.004 in. If the endplay is excessive, replace the locating plate. New plates are available in several sizes.

11. If the crankshaft or camshaft has been replaced, install the sprockets temporarily and make sure that they are parallel. Adjust by shimming under the crankshaft sprocket.

12. Assemble the sprockets and chain, aligning them.

13. Turn the crankshaft until the keyway and the No. 1 piston is at top dead center. Install the sprockets and chain. The oil slinger behind the crankshaft sprocket must be replaced with the concave surface to the front. If the chain and sprocket installation is correct, the sprocket marks must be aligned between the shaft centers when the No. 1 piston is at top dead center. Engine camshaft sprocket retaining bolt torque is 33–36 ft.lb.

14. The rest of the reassembly procedure is the reverse of disassembly. Engine chain tensioner bolt torque is 4–6 ft.lb.

Camshaft and Timing Belt
REMOVAL AND INSTALLATION
E series Overhead Cam Engines

1. Removal of the cylinder head from the engine is optional. Crank the engine until the No. 1 piston is at Top Dead Center on its compression stroke.

2. Follow the "Timing Belt Cover" removal procedure and remove the cover. Mark the relationship of the camshaft sprocket to the timing belt and the crankshaft sprocket to the timing belt with paint or grease pencil. This will make setting everything up during reassembly much easier, if the engine is disturbed during assembly.

3. Remove the distributor.

4. Remove the thermostat housing.

5. Remove the timing belt from the sprockets, after loosening the belt tensioner pulley.

6. Remove the rocker cover and remove the rocker shaft.

7. Loosen and remove the cam drive sprocket.

8. Remove the camshaft front retainer plate.

NOTE: *Be careful not to damage the oil seal*

CAMSHAFT PULLEY MARK (E15 ENGINE) — ALIGN

— ALIGN

Camshaft and crankshaft sprocket alignment marks, E-series engine

Remove three cam sprocket bolts and pull off sprocket, E-series

E-series front camshaft retainer screws

lip between the front retainer plate and the end of the camshaft.

9. Squirt a small amount of clean oil around the camshaft bearings. Carefully slide the camshaft out of the carrier in the cylinder head.

10. To install, lightly oil the camshaft bear-

Use care in removing camshaft from head, E-series

ings with clean motor oil and slowly slide the cam into place in the cylinder head.

11. Install the camshaft front retainer plate on the cylinder head.

12. Reassemble the remainder of the head assembly in the reverse order of removal. Check the valve timing after all sprockets and timing belt are installed. Tighten the camshaft drive sprocket to 4.3–5.8 ft.lb. Install a new gasket behind the thermostat housing. Adjust the valves, and adjust all drive belts.

CD 17 Diesel

NOTE: *The camshaft is normally removed with the cylinder head removed from the engine. Follow the procedure below for timing belt removal, then follow the "Cylinder Head Removal" procedure earlier in this section; the camshaft removal procedure follows timing belt removal. The injection pump has its own belt drive and is covered later in this section.*

1. Support the engine with a jack and remove the right side engine mount, then jack the engine up to allow working clearance.

2. Set the No. 1 cylinder at TDC on its compression stroke.

3. Remove the alternator and A/C cmpressor (if equipped) drive belts.

4. Using a puller, remove the crankshaft damper pulley.

5. Loosen the tensioner pulley and set it to the "free" position. Remove the idler pulley.

6. Remove the crankshaft pulley with the timing belt.

7. Check the belt for damage, missing teeth, wear or saturation with oil or grease. If damage is evident or if you are in doubt as to the belt's condition, replace the belt.

NOTE: *Do not bend, twist or turn the timing belt inside out. Do not allow the belt to come into contact with any grease, oil or solvents.*

8. Remove the cylinder head and manifolds.

9. Remove the camshaft bearing caps and check the clearance with Plastigage®. Do not

CD17 camshaft bearing cap torque sequence

turn the camshaft. If the bearing clearance exceeds 0.1 mm (0.004 in.) replace the bearing caps, camshaft or cylinder head.

10. After checking clearances, remove the bearing caps and remove the camshaft with both oil seals. Have the camshaft runout and lobe height checked; if worn beyond specification, replace the camshaft.

11. To install the camshaft, assemble in the reverse order of removal. Before installing the oil seals, lubricate with clean engine oil. Reinstall the cylinder head and check valve clearances; adjust if necessary.

NOTE: *There are two different diameter seals used on the camshaft front and rear. Be sure to use the correct seal when installing. (The front seal has an arrow on the outer edge facing clockwise; the rear seal arrow points counterclockwise). If you are replacing the oil seals without removing the camshaft, remove the pulleys and carefully pry the seals out using a small pry bar or an old screwdriver covered with tape. Use care not to scratch the camshaft, cylinder head or bearing cap.*

12. Install the timing belt assembly in the reverse order of removal. Align the marks on the timing belt with those on the camshaft and crankshaft pulleys. When tensioning the belt, loosen the tensioner bolt and turn the crankshaft pulleys. When tensioning the belt, loosen the tensioner bolt and turn the crankshaft two times in its normal rotating direction, then tighten the tensioner while holding it. Do not allow the tensioner to rotate when tightening, and NEVER turn the engine against its normal rotating direction

CHECKING CAMSHAFT

Place the camshaft on a set of V-blocks, supported by the outermost bearing surfaces. Place a dial micrometer, with it's finger resting on the center bearing surface, then turn the camshaft to check the bearing runout; the runout should not exceed 0.0039 in., if it does exceed the limit, replace the camshaft.

Check the camshaft bearing surfaces (in the engine) with an internal micrometer and the bearing surfaces (of the camshaft) with a micrometer.

Jack Shaft

REMOVAL AND INSTALLATION

E-Series Engine

1. Refer to the Timing Belt and/or Chain, Removal and Installation procedures in this section and remove the timing belt.

2. Pull the crankshaft sprocket from the crankshaft. Remove the jackshaft sprocket bolts, then separate the sprocket from the jackshaft.

3. Remove the lower locating plate from the cylinder block. Remove the jackshaft and the crankshaft oil seals from the locating plate.

4. Remove the jackshaft locating plate, then pull the shaft out through the front of the cylinder block.

5. Check the jackshaft bearing diameters (in the cylinder block) with an internal micrometer and the bearing diameters (of the jackshaft) with a micrometer; the clearance should not exceed 0.0059 in., if it does exceed the limit, replace the jackshaft bearings.

6. Use a hammer and a brass drift, to remove and install the jackshaft bearings in the cylinder block.

NOTE: *Be sure to align the oil hole in the bearing with the hole in the cylinder block. After installation, check the bearing clearances. Using sealant, install a new welch plug into the cylinder block.*

7. To install, use new oil seals, gaskets and

Checking the jackshaft bearing diameters with an internal micrometer

Installing the welch plug into the cylinder block

reverse the removal procedures. Torque the jackshaft sprocket bolts to 6.5–9 ft.lb., the oil pump bolts to 5.8–7.2 ft.lb., the tensioner pulley bolts to 12–15 ft.lb., the timing cover bolts to 2.5–4 ft.lb., the crankshaft pulley bolt to 83–108 ft.lb. Adjust the timing belt and the drive belt tensions.

Pistons and Connecting Rods

REMOVAL AND INSTALLATION

It is recommended that the engine be removed from the vehicle and mount it on an engine stand, before removing the pistons and connecting rods from the engine.

1. Refer to the Cylinder Head, Removal and Installation procedures in this section and remove the cylinder head.

2. Using a ridge reamer tool, remove the carbon buildup from the top of the cylinder wall.

3. Drain the lubricant from the engine. Invert the engine on the stand, then remove the oil pan, the oil strainer and the pickup tube.

4. Position the piston to be removed at the bottom of its stroke, so that the connecting rod bearing cap can be easily reached.

5. Remove the connecting rod bearing cap nuts and the cap and the lower half of the bearing. Cover the rod bolts with lengths of rubber tubing to protect the cylinder walls when the rod and piston assembly is driven out.

6. Push the piston/connecting rod assembly, out through the top of the cylinder block with a length of wood or a wooden hammer handle.

CAUTION: *When removing the piston/connecting rod assembly, be careful not to scratch the cylinder wall with the connecting rod.*

7. Keep all of the components from each cylinder together and install them in the cylinder from which they were removed.

8. Lubricate all of the piston/connecting rod components with engine oil, including the bearing face of the connecting rod and the outer face of the pistons with engine oil.

NOTE: *See the illustrations for the correct positioning of the piston rings.*

9. Turn the crankshaft until the rod journal of the particular cylinder you are working on is brought to the TDC position.

10. Clamp the piston/ring assembly into a ring compressor, the notched mark or number (on the piston head) must face the front of the engine and the oil hole (on the side of the connecting rod) must face the rightside of the engine; push the piston/connecting rod assembly into the cylinder bore until the big bearing end

Piston and rod positioning—A-series engines

Piston and rod positioning, E-series

Ring positioning, E-series

Piston ring placement—A-series engines

of the connecting rod seats on the rod journal of the crankshaft.

CAUTION: *Use care not to scratch the cylinder wall with the connecting rod.*

11. Push down on the piston/connecting rod assembly, while turning the crankshaft (the connecting rod rides around on the crankshaft

Space CD17 ring gaps 120° apart when installing piston

CD17 piston identification marks

rod journal), until the crankshaft rod journal is at the BDC (bottom dead center).

12. Align the mark on the connecting rod bearing cap with that on the connecting rod and torque the connecting rod bearing cap bolts to 24–27 ft.lb.

13. To complete the installation, reverse the removal procedures.

IDENTIFICATION AND POSITIONING

The pistons are marked with a notch or a number stamped on the piston head. When installed in the engine the notch or number markings must be facing the front of the engine.

The connecting rods are installed in the engine with the oil hole facing the right side of the engine.

NOTE: *It is advisable to number the pistons, connecting rods and bearing caps in some manner so that they can be reinstalled in the same cylinder, facing in the same direction from which they are removed.*

PISTON RING REPLACEMENT

A piston ring expander is necessary for removing and installing the piston rings (to avoid damaging them). When the rings are removed, clean the ring grooves using an appropriate ring groove cleaning tool, using care not to cut

too deeply. Use solvent to thoroughly remove all of the carbon and varnish deposits.

When installing the rings, make sure that the stamped mark on the ring is facing upwards. Install the bottom rings first, then the upper ones last. Be sure to use a ring expander, to keep from breaking the rings.

CLEANING AND INSPECTION

Clean the piston after removing the rings (Refer to Piston Ring Replacement), by scraping the carbon from the top of the piston (DO NOT scratch the piston surface). Use a broken piston ring or a ring cleaning tool, to clean out the ring grooves. Clean the entire piston with solvent and a brush (NOT a wire brush).

With the piston thoroughly cleaned, place both compression rings on each piston. Using a feeler gauge, check the side clearance of the piston rings. If the side clearance is too large, replace the piston; if the side clearance is too small, cut the land areas a little larger.

Using a feeler gauge to check the ring end gap, lubricate the cylinder wall, then (using an inverted piston) drive the new ring(s) approximately 1–2 inches below the top of the cylinder bore.

NOTE: *If the ring gap is too small, carefully remove the rings and file the ends until the proper gap is acquired.*

PISTON PIN REPLACEMENT

The piston pin, the piston and the connecting rod are held together as an assembly, by pressing piston pin into the connecting rod. An arbor press and a special pin removing stand tool No. ST13040000 (1973–78), KV10105300 (1979–81), or KV10107400 (1982 and later), are used for removing and installing the piston pin.

NOTE: *The piston pin should slide smoothly into the piston, using hand pressure, at room temperature.*

ROD BEARING REPLACEMENT

The connecting rod side clearance and the big-end bearing inspection should be performed while the rods are still installed in the engine. Determine the clearance between the connecting rod sides and the crankshaft, using a feeler gauge. If the side clearance is below the minimum tolerance, have a machine shop correct the tolerance; if the clearance is excessive, substitute an unworn rod and recheck the clearance.

To check the connecting rod big-end bearing clearances, remove the rod bearing caps one at a time. Using a clean, dry shop rag, thoroughly clean all of the oil from the crank journal and the bearing insert in the cap.

NOTE: *The Plastigage® gauging material you will be using to check the clearances with, is soluble in oil; therefore any oil on the journal or bearing could result in an incorrect reading.*

Lay a strip of Plastigage® across the bearing insert. Reinsert the bearing cap and retorque to specifications.

Remove the rod cap and determine the bearing clearance by comparing the width of the now flattened Plastigage® to the scale on the Plastigage® envelope. The journal taper is determined by comparing the width of the strip near its ends. Rotate the crankshaft 90° and retest, to determine the journal eccentricity.

CAUTION: *DO NOT rotate the crankshaft with Plastigage® installed, for an incorrect reading will result.*

If the clearances are not within the tolerances, the bearing inserts must be replaced with ones of the correct oversize or undersize and/or the crankshaft must be ground. If installing new bearing inserts, make sure that the tabs fit correctly into the notch of the bearing cap and rod. Lubricate the face of each insert before installing them onto the crankshaft.

Crankshaft and Main Bearing

REMOVAL AND INSTALLATION

1. Refer to the Piston and Connecting Rod, Removal and Installation procedures, in this section and remove the connecting rod bearings from the crankshaft.

NOTE: *It may not be necessary to remove the piston/connecting rod assemblies from the cylinder block.*

2. On the A-series engine, remove the timing chain and the flywheel from the engine. On the E-series engine, remove the jackshaft sprocket, the crankshaft sprocket, the frontside rear timing plate, then the clutch/flywheel assembly (M/T) or driveplate (A/T), the rear oil seal retainer and the rear plate.

3. Check the crankshaft thrust clearance (end play) before removing the crankshaft from the engine block. Using a pry bar, pry the crankshaft forward to the extent of its travel and measure the clearance at the No. 3 main bearing. Pry the crankshaft rearward to the extent of its travel and measure the clearance on the other side of the bearing.

NOTE: *If the clearance is greater than specified, the thrust bearing must be replaced. When removing the crankshaft bearing caps, be sure to keep the bearing together with the caps, unless new bearings are going to be installed.*

4. Remove the crankshaft bearing caps, the cap bearings and the crankshaft from the engine.

5. To install, check the clearances with the Plastigage® method, then replace the bearings (if necessary) and reverse the removal procedures. Torque the crankshaft bearing cap bolts to 36–43 ft.lb. (A and E-series engines), 33–40 ft.lb. (CD-series engines).

6. To complete the installation, reverse the removal procedures.

NOTE: *When torquing the main bearing caps, start with the center bearing and work towards both ends at the same time.*

INSPECTION

The crankshaft inspection and servicing should be handled exclusively by a reputable machinist, for most necessary procedures require a dial indicator, fixing jigs and a large micrometer; also machine tools, such as: crankshaft grinder. The crankshaft should be throughly cleaned (especially the oil passages), Magnafluxed (to check for minute cracks) and the following checks made: Main journal diameter, crank pin (connecting rod journal) diameter, taper, out-of-round and runout. Wear, beyond the specification limits, in any of these areas means the crankshaft must be reground or replaced.

MAIN BEARING CLEARANCE CHECK

Checking the main bearing clearances is done in the same manner as checking the connecting rod big-end clearances.

1. With the crankshaft installed, remove the main bearing cap. Clean all of the oil from the bearing insert (in the cap and the crankshaft journal), for the Plastigage® material is oil-soluble.

2. Lay a strip of Plastigage® across the full width of the bearing cap and install the bearing cap, then torque the cap to specifications.

NOTE: *DO NOT rotate the crankshaft with the Plastigage® installed.*

3. Remove the bearing cap and compare the scale on the Plastigage® envelope with the flattened Plastigage® material in the bearing. The journal taper is determined by comparing the width of both ends of the Plastigage® material. Rotate the crankshaft 90° and retest, to determine eccentricity.

4. Repeat the procedure for the remaining bearings. If the bearing journal and insert appear to be in good shape (with no unusual wear visible) and are within tolerances, no further main bearing service is required. If unusual wear is evident and/or the clearances are outside specifications, the bearings must be replaced and the cause of their wear determined.

Rear Main Oil Seal

REPLACEMENT

A Series And CD 17 (Diesel) Engines

In order to replace the rear main oil seal, the rear main bearing cap must be removed. Removal of the rear main bearing cap requires the use of a special rear main bearing cap puller. Also, the oil seal is installed with a special crankshaft rear oil seal drift. Unless these or similar tools are available to you, it is recommended that the oil seal be replaced by a Datsun service center.

1. Remove the engine and transmission assembly from the vehicle.
2. Remove the transmission from the engine. Remove the oil pan.
3. Remove the clutch from the flywheel.
4. Remove the flywheel from the crankshaft.
5. Except on the CD 17, remove the rear main bearing cap together with the bearing cap side seals.
6. Remove the rear main oil seal from around the crankshaft. On the CD 17, pry the old seal from around the crankshaft with a small prybar.
7. Apply lithium grease around the sealing lip of the oil seal and install the seal around the crankshaft using a suitable tool.
8. Apply sealer to the rear main bearing cap as indicated, install the rear main bearing cap, and tighten the cap bolts to 33–40 ft.lb.

Installing A-series rear oil seal using drift

9. Apply sealant to the rear main bearing cap side seals and install the side seals, driving the seals into place with a suitable drift.
10. Assemble the engine and install it in the vehicle in the reverse order of removal.

E Series Engines

In order to replace the rear main oil seal in the E series engines, the transaxle must be removed, or the engine and transaxle assembly must be removed.

Prying out the oil seal on the CD-17 series engine using a suitable tool

Drive in the new oil seal—CD-17 series engines

Installing E-series rear oil seal retainer

1. Remove the transaxle from the car.
2. Remove the clutch from the flywheel.
3. Unbolt and remove the flywheel from the end of the crankshaft.
4. Unbolt the two bolts attaching the oil seal retainer to the oil pan.
5. Remove the three Phillips head screws that attach the oil seal retainer to the engine block, and remove the oil seal.
6. During installation of the new oil seal, apply a coating of clean oil to the outside edge of the seal. Install the new seal in the direction that the dust seal lip faces (to the outside of the crankcase). Coat the mating shaft with clean oil also, when installing the oil seal retainer, to prevent scratches and a folded lip.

Emission Controls and Fuel System

4

EMISSION CONTROLS

There are three types of automotive pollutants; crankcase fumes, exhaust gases and gasoline evaporation. The equipment that is used to limit these pollutants is commonly called emission control equipment.

Crankcase Emission Controls

The crankcase emission control equipment consists of a positive crankcase ventilation valve (PCV), a closed or open oil filler cap, and hoses to connect this equipment.

When the engine is running, a small portion of the gases which are formed in the combustion chamber during combustion leak by the piston rings and enter the crankcase. Since these gases are under pressure they tend to escape from the crankcase and enter into the atmosphere. If these gases were allowed to remain in the crankcase, they would contaminate the engine oil and cause sludge to build up. If the gases are allowed to escape into the atmosphere, they would pollute the air, as they contain unburned hydrocarbons. The crankcase emission control equipment recycles these gases back into the engine combustion chamber where they are burned.

Crankcase gases are recycled in the following manner: while the engine is running, clean filtered air is drawn into the crankcase through the carburetor air filter and then through a hose lading to the rocker cover. As the air passes through the crankcase it picks up the combustion gases and carries them out of the crankcase, up through the PCV valve and into the intake manifold. After they enter the intake manifold they are drawn into the combustion chamber and burned.

The most critical component in the system is the PCV valve. This vacuum controlled valve regulates the amount of gases which are recycled into the combustion chamber. At low engine speeds the valve is partially closed, limiting the flow of gases into the intake manifold. As engine speed increases, the valve opens to admit greater quantities of the gases into the intake manifold. If the valve should become blocked or plugged, the gases will be prevented from escaping from the crankcase by the normal route. Since these gases are under pressure, they will find their own way out of the crankcase. This alternate route is usually a weak oil seal or gasket in the engine. As the gas escapes by the gasket, it also creates an oil leak. Besides causing oil leaks, a clogged PCV valve also allows these gases to remain in the crankcase, promoting the formation of sludge in the engine.

The above explanation and the troubleshooting procedure which follows applies to all engines with PCV systems.

TESTING

Check the PCV system hoses and connections, to see that there are no leaks; then replace or tighten, as necessary.

To check the valve, remove it and blow through both of its ends. When blowing from the side which goes toward the intake manifold, very little air should pass through it. When blowing from the crankcase (valve cover) side, air should pass through freely.

Replace the valve with a new one, if the valve fails to function as outlined.

NOTE: *Do not attempt to clean or adjust the valve; replace it with a new one.*

REMOVAL AND INSTALLATION

To remove the PCV valve, simply loosen the hose clamp and remove the valve from the manifold-to-crankcase hose and intake manifold. Install the PCV valve in the reverse order of removal.

1. Seal type oil level gauge
2. Baffle plate
3. Flame arrester
4. Filter
5. P.C.V. valve
6. Steel net
7. Baffle plate

⇒ FRESH AIR
➡ BLOW-BY GAS

Crankcase emissions control system, A-series. E-series similar

PCV FILTER

Replace the PCV filter inside the air cleaner when you replace the PCV valve, or more frequently if operating in dusty or smoggy conditions.

Evaporative Emission Control System

When raw fuel evaporates, the vapors contain hydrocarbons. To prevent these nasties from escaping into the atmosphere, the fuel evaporative emission control system was developed.

There are two different evaporative emission control systems used on Datsuns.

The system used through 1974 consists of a sealed fuel tank, a vapor-liquid separator, a flow guide (check) valve, and all of the hoses connecting these components, in the above order, leading from the fuel tank to the PCV hose, which connects the crankcase to the PCV valve.

In operation, the vapor formed in the fuel tank passes through the vapor separator, onto the flow guide valve and the crankcase. When the engine is not running, if the fuel vapor pressure in the vapor separator goes above 0.4 in. Hg., the flow guide valve opens and allows the vapor to enter the engine crankcase. Otherwise the flow guide valve is closed to the vapor separator while the engine is not running. When the engine is running, and a vacuum is developed in the fuel tank or in the engine crankcase and the difference of pressure between the relief side and the fuel tank or crankcase becomes 2 in. Hg., the relief valve opens and allows ambient air from the air cleaner into the fuel tank or the engine crankcase. This ambient air replaces the vapor within the fuel tank or crankcase, bringing the fuel tank or crankcase back into a neutral or positive pressure range.

The system used on 1975 and later models consists of sealed fuel tank, vapor-liquid separator (certain models only), vapor vent line, carbon canister, vacuum signal line and a canister purge line.

In operation, fuel vapors and/or liquid are routed to the liquid/vapor separator or check

1. Carbon canister
2. Vacuum signal line
3. Canister vent line
4. Vapor vent line
5. Fuel filler cap with vacuum relief valve
6. Fuel check valve
7. Fuel tank

Evaporative emission control system schematic

valve where liquid fuel is directed back into the fuel tank as fuel vapors flow into the charcoal filled canister. The charcoal absorbs and stores the fuel vapors when the engine is not running or is at idle. When the throttle valves in the carburetor (or air intakes for fuel injection) are opened, vacuum from above the throttle valves is routed through a vacuum signal line to the purge control valve on the canister. The control valve opens and allows the fuel vapors to be drawn from the canister through a purge line and into the intake manifold and the combustion chambers.

INSPECTION AND SERVICE

Check the hoses for proper connections and damage. Replace as necessary. Check the vapor separator tank for fuel leaks, distortion and dents, and replace as necessary.

Flow Guide Valve – Through 1974

Remove the flow guide valve and inspect it for leakage by blowing air into the ports in the valve. When air is applied from the fuel tank side, the flow guide valve is normal if the air passes into the check side (crankcase side), but not into the relief side (air cleaner side). When air is applied from the check side, the valve is normal if the passage of air is restricted. When air is applied from the relief side (air cleaner side), the valve is normal if air passes into the fuel tank side or into the check side.

Carbon Canister and Purge Control Valve – 1975 and Later

To check the operation of the carbon canister purge control valve, disconnect the rubber hose between the canister control valve and the T-fitting, at the T-fitting. Inhale air on the hose leading to the control valve. Make sure there are no leaks. If the control valve leaks, remove the top cover of the valve and check for a dislocated or cracked diaphragm. If the diaphragm is damaged, a repair kit containing a

Applying vacuum to carbon canister

new diaphragm, retainer, and spring is available and should be installed.

The carbon canister has an air filter in the bottom of the canister. The filter element should be checked once a year or every 12,000 miles; more frequently if the car is operated in dusty areas. Replace the filter by pulling it out of the bottom of the canister and installing a new one.

REMOVAL AND INSTALLATION

Removal and installation of the various evaporative emission control system components consists of disconnecting the hoses, loosening retaining screws, and removing the part which is to be replaced or checked. Install in the reverse order. When replacing hose, make sure that it is fuel and vapor resistant.

Spark Timing Control System

The spark timing control system has been used in different forms on Datsuns since 1972. The first system, Transmission Controlled Spark System (TCS) was used on most Datsuns through 1979. This system consists of a thermal vacuum valve, a vacuum switching valve, a high gear detecting switch, and a number of vacuum hoses. Basically, the system is designed to retard full spark advance except when the car is in high gear and the engine is at normal operating temperature. At all other times, the spark advance is retarded to one degree or another.

The 1980–83 Spark Timing Control System replaces the TCS system. The major difference is that it works solely from engine water temperature changes rather than a transmission-mounted switch. The system includes a thermal vacuum valve, a vacuum delay valve, and attendant hoses. It performs the same function as the earlier TCS system; to retard full spark advance at times when high levels of pollutants would otherwise by given off.

On 1984 and later models the ignition timing is controlled by the central electronic control unit adjusting the engine operating conditions: as the best ignition timing in each driving condition and is determined by the electric signal calculated in the unit.

The information signals (used to determine the engine timing) are received from the water temperature, the engine rpm, the engine load and etc. The electronic control unit sends signals to the power transistor (of the ignition coil) and controls the ignition timing.

The distributor is equipped with a sensor and a signal rotor plate (photo-electric), which detects the position of the crankshaft and sends a signal to the control unit to control the various operations. The signal rotor plate has 360 (at 1° intervals) slots surrounding the outer edge (for detecting the rpm and ignition timing control) and 4 (at 90° intervals) slots on a inner circle (for detecting the piston TDC). When the signal rotor plate cuts the light signal between the Light Emitting Diode (LED) and the Photo Diode, an alternate voltage is created and sent to the control unit.

INSPECTION AND ADJUSTMENTS

Through 1983

Normally the TCS and Spark Timing Control systems should be trouble-free. However, if you suspect a problem in the system, first check to make sure all wiring (if so equipped) and hoses are connected and free from dirt. Also check to make sure the distributor vacuum advance is working properly. If everything appears all right, connect a timing light to the engine and make sure the initial timing is correct. On vehicles with the TCS system, run the engine until it reaches normal operating temperature, and then have an assistant sit in the car and shift the transmission through all the gears slowly. If the system is functioning properly, the timing will be 10 to 15 degrees advanced in high gear (compared to the other gear positions). If the system is still not operating correctly, you will have to check for continuity at all the connections with a test light.

To test the Spark Timing Control System, connect a timing light and check the ignition timing while the temperature gauge is in the "cold" position. Write down the reading. Allow the engine to run with the timing light attached until the temperature needle reaches the center of the gauge. As the engine is warming up, check with the timing light to make sure the ignition timing retards. When the temperature needle is in the middle of the gauge, the ignition timing should advance from its previous position. If the ignition timing does not change, replace the thermal vacuum valve.

1984 and Later

The ignition timing is automatically controlled by the control unit and adjustment is unnecessary.

Early Fuel Evaporation System

The Early Fuel Evaporation System is used on the A-series engines. The system's purpose is to heat the air/fuel mixture when the engine is below normal operating temperature. The 1973–79 engines use a system much akin to the old style exhaust manifold heat riser. The only adjustment necessary is to occasionally lubricate the counterweight, with a spray-type heat riser lubricant. Other than that, the system should be trouble-free.

The 1980 and later engines use coolant water instead of exhaust gas heat to pre-warm the fuel mixture. This system should be trouble-free.

Throttle Opener Control System (TOCS)

The Throttle Opener Control System (TOCS) used on the A-series engines (except 1980 and later California cars) and Canadian Sentras is designed to reduce hydrocarbon emissions during coasting conditions.

During coasting, high manifold vacuum prevents the complete combustion of the air/fuel mixture because of the reduced amount of air. This condition will result in a large amount of hydrocarbon (HC) emissions. Enriching the air/fuel mixture for a short time (during the high vacuum condition) will reduce the emission of the HC. However, enriching the air/fuel mixture with only the mixture adjusting screw will cause poor engine idle or invite an increase in the carbon monoxide (CO) content of the exhaust gases.

The TOCS system used on the 1980 and later A-series non-California cars and Canadian Sentras consists of a servo diaphragm, vacuum control valve, throttle opener solenoid valve, speed detecting switch and amplifier (on manual transmission models). Automatic transmission models use the speed detecting switch and amplifier. At the moment when manifold vacuum increases, as during deceleration, the vacuum control valve opens to transfer the manifold vacuum to the servo diaphragm chamber, and the carburetor throttle valve opens slightly. Under this condition, the proper amount of fresh air is sucked into the combustion chamber, resulting in a more thorough ignition and more complete burning of the HC in the exhaust gases.

Connect a quick response vacuum gauge to intake manifold when checking Throttle Opener Control System (TOCS)

1. Adjusting nut   2. Lock spring

TOCS location and adjustment

Adjusting the TOCS pressure

ADJUSTMENT – TOCS

1. Connect a tachometer to the engine.

2. Connect a quick-response vacuum gauge to the intake manifold.

3. Disconnect the solenoid valve electrical leads.

4. Start and warm up the engine until it reaches normal operating temperature.

5. Adjust the idle speed to the proper specification (see Tune Up Specifications chart).

6. Raise the engine speed to 3,000–3,500 rpm under no-load (transmission in Neutral or Park), then allow the throttle to snap closed quickly. Take notice as to whether or not the engine rpm returns to idle speed and if it does,

how long the fall in rpm is interrupted before it reaches idle speed.

At the moment the throttle is snapped shut at high engine rpm, the vacuum in the intake manifold reaches between –23.6 in. Hg. or above, then gradually decreases to idle level.

The pressure of the TOCS while operating should be –22.05 ± 0.79 in. Hg.

Turning the adjusting screw clockwise raises the vacuum level. Turning the screw counterclockwise lowers the vacuum level.

NOTE: *When adjusting the TOCS, turn the adjusting nut in or out with the lock spring in place. Always set the lock spring properly to prevent changes in the set pressure.*

Automatic Temperature Controlled Air Cleaner

The rate of fuel atomization (the process where the liquid gasoline is changed into a very fine mist) varies with the temperature of the air with which the fuel is being mixed. Because your car operates in a wide range of air temperatures, this air/fuel ratio cannot be held constant for efficient fuel combustion. Cold air drawn into the engine causes a denser and richer air/fuel mixture, inefficient fuel atomization, and thus, more hydrocarbons in the exhaust gas. Hot air drawn into the engine causes a leaner air/fuel mixture and more efficient atomization and combustion for less hydrocarbons in the exhaust gases.

The automatic temperature controlled air cleaner is designed so that the temperature of the ambient air being drawn into the engine is automatically controlled, to hold the temperature of the air and, consequently, the fuel/air ratio at a constant rate for efficient fuel combustion.

A temperature sensing vacuum switch controls vacuum applied to a vacuum motor operating a valve in the intake snorkle of the air cleaner. When the engine is cold or the air being drawn into the engine is cold, the vacuum motor opens the valve, allowing air heated by the exhaust manifold to be drawn into the engine. As the engine warms up, the temperature sensing unit shuts off the vacuum applied to the vacuum motor which allows the valve to close, shutting off the heated air and allowing cooler, outside (under hood) air to be drawn into the engine.

TESTING

When the air around the temperature sensor of the unit mounted inside the air cleaner housing reaches 100°F, the sensor should block the flow of vacuum to the air control valve vacuum motor. When the temperature around the tem-

1. Air inlet pipe
2. Vacuum motor ass'y
3. Temperature sensor ass'y
4. Hot air pipe
5. Air control valve
6. Idle compresator

Automatic temperature controlled air cleaner, B210 and 210. Sentra similar

perature sensor is below 100°F, the sensor should allow vacuum to pass into the air valve vacuum motor thus blocking off the air cleaner snorkle to under hood (unheated) air.

When the temperature around the sensor is above 118°F, the air control valve should be completely open to under hood air.

If the air cleaner fails to operate correctly, check for loose or broken vacuum hoses. If the hoses are not the cause, replace the vacuum motor in the air cleaner.

Exhaust Gas Recirculation (EGR)

The EGR system is used on all 1974 and later B210 and 210 model Datsuns and Nissan Sentras. Exhaust gas recirculation is used to reduce combustion temperatures in the engine, thereby reducing the oxides of nitrogen emissions.

An EGR valve is mounted on the center of the intake manifold. The recycled exhaust gas is drawn into the bottom of the intake manifold riser portion through the exhaust manifold heat stove and EGR valve. A vacuum diaphragm is connected to a timed signal port at the carburetor flange.

As the throttle valve is opened, vacuum is applied to the EGR valve vacuum diaphragm. When the vacuum reaches about 2 in. Hg. the diaphragm moves against spring pressure and is in a fully up position at 8 in. Hg. of vacuum. As the diaphragm moves up, it opens the exhaust gas metering valve which allows exhaust gas to be pulled into the engine intake manifold. The system does not operate when the engine is idling because the exhaust gas recirculation would cause a rough idle.

On 1975 and later models, a thermal vacu-

um valve inserted in the engine thermostat housing controls the application of the vacuum to the EGR valve. When the engine coolant reaches a predetermined temperature, the thermal vacuum valve opens and allows vacuum to be routed to the EGR valve. Below the predetermined temperature, the thermal vacuum valve closes and blocks vacuum to the EGR valve.

All 1978–80 B210 and 210 models have a B.P.T. (Back Pressure Transducer) valve installed between the EGR valve and the thermal vacuum valve. The B.P.T. valve monitors exhaust pressure in order to control, through its diaphragm, carburetor throttle vacuum applied to the EGR valve. The diaphragm opens and closes an air bleed, which is connected into the EGR vacuum line. High pressure results in higher levels of exhaust recirculation, because the diaphragm is raised, closing off the air bleed, and allowing more vacuum to reach and open the EGR valve. Thus, the amount of recirculated exhaust gas varies with exhaust pressure.

The 1980 California 210 and all 1981 and later U.S. 210s and Nissan Sentras use a V.V.T. valve (venturi vacuum transducer) in place of the B.P.T. valve. The V.V.T. monitors exhaust pressure and carburetor vacuum in order to activate the diaphragm which controls the throttle vacuum applied to the EGR control valve. This system expands the operating range of the EGR unit, as well as increasing the EGR flow rate as compared to the B.P.T. unit.

Many 1975 and later Datsuns are equipped with an EGR warning system which signals via a light in the dashboard that the EGR sys-

1980 210 Thermal Vacuum Valve

E-series EGR location on side of intake manifold

tem may need service. The EGR warning light should come on every time the starter is engaged as a test to make sure the bulb is not blown. The system uses a counter which works in conjunction with the odometer, and lights the warning signal after the vehicle has traveled a pre-determined number of miles.

To reset the counter, which is mounted in the engine compartment, remove the grommet installed in the side of the counter and insert the tip of a small screwdriver into the hole. Press down on the knob inside the hole. Reinstall the grommet.

TESTING

Pre–1975

Check the operation of the EGR system as follows:

1. Visually inspect the entire EGR control system. Clean the mechanism free of oil and dirt. Replace any rubber hoses found to be cracked or broken.

2. Make sure that the EGR solenoid valve is properly wired.

3. Increase the engine speed from idling to 2,000–3,500 rpm. The plate of the EGR control valve diaphragm and the valve shaft should move upward as the engine speed is increased.

4. Disconnect the EGR solenoid valve elec-trical leads and connect them directly to the vehicle's 12 volt electrical supply (battery). Race the engine again with the EGR solenoid valve connected to a 12 volt power source. The EGR control valve should remain stationary.

5. With the engine running at idle, push up on the EGR control valve diaphragm with your finger. When this is done, the engine idle should become rough and uneven.

6. Inspect the two components of the EGR system as necessary in the following manner:

a. Remove the EGR control valve from the intake manifold.

b. Apply 4.7–5.1 in. Hg. of vacuum to the EGR control valve by sucking on a tube attached to the outlet on top of the valve. The valve should move to the full up position. The valve should remain open for more than 30 seconds after the application of vacuum is discontinued and the vacuum hose is blocked.

c. Inspect the EGR valve for any signs of warpage or damage.

d. Clean the EGR valve seat with a brush and compressed air to prevent clogging.

e. Connect the EGR solenoid valve to a 12 volt DC power source and notice if the valve clicks when intermittently electrified. If the valve clicks, it is considered to be working properly.

f. Check the EGR temperature sensing switch by removing it from the engine and placing it in a container of water together with a thermometer. Connect a self-powered test light to the two electrical leads of the switch.

g. Heat the container of water.

h. The switch should conduct current when the water temperature is below 77°F and stop conducting current when the water reaches a temperature somewhere between 88°–106°F. Replace the switch if it functions otherwise.

1975 and Later

1. Remove the EGR valve and apply enough vacuum to the diaphragm to open the valve.

2. The valve should remain open for over 30 seconds after the vacuum is removed.

3. Check the valve for damage, such as warpage, cracks, and excessive wear around the valve and seat.

4. Clean the seat with a brush and compressed air and remove any deposits from around the valve and port (seat).

5. To check the operation of the thermal vacuum valve, remove the valve from the engine and apply vacuum to the ports of the valve. The valve should not allow vacuum to pass.

6. Place the valve in a container of water with a thermometer and heat the water. When the temperature of the water reaches 134°–145°F, remove the valve and apply vacuum to the ports; the valve should allow vacuum to pass through it.

7. To test the B.P.T. valve installed on 1978 and later models, disconnect the two vacuum hoses from the valve. Plug one of the ports. While applying pressure to the bottom of the valve, apply vacuum to the unplugged port and check for leakage. If any exists, replace the valve.

8. To test the check valve installed in some 1978 and later models, remove the valve and blow into the side which connects to the EGR valve. Air should flow. When air is applied in the other side, air flow resistance should be greater. If not, replace the valve.

9. To check the V.V.T. valve which replaces the B.T.P. valve on some 1980 and later models, disconnect the top and bottom center hoses and apply a vacuum to the top hose. Check for leaks. If a leak is present, replace the valve.

Mixture Ratio Rich-Lean and EGR Large-Small Exchange Systems

1980 California and all 1981 and later models; California Sentra

These systems control the air-fuel mixture ratio and the amount of recirculated exhaust gas (manual transmission models only) in accordance with the engine coolant temperature and speed of the car. The systems consist of a vacuum switching valve, a power valve, a speed detecting switch amplifier and a water temperature switch.

When the coolant temperature is above 122°F and the car is traveling at least 40 mph, the vacuum switching valve is on and acts to lean down the fuel mixture. It also allows a small amount of EGR to be burned on manual transmission cars. When the coolant temperature is above 122°F but the vehicle is traveling less than 40 miles per hour, the vacuum switching valve is off and allows the mixture to richen. It also allows a large amount of EGR to be burned in manual transmission models. When coolant temperature is below 122°F the vacuum switching valve is always on and acts to lean down the fuel mixture.

TESTING

1. Warm the engine up to operating temperature.

2. Shut off the engine and jack up the drive wheels of the vehicle just far enough that they clear the ground.

CAUTION: *Make sure the front wheels are chocked when raising the rear end of the car. When you have jacked the car to the desired height, support it with jackstands. DO NOT get in the car and attempt the following procedure with the car on a jack.*

3. Start the engine and shift the transmission into HIGH (top) gear and maintain the indicated speed above 50 mph.

4. Pinch the hose running from the vacuum switching valve to the air cleaner and see if the engine speed decreases and operates erratically.

5. Shift the transmission into the next lowest gear and run the indicated speed lower than 30 mph.

6. Disconnect the vacuum hose running between the vacuum switching valve and the power valve, by detaching it at the power valve and blocking its open end with your finger. The engine should operate erratically. If the expected engine reaction in both of these tests does not happen, check all wiring connections and hoses for breaks and blockage.

Air Injection System

It is difficult for an engine to completely burn the air/fuel mixture through the normal combustion in the combustion chambers. Under certain operating conditions, unburned fuel is exhausted into the atmosphere. Air injection is one answer to the pollution problem of unburned exhaust gases.

The air injection system used on 1975–80 B210 and 210 Datsuns is designed so that ambient air, pressurized by a belt-driven air pump, is injected through the injection nozzles into the exhaust ports near each of the four exhaust valves. The exhaust gases are at high temperatures and ignite when brought into contact with the oxygen. The unburned fuel is then burned in the exhaust ports and manifold.

California B210 models began utilizing a secondary system in 1976 consisting of an air control valve which limits injection of secondary air and an emergency relief valve which controls the supply of secondary air. This system protects the catalytic converter from overheating. In 1977 through 1980, the function of these two valves was taken by a single combined air control (C.A.C.) valve.

All engines with the air pump system have a series of minor alterations to accomodate the system. These are:

1. Special close-tolerance carburetor. Most engines require a slightly rich idle mixture adjustment.

2. Distributor with special advance curve. Ignition timing is retarded about 10° at idle in most cases.

Air pump (arrow)

3. Cooling system changes such as larger fan, higher fan speed, and thermostatic fan clutch. This is required to offset the increase in temperature caused by retarded timing at idle.

4. Faster idle speed.

5. Heated air intake on some engines.

The only periodic maintenance required on the air pump system is replacement of the air filter element and adjustment of the drive belt.

TESTING

Air Pump

If the air pump makes an abnormal noise and cannot be corrected without removing the pump from the car, the following check is the only one the owner/mechanic should make. Disassembly of the pump and replacement of any internal parts requires (in most cases) spe-

1. Air pump
2. Air pump air cleaner
3. 4-way connector
4. Air relief valve
5. Air cleaner
6. Check valve
7. Air gallery pipe
8. Carburetor
9. Air control valve
10. Injection nozzle
11. A.B. valve

Air injection system schematic—typical

cial tools, and knowledge generally outside the realm of the owner/mechanic. Major pump problems should be handled by a professional.

Check belt tension on the air pump drive belt. There should be about ¼ in. play in the belt at its center point; too tight a belt will wear out the pump bearings quickly (and cause a noise), and a belt too loose will slip around on the pulley (causing the pump to operate inefficiently).

Turn the pump pulley ¾ of a turn in the clockwise direction and ¼ of a turn in the counterclockwise direction. If the pulley is binding and if rotation is not smooth, this could indicate a defective bearing.

Check Valve

Remove the check valve from the air pump discharge line. Test it for leakage by blowing air into the valve from the air pump side and from the manifold side. Air should only pass through the valve from the air pump side if the valve is functioning normally. A small amount of air leakage from the manifold side can be overlooked. Replace the check valve if it is found to be defective.

Air pump system check valve

Anti-Backfire Valve

Disconnect the rubber hose connecting the mixture control valve with the intake manifold and plug the hose. If the mixture control

Removing anti-backfire (AB) valve, 210. Sentra location similar

valve is operating correctly, air will continue to blow out the mixture control valve for a few seconds after the accelerator pedal is fully depressed (engine running) and released quickly. If air continues to blow out for more than five seconds, replace the mixture control valve.

Air Pump Relief Valve

Disconnect the air pump discharge hose leading to the exhaust manifold. With the engine running, restrict the air-flow coming from the pump. The air pump relief valve should vent the pressurized air to the atmosphere if it is working properly.

NOTE: *When performing this test do not completely block the discharge line of the air pump as damage may result if the relief valve fails to function properly.*

Removing air pump relief valve, B210 and 210 to 1980

Air Injection Nozzles

Check around the air manifold for air leakage with the engine running at 2,000 rpm. If air is leaking from the eye joint bolt, retighten or replace the gasket. Check the air nozzles for restrictions by blowing air into the nozzles.

Hoses

Check and replace hoses if they are found to be weakened or cracked. Check all hose connections and clips. Be sure that the hoses are not in contact with other parts of the engine.

Emergency Air Relief Valve

1. Warm up the engine.
2. Check all hoses for leaks, kinks, improper connections, etc.
3. Run the engine up to 2000 rpm under no load. No air should be discharged from the valve.
4. Disconnect the vacuum hose from the valve. This is the hose which runs to the intake manifold. Run the engine up to 2000 rpm. Air should be discharged from the valve. If not, replace it.

Combined Air Control Valve

1. Check all hoses for leak, kinks, and improper connections.

2. Thoroughly warm up the engine.

3. With the engine idling, check for air discharge from the relief opening in the air cleaner case.

4. Disconnect and plug the vacuum hose from the valve. Air should be discharged from the valve with the engine idling. If the disconnected vacuum hose is not plugged, the engine will stumble.

5. Connect a hand operated vacuum pump to the vacuum fitting on the valve and apply 7.8–9.8 in. Hg. of vacuum. Run the engine speed up to 3000 rpm. No air should be discharged from the valve.

6. Disconnect and plug the air hose at the check valve, with the conditions as in the preceding step. This should cause the valve to discharge air. If not, or if any of the conditions in this procedure are not met, replace the valve.

Combined Air Control valve mounting, California models

Air Induction System (A.I.S.)

The air induction system (A.I.S.) is designed to send secondary air to the exhaust manifold, utilizing a vacuum caused by exhaust pulsation in the exhaust manifold.

The exhaust pressure in the exhaust manifold usually pulsates in response to the opening and closing of the exhaust valve and it decreases below atmospheric pressure periodically.

If a secondary air intake is opened to the atmosphere under vacuum conditions, secondary air can be drawn into the exhaust manifold in proportion to the vacuum. Therefore, the A.I.S. system reduces carbon monoxide (CO) and HC emissions in exhaust gases.

The A.I.S. system has been used in conjunction with the air injection (air pump) system in B210 and 210 Datsuns from the mid 1970s up until 1979. In 1980, only the California model 210s used both systems together, the air pump having been dropped from the non-California

Sentra Air Induction connections. A-series similar

cars. The 1981 and later model 210s and Nissan Sentras use just the A.I.S. system, as they employ no air pump.

Electric Choke

Gasoline engines produce most of their hydrocarbon (HC) emissions during warmup and at low rpm running. The purpose of the electric choke is to shorten the time the choke is in operation, thus shortening the time of the greatest HC output.

An electric heater warms the bimetal spring (typical spring found on most chokes) which controls the opening and closing of the choke valve. The heater begins to heat as soon as the engine starts.

Electric choke (arrow)

Catalytic Converter

This system is used on all 1975 (California) and later models. In addition to the air injection system, EGR and the engine modifications, the catalyst further reduces pollutants. Through catalytic action, it changes residual hydrocarbons and carbon monoxide the the exhaust gas into carbon dioxide and water before the exhaust gas is discharged into the atmosphere.

NOTE: *Only unleaded fuel must be used with catalytic converters; lead in fuel will quickly pollute the catalyst and render it useless.*

The emergency air relief valve is used as a catalyst protection device. When the temperature of the catalyst goes above maximum operating temperature, the temperature sensor signals the switching module to activate the emergency air relief valve. This stops air injection into the exhaust manifold and lowers the temperature of the catalyst.

Certain late 1970's catalyst equipped models have a floor temperature warning system which emits a warning if the catalytic converter or engine becomes overly hot or malfunctions, causing floor temperature to rise.

Vacuum Hoses of Emission Control System

1982 AND LATER SENTRA

The following show the various color coding for connecting emission control vacuum hoses and air hoses. Careful attention should be paid to the proper location and hook-up of the hoses.

Yellow: Vacuum line to distributor
White: Vacuum line for EGR system
Green: Manifold vacuum line
Pink: Atmospheric pressure
Blue: Venturi vacuum line to VVT valve

GASOLINE FUEL SYSTEM

Fuel Pump

The fuel pump is a mechanically operated diaphragm-type pump driven by the fuel pump eccentric on the camshaft. It is mounted on the side of the engine block.

Design of the fuel pump permits disassembly, cleaning, and repair or replacement of defective parts.

TESTING

1. Disconnect the line between the carburetor and the pump at the carburetor.

2. Connect a rubber hose to each open end of the T-connector, and connect this connector-hose assembly between carburetor and fuel pump.

NOTE: *Locate this T-connector as close to the carburetor as possible.*

3. Connect a suitable pressure gauge to the opening of the T-connector, and fasten the hose between the carburetor and T-connector securely with a hose clamp.

4. Start the engine and run at various speeds.

5. The pressure gauge indicates static fuel pressure in the line. The gauge reading should be within 3.0 to 3.9 psi. There is usually enough gas in the float bowl to perform this test.

CAPACITY TEST

The capacity test is conducted if the static pressure of the pump is ok.

1. Packing
2. Valve assembly
3. Retainer
4. Screw
5. Diaphragm assembly
6. Diaphragm spring
7. Retainer
8. Diaphragm assembly
9. Complete-body lower
10. Screw
11. Washer-spring
12. Fuel pump cap
13. Cap gasket
14. Connector-inlet
15. Connector-outlet
16. Rocker arm spring
17. Nut
18. Washer-spring
19. Washer-plain
20. Gasket
21. Spacer
22. Rocker pin
23. Spacer
24. Rocker arm

A-series fuel pump. E-series similar type

1. Disconnect the pressure gauge from the line. In place of the gauge, install a container suitable to collect the fuel (a graduated container works well here, as you can measure the amount of fuel immediately).

2. Make sure the carburetor float bowl is full of gas. Start the engine and run at about 1,000 rpm for one minute.

3. The fuel pump should deliver 450 cc (15.2 US fl. oz.) of fuel per minute for all 1973–81 1200, B210 and 210 models. The delivery rate

for 1982 210 fuel pumps is 1300 cc (44.0 U.S. fl. oz.) per minute at 1000 rpm; 1982 and later Sentra pumps deliver the same amount at 600 rpm.

REMOVAL AND INSTALLATION

1. Disconnect the two fuel lines from the fuel pump. Be sure to keep the line leading from the fuel tank up high to prevent the excess loss of fuel.

Exploded view '82 210 carburetor. Other A-series and E-series Sentra similar

2. Remove the two fuel pump mounting nuts and remove the fuel pump assembly from the side of the engine.

3. Install the fuel pump in the reverse order of removal, using a new gasket and sealer on the mating surface.

Carburetor

The carburetor used on all models is a two-barrel downdraft type with a low speed (primary) side and a high speed (secondary) side.

All models have an electrically operated anti-dieseling solenoid. As the ignition switch is turned off, the valve is energized and shuts off the supply of fuel to the idle circuit of the carburetor

All 1984 and later U.S.A. models are equipped with the E.C.C. System (Electronic Controlled Carburetor). The E.C.C control unit consists of a microcomputer, connectors for signal input and output and power supply, an exhaust gas sensor monitor lamp. The control unit senses and controlls various carburetor operations.

On all non-California models instead of a choke valve and fast idle cam of a conventional carburetor, this system utilizes a duty-controlled solenoid valve for fuel enrichment and an idle speed control actuator (ISCA) for the basic controls. These devices are controlled according to the engine speed , amount of intake air, and objective engine speed. Also, the air-fuel ratio and ignition timing are controlled according to the engine water temperature, atmospheric pressure, vehicle speed and transaxle gear position. In addition, this system controls the ignition timing and the idle speed according to applied electric loads such as A cooler, thereby achieving better emission control, fuel economy etc.

On California models the carburetor is equipped with an air-fuel ratio control on-off valve instead of a power valve. This on-off valve opens or closes the compensating air bleed and main jet to compensate for rich/lean air-fuel ratio, depending on varying conditions, such as acceleration, deceleration, low coolant temperature, low voltage, etc. These varying conditions are detected by various sensors which transmit corresponding signals to provide air-fuel ratio compensation.

REMOVAL AND INSTALLATION

1. Remove the air cleaner.
2. Disconnect the fuel and vacuum lies from the carburetor.
3. Remove the throttle lever.
4. Remove the four nuts and washers retaining the carburetor to the manifold.

5. Lift the carburetor from the manifold.
6. Remove and discard the gasket used between the carburetor and he manifold.
7. Install the carburetor in the reverse order of removal, using a new carburetor base gasket.

THROTTLE LINKAGE ADJUSTMENT

On all models, make sure the throttle is wide open when the accelerator pedal is floored. Some models have an adjustable accelerator pedal stop to prevent strain on the linkage.

PRIMARY AND SECONDARY THROTTLE VALVE INTERLOCK OPENING ADJUSTMENT

With the carburetor removed from the engine, turn the throttle arm intil the adjusting plate comes in contact with the lock lever at point "A" and Check clearance "G". Clearance should be 0.2472 in.

Interlock opening adjustment

DASHPOT ADJUSTMENT

A dashpot is used on carburetors of all cars with automatic transmissions and many late model manual transmission models. The dashpot slowly closes the throttle on automatic transmissions to prevent stalling and serves as an emission control device on all late model vehicles.

NOTE: *This adjustment does not apply to 1984 and later non-California U.S.A. models*

The dashpot should be adjusted to contact the throttle lever on deceleration at approximately 2,000–2,300 rpm for all models of the A-series and E 16 Automatics engines, and 2,300 to 2,500 rpm for all E 15 series engines.

Dashpot adjustment

NOTE: *Before attempting to adjust the dashpot, make sure the idle speed, timing and mixture adjustments are correct.*

FLOAT LEVEL ADJUSTMENT

The fuel level is normal if it is within the lines on the window glass of the float chamber (or the sight glass) when the vehicle is resting on level ground and the engine is off.

If the fuel level is outside the lines, remove the float housing cover. Have an absorbent cloth under the cover to catch the fuel from the fuel bowl. Adjust the float level by bending the needle seat on the float.

The needle valve should have an effective stroke of about 0.0591 in. When necessary, the

Float level adjustment

Close-up of float level sight window

needle valve stroke can be adjusted by bending the float stopper.

NOTE: *Be careful not to bend the needle valve rod when installing the float and baffle plate, if removed.*

FAST IDLE ADJUSTMENT

NOTE: *This adjustment does not apply to non-California U.S.A. models.*

1. With the carburetor removed from the engine, place the adjusting screw on the upper step of the fast idle cam and measure the clearance between the throttle valve and the wall of the throttle valve chamber at the center of the valve. Check it against the following specifications:

1973 1200, 1974–76 B210
  MT: 0.0315–0.0346 in.
  AT: 0.0421–0.0461
1977–78 B210
  MT: 0.0287–0.0343 in.
  AT: 0.0394–0.0449 in.
1979–82 210
  A12 engine: 0.0248–0.0315 in.
  A14 engine: 0.0283–0.0350 in.
  A15 engine: 0.0386–0.0461 in.
1982-86 Sentra
  MT: 0.0315–0.0343 in.
  AT: 0.0421–0.0449 in.
NOTE: *MT is Manual Transmission; AT is Automatic Transmission.*

2. Install the carburetor on the engine.

3. Start the engine and check the fast idle rpm at operating temperature, and the adjusting screw on the second step of the fast idle cam.

1973 1200, 1974 B210
  MT: 1,720–2.050 rpm
  AT: 2,650–2,950 rpm
1975–76 B210
  MT: 2,450–2,650 rpm
  AT: 2,700–2,900 rpm
1977–78 B210
  MT: 1,900–2,700 rpm
  AT: 2,400–3,200 rpm
1980 and later 210 w/A12, 14
  49s: 2,400–3,200 rpm
  Cal.: 2,300–3,100 rpm
1980 and later 210 w/A15
  MT: 2,300–3,100 rpm
  AT: 2,700–3,500 rpm
1982–83 Sentra E15
  49s: 2,400–3,200 rpm
  Cal.: 2,300–3,100 rpm
  Canada MT: 1,900–2,700 rpm
  Canada AT: 2,400–3,200 rpm
1984-86 Sentra E16
  49s: Not adjustable
  Cal. MT: 2,600–3,400 rpm

Fast idle adjustment, all models similar

Cal. AT: 2,900–3,700 rpm
Canada MT: 1,900–2,700 rpm
Canada AT: 2,400–3,200 rpm
4. To adjust the fast idle speed, turn the fast idle adjusting screw counterclockwise to increase the speed; clockwise to decrease the speed.

AUTOMATIC CHOKE ADJUSTMENT

NOTE: *This adjustment does not apply to 1984 and later non-California U.S.A. models*
1. With the engine cold, make sure the choke is fully closed (press the gas pedal all the way to the floor and release).
2. Check the choke linkage for binding. The choke plate should be easily opened and closed with your finger. If the choke sticks or binds, it can usually be freed with a liberal application of a spray-type carburetor cleaner made for the purpose. A couple of quick squirts on the linkage and choke plate normally does the trick. If not, the carburetor will have to be disassembled for repairs.
3. The choke is correctly adjusted when the index mark on the choke housing (notch)

Adjusting choke unloader gap "C" to specifications

aligns with the center mark on the carburetor body. If the setting is incorrect, loosen the three screws clamping the choke body in place and rotate the choke cover left or right until the marks align. Tighten the screws carefully to avoid cracking the housing.

CHOKE UNLOADER ADJUSTMENT

NOTE: *This adjustment does not apply to 1984 and later non-California U.S.A. models.*
1. Close the choke valve completely.
2. Hold the choke valve closed by stretching a rubber band between the choke piston lever and a stationary part of the carburetor.
3. Open the throttle lever fully.
4. Adjust the gap between the choke plate and the carburetor body to:
A-series engines: 1973–77: 0.0791 in.
1978–80: 0.0929 in. except:
1978 and later: Non-Cal. 5 speed hatchback 210, B210 and 1980 and later Canada manual trans. A12A: 0.0854 in.
E-series engines: 1982–83: 0.0929 in.
1984–86: 0.1165 in.

OVERHAUL

Efficient carburetion depends greatly on careful cleaning and inspection during overhaul, since dirt, gum, water, or varnish in or on the carburetor parts are often responsible for poor performance.

Overhaul your carburetor in a clean, dust-free area. Carefully disassemble the carburetor, referring often to the exploded views. Keep all similar and look-alike parts segregated during disassembly and cleaning to avoid accidental interchange during assembly. Make a note of all jet sizes.

When the carburetor is disassembled, wash all parts (except diaphragms, electric choke units, pump plunger, and any other plastic, leather, fiber, or rubber parts) in clean carburetor solvent. Do not leave parts in the solvent any longer than is necessary to sufficiently loosen the deposits. Excessive cleaning may remove the special finish from the float bowl and choke valve bodies, leaving these parts unfit for service. Rinse all parts in clean solvent and blow them dry with compressed air to allow them to air dry. Wipe clean all cork, plastic, leather, and fiber parts with a clean, lint-free cloth.

NOTE: *Carburetor solvent is available in various sized solvent cans, which are designed with a removable small parts basket in the top. The carburetor choke chamber and body, and all small parts can be soaked in this can until clean. These solvent cans are available at most auto parts stores, and are quite handy for soaking other small engine parts.*

Blow out all passages and jets with compressed air and be sure that there are no restrictions or blockages. Never use wire or similar tools to clean jets, fuel passages, or air bleeds. Clean all jets and valves separately to avoid accidental interchange.

Check all parts for wear or damage. If wear or damage is found, replace the defective parts. Especially check the following:
1. Check the float needle and seat for wear. If wear is found, replace the complete assembly.
2. Check the float hinge pin for wear and the float(s) for dents or distortion. Replace the float if fuel has leaked into it.
3. Check the throttle and choke shaft bores for wear or an out-of-round condition. Damage or wear to the throttle arm, shaft, or shaft bore will often require replacement of the throttle body. These parts require a close tolerance of fit; wear may allow air leakage, which could affect starting and idling.
NOTE: *Throttle shafts and bushings are not included in overhaul kits. They can be purchased separately.*
4. Inspect the idle mixture adjusting needles for burrs or grooves. Any such condition requires replacement of the needle, since you will not be able to obtain a satisfactory idle.
5. Test the accelerator pump check valves. They should pass air one way but not the other. Test for proper seating by blowing and sucking on the valve. Replace the valve if necessary. If the valve is satisfactory, wash the valve again to remove breath moisture.
6. Check the bowl cover for warped surfaces with a straightedge.
7. Closely inspect the valves and seats for wear and damage, replacing as necessary.
8. After the carburetor is assembled, check the choke valve for freedom of operation.

Carburetor overhaul kits are recommended for each overhaul. These kits contain all gaskets and new parts to replace those that deteriorate most rapidly. Failure to replace all parts supplied with the kit (especially gaskets) can result in poor performance and a leaky carburetor later.

Some carburetor manufacturers supply overhaul kits of three basic types: minor repair; major repair; and gasket kits. Basically, they contain the

Repair Kits:
All gaskets
Float needle valve
Volume control screw
All diaphragms

Carburetor Specifications

Year	Model	Vehicle Model	Carb Model	Main Jet # Primary	Main Jet # Secondary	Main Air Bleed # Primary	Main Air Bleed # Secondary	Slow Jet # Primary	Slow Jet # Secondary	Float Level (in.)	Power Jet #
1973	A12	1200	DCH 306-4 ① DCH 306-5 ②	95	140	80	80	43③	50③	0.709 0.748	60
1974	A13	B210	DCH 306-6 ① DCH 306-7 ②	140	145	65	80	43④	50④	0.709 0.748	55
1975	A14 (Federal)	B210	DCH 306-10 ① DCH 306-14 ②	102	150	95	80	45	50	0.75	45
	A14 (California)	B210	DCH 306-11 ① DCH 306-15 ②	104	150	95	80	45	50	0.75	43
1976–77	A14 (Federal)	B210	DCH 306-10A ① DCH 306-14A ②	102	145	95	80	45	50	0.75	45
1978	A14 (Federal)	B210	DCH 306-60 ① DCH 306-14 ②	104	145	110 95	80	45	50	0.75	48 40
	A14 (California)	B210	DCH 306-11 ① DCH 306-15 ②	105 104	145	95	80	45	50	0.75	40 48
	A14 (FU Model)	B210	DCH 306-37	107	145	65	60	46	50	0.75	48
1979	A14, A15 (Federal)	210	DCH 306-60E ① DCH 306-68 ②	106 105	145	110 95	80	45	50	0.75	43
	A14, A15 (California)	210	DCH 306-61 ① DCH 306-63 ②	107	145	95	80	45	50	0.75	43
	A14 (FU Model)	210	DCH 306-67	107	145	65	60	46	50	0.75	48
1980	A14, A15 (Federal)		DCH 306-100 ① DCH 306-101 ②	107	143	65	60	45	50	0.75	43
	A12A (Federal)		DCH 306-105	95	138	65	60	45	50	0.75	35
	A14, A15 (California)		DCH 306-110 ① DCH 306-111 ②	107	145	80	80	45	50	0.75	38
	A12A (California)		DCH 306-15	94	145	95	80	45	50	0.75	38

Year	Engine	Carburetor Number								
	A12A (Canada)	DCH 306-70①	96	140	70	60	43	50	0.75	50
	A14, A15 (Canada)	DCH 306-60① DCH 306-12②	104	145	110 95	80	45	50	0.75	48 50
1981	A12A (Federal)	DCR 306-100	105	125	95	80	45	50	0.75	35
	A14, A15 (Federal)	DCR 306-104① DCR 306-101① DCR 306-102②	115	125	80	80	45	50	0.75	35
	A12A (California)	DCR 306-110	103	125	60	80	45	50	0.75	35
	A15 (California)	DCR 306-111① DCR 306-112②	114	125	60	80	45	50	0.75	35
	A12A⑤ (Canada)	DCR 306-120	100	145	70	80	43	50	0.75	35
	A15⑥ (Canada)	DCR 306-121① DCR 306-122②	100	145	70	80	43	70	0.75	35
1982	A12A (Federal)	DCR 306-106	105	125	95	80	45	50	0.75	35
	A14② (MPG)	DCR 306-109	117	125	80	80	45	50	0.75	35
	A15 (Federal)	DCR 306-107① DCR 306-108②	115 116	125	80	80	45	50	0.75	35
	A12A (California)	DCR 306-116	103	125	60	80	45	50	0.75	35
	A15 (California)	DCR 306-117 DCR 306-118	115 116	125	80	80	45	50	0.75	35
1982–83	E15 (Federal)	DCR 306-132① DCR 306-133②	117 115	125 125	60 60	80 80	45 45	50 50	N.A.	38 38
	E15 (California)	DCR 306-142① DCR 306-143②	115 114	125 125	80 80	80 80	45 45	50 50	N.A.	38 35
	E15 (Canada)	DCR 306-152① DCR 306-153②	100 100	130 130	70 70	60 60	43 43	80 80	N.A.	40 40
	E15 (MPG)	DFP 306-2	98	135	60	80	43	55	N.A.	—

Carburetor Specifications (cont.)

Year	Model	Vehicle Model	Carb Model	Main Jet # Primary	Main Jet # Secondary	Main Air Bleed # Primary	Main Air Bleed # Secondary	Slow Jet # Primary	Slow Jet # Secondary	Float Level (in.)	Power Jet #
1982–83	A12A (Canada)		DCH 306-70 ①	96	140	70	60	43	50	0.75	50
	A14, A15 (Canada)		DCH 306-60 ① DCH 306-12 ②	104	145	110 95	80	45	50	0.75	48 50
1981	A12A (Federal)		DCR 306-100	105	125	95	80	45	50	0.75	35
	A14, A15 (Federal)		DCR 306-104 ① DCR 306-101 ① DCR 306-102 ②	115	125	80	80	45	50	0.75	35
	A12A (California)		DCR 306-110	103	125	60	80	45	50	0.75	35
	A15 (California)		DCR 306-111 ① DCR 306-112 ②	114	125	60	80	45	50	0.75	35
	A12A ⑤ (Canada)		DCR 306-120	100	145	70	80	43	50	0.75	35
	A15 ⑤ (Canada)		DCR 306-121 ① DCR 306-122 ②	100	145	70	80	43	70	0.75	35
1982	A12A (Federal)		DCR 306-106	105	125	95	80	45	50	0.75	35
	A14 ② (MPG)		DCR 306-109	117	125	80	80	45	50	0.75	35
	A15 (Federal)		DCR 306-107 ① DCR 306-108 ②	115 116	125	80	80	45	50	0.75	35
	A12A (California)		DCR 306-116	103	125	60	80	45	50	0.75	35
	A15 (California)		DCR 306-117 DCR 306-118	115 116	125	80	80	45	50	0.75	35

CHILTON'S
FUEL ECONOMY
& TUNE-UP TIPS

55 WAYS TO IMPROVE FUEL ECONOMY

Tune-up • Spark Plug Diagnosis • Emission Controls

Fuel System • Cooling System • Tires and Wheels

General Maintenance

CHILTON'S FUEL ECONOMY & TUNE-UP TIPS

Fuel economy is important to everyone, no matter what kind of vehicle you drive. The maintenance-minded motorist can save both money and fuel using these tips and the periodic maintenance and tune-up procedures in this Repair and Tune-Up Guide.

There are more than 130,000,000 cars and trucks registered for private use in the United States. Each travels an average of 10-12,000 miles per year, and, and in total they consume close to 70 billion gallons of fuel each year. This represents nearly ⅔ of the oil imported by the United States each year. The Federal government's goal is to reduce consumption 10% by 1985. A variety of methods are either already in use or under serious consideration, and they all affect you driving and the cars you will drive. In addition to "down-sizing", the auto industry is using or investigating the use of electronic fuel delivery, electronic engine controls and alternative engines for use in smaller and lighter vehicles, among other alternatives to meet the federally mandated Corporate Average Fuel Economy (CAFE) of 27.5 mpg by 1985. The government, for its part, is considering rationing, mandatory driving curtailments and tax increases on motor vehicle fuel in an effort to reduce consumption. The government's goal of a 10% reduction could be realized — and further government regulation avoided — if every private vehicle could use just 1 less gallon of fuel per week.

How Much Can You Save?

Tests have proven that almost anyone can make at least a 10% reduction in fuel consumption through regular maintenance and tune-ups. When a major manufacturer of spark plugs sur-

TUNE-UP

1. Check the cylinder compression to be sure the engine will really benefit from a tune-up and that it is capable of producing good fuel economy. A tune-up will be wasted on an engine in poor mechanical condition.

2. Replace spark plugs regularly. New spark plugs alone can increase fuel economy 3%.

3. Be sure the spark plugs are the correct type (heat range) for your vehicle. See the Tune-Up Specifications.

Heat range refers to the spark plug's ability to conduct heat away from the firing end. It must conduct the heat away in an even pattern to avoid becoming a source of pre-ignition, yet it must also operate hot enough to burn off conductive deposits that could cause misfiring.

The heat range is usually indicated by a number on the spark plug, part of the manufacturer's designation for each individual spark plug. The numbers in bold-face indicate the heat range in each manufacturer's identification system.

Manufacturer	Typical Designation
AC	R **45** TS
Bosch (old)	WA **145** T30
Bosch (new)	HR **8** Y
Champion	RBL **15** Y
Fram/Autolite	41**5**
Mopar	P-**62** PR
Motorcraft	BRF-**42**
NGK	BP **5** ES-15
Nippondenso	W **16** EP
Prestolite	14GR **5** 2A

Periodically, check the spark plugs to be sure they are firing efficiently. They are excellent indicators of the internal condition of your engine.

On AC, Bosch (new), Champion, Fram/Autolite, Mopar, Motorcraft and Prestolite, a higher number indicates a hotter plug. On Bosch (old), NGK and Nippondenso, a higher number indicates a colder plug.

4. Make sure the spark plugs are properly gapped. See the Tune-Up Specifications in this book.

5. Be sure the spark plugs are firing efficiently. The illustrations on the next 2 pages show you how to "read" the firing end of the spark plug.

6. Check the ignition timing and set it to specifications. Tests show that almost all cars have incorrect ignition timing by more than 2°.

veyed over 6,000 cars nationwide, they found that a tune-up, on cars that needed one, increased fuel economy over 11%. Replacing worn plugs alone, accounted for a 3% increase. The same test also revealed that 8 out of every 10 vehicles will have some maintenance deficiency that will directly affect fuel economy, emissions or performance. Most of this mileage-robbing neglect could be prevented with regular maintenance.

Modern engines require that all of the functioning systems operate properly for maximum efficiency. A malfunction anywhere wastes fuel. You can keep your vehicle running as efficiently and economically as possible, by being aware of your vehicle's operating and performance characteristics. If your vehicle suddenly develops performance or fuel economy problems it could be due to one or more of the following:

PROBLEM	POSSIBLE CAUSE
Engine Idles Rough	Ignition timing, idle mixture, vacuum leak or something amiss in the emission control system.
Hesitates on Acceleration	Dirty carburetor or fuel filter, improper accelerator pump setting, ignition timing or fouled spark plugs.
Starts Hard or Fails to Start	Worn spark plugs, improperly set automatic choke, ice (or water) in fuel system.
Stalls Frequently	Automatic choke improperly adjusted and possible dirty air filter or fuel filter.
Performs Sluggishly	Worn spark plugs, dirty fuel or air filter, ignition timing or automatic choke out of adjustment.

Check spark plug wires on conventional point type ignition for cracks by bending them in a loop around your finger.

Be sure that spark plug wires leading to adjacent cylinders do not run too close together. (Photo courtesy Champion Spark Plug Co.)

7. If your vehicle does not have electronic ignition, check the points, rotor and cap as specified.

8. Check the spark plug wires (used with conventional point-type ignitions) for cracks and burned or broken insulation by bending them in a loop around your finger. Cracked wires decrease fuel efficiency by failing to deliver full voltage to the spark plugs. One misfiring spark plug can cost you as much as 2 mpg.

9. Check the routing of the plug wires. Misfiring can be the result of spark plug leads to adjacent cylinders running parallel to each other and too close together. One wire tends to pick up voltage from the other causing it to fire "out of time".

10. Check all electrical and ignition circuits for voltage drop and resistance.

11. Check the distributor mechanical and/or vacuum advance mechanisms for proper functioning. The vacuum advance can be checked by twisting the distributor plate in the opposite direction of rotation. It should spring back when released.

12. Check and adjust the valve clearance on engines with mechanical lifters. The clearance should be slightly loose rather than too tight.

SPARK PLUG DIAGNOSIS

Normal

APPEARANCE: This plug is typical of one operating normally. The insulator nose varies from a light tan to grayish color with slight electrode wear. The presence of slight deposits is normal on used plugs and will have no adverse effect on engine performance. The spark plug heat range is correct for the engine and the engine is running normally.

CAUSE: Properly running engine.

RECOMMENDATION: Before reinstalling this plug, the electrodes should be cleaned and filed square. Set the gap to specifications. If the plug has been in service for more than 10-12,000 miles, the entire set should probably be replaced with a fresh set of the same heat range.

Oil Deposits

APPEARANCE: The firing end of the plug is covered with a wet, oily coating.

CAUSE: The problem is poor oil control. On high mileage engines, oil is leaking past the rings or valve guides into the combustion chamber. A common cause is also a plugged PCV valve, and a ruptured fuel pump diaphragm can also cause this condition. Oil fouled plugs such as these are often found in new or recently overhauled engines, before normal oil control is achieved, and can be cleaned and reinstalled.

RECOMMENDATION: A hotter spark plug may temporarily relieve the problem, but the engine is probably in need of work.

Incorrect Heat Range

APPEARANCE: The effects of high temperature on a spark plug are indicated by clean white, often blistered insulator. This can also be accompanied by excessive wear of the electrode, and the absence of deposits.

CAUSE: Check for the correct spark plug heat range. A plug which is too hot for the engine can result in overheating. A car operated mostly at high speeds can require a colder plug. Also check ignition timing, cooling system level, fuel mixture and leaking intake manifold.

RECOMMENDATION: If all ignition and engine adjustments are known to be correct, and no other malfunction exists, install spark plugs one heat range colder.

Carbon Deposits

APPEARANCE: Carbon fouling is easily identified by the presence of dry, soft, black, sooty deposits.

CAUSE: Changing the heat range can often lead to carbon fouling, as can prolonged slow, stop-and-start driving. If the heat range is correct, carbon fouling can be attributed to a rich fuel mixture, sticking choke, clogged air cleaner, worn breaker points, retarded timing or low compression. If only one or two plugs are carbon fouled, check for corroded or cracked wires on the affected plugs. Also look for cracks in the distributor cap between the towers of affected cylinders.

RECOMMENDATION: After the problem is corrected, these plugs can be cleaned and reinstalled if not worn severely.

MMT Fouled

APPEARANCE: Spark plugs fouled by MMT (Methycyclopentadienyl Maganese Tricarbonyl) have reddish, rusty appearance on the insulator and side electrode.

CAUSE: MMT is an anti-knock additive in gasoline used to replace lead. During the combustion process, the MMT leaves a reddish deposit on the insulator and side electrode.

RECOMMENDATION: No engine malfunction is indicated and the deposits will not affect plug performance any more than lead deposits (see Ash Deposits). MMT fouled plugs can be cleaned, regapped and reinstalled.

High Speed Glazing

APPEARANCE: Glazing appears as shiny coating on the plug, either yellow or tan in color.

CAUSE: During hard, fast acceleration, plug temperatures rise suddenly. Deposits from normal combustion have no chance to fluff-off; instead, they melt on the insulator forming an electrically conductive coating which causes misfiring.

RECOMMENDATION: Glazed plugs are not easily cleaned. They should be replaced with a fresh set of plugs of the correct heat range. If the condition recurs, using plugs with a heat range one step colder may cure the problem.

Ash (Lead) Deposits

APPEARANCE: Ash deposits are characterized by light brown or white colored deposits crusted on the side or center electrodes. In some cases it may give the plug a rusty appearance.

CAUSE: Ash deposits are normally derived from oil or fuel additives burned during normal combustion. Normally they are harmless, though excessive amounts can cause misfiring. If deposits are excessive in short mileage, the valve guides may be worn.

RECOMMENDATION: Ash-fouled plugs can be cleaned, gapped and reinstalled.

Detonation

APPEARANCE: Detonation is usually characterized by a broken plug insulator.

CAUSE: A portion of the fuel charge will begin to burn spontaneously, from the increased heat following ignition. The explosion that results applies extreme pressure to engine components, frequently damaging spark plugs and pistons.

Detonation can result by over-advanced ignition timing, inferior gasoline (low octane) lean air/fuel mixture, poor carburetion, engine lugging or an increase in compression ratio due to combustion chamber deposits or engine modification.

RECOMMENDATION: Replace the plugs after correcting the problem.

EMISSION CONTROLS

13. Be aware of the general condition of the emission control system. It contributes to reduced pollution and should be serviced regularly to maintain efficient engine operation.

14. Check all vacuum lines for dried, cracked or brittle conditions. Something as simple as a leaking vacuum hose can cause poor performance and loss of economy.

15. Avoid tampering with the emission control system. Attempting to improve fuel econ-

FUEL SYSTEM

Check the air filter with a light behind it. If you can see light through the filter it can be reused.

Extremely clogged filters should be discarded and replaced with a new one.

18. Replace the air filter regularly. A dirty air filter richens the air/fuel mixture and can increase fuel consumption as much as 10%. Tests show that ⅓ of all vehicles have air filters in need of replacement.

19. Replace the fuel filter at least as often as recommended.

20. Set the idle speed and carburetor mixture to specifications.

21. Check the automatic choke. A sticking or malfunctioning choke wastes gas.

22. During the summer months, adjust the automatic choke for a leaner mixture which will produce faster engine warm-ups.

COOLING SYSTEM

29. Be sure all accessory drive belts are in good condition. Check for cracks or wear.

30. Adjust all accessory drive belts to proper tension.

31. Check all hoses for swollen areas, worn spots, or loose clamps.

32. Check coolant level in the radiator or expansion tank.

33. Be sure the thermostat is operating properly. A stuck thermostat delays engine warm-up and a cold engine uses nearly twice as much fuel as a warm engine.

34. Drain and replace the engine coolant at least as often as recommended. Rust and scale

TIRES & WHEELS

38. Check the tire pressure often with a pencil type gauge. Tests by a major tire manufacturer show that 90% of all vehicles have at least 1 tire improperly inflated. Better mileage can be achieved by over-inflating tires, but never exceed the maximum inflation pressure on the side of the tire.

39. If possible, install radial tires. Radial tires deliver as much as ½ mpg more than bias belted tires.

40. Avoid installing super-wide tires. They only create extra rolling resistance and decrease fuel mileage. Stick to the manufacturer's recommendations.

41. Have the wheels properly balanced.

omy by tampering with emission controls is more likely to worsen fuel economy than improve it. Emission control changes on modern engines are not readily reversible.

16. Clean (or replace) the EGR valve and lines as recommended.

17. Be sure that all vacuum lines and hoses are reconnected properly after working under the hood. An unconnected or misrouted vacuum line can wreak havoc with engine performance.

23. Check for fuel leaks at the carburetor, fuel pump, fuel lines and fuel tank. Be sure all lines and connections are tight.

24. Periodically check the tightness of the carburetor and intake manifold attaching nuts and bolts. These are a common place for vacuum leaks to occur.

25. Clean the carburetor periodically and lubricate the linkage.

26. The condition of the tailpipe can be an excellent indicator of proper engine combustion. After a long drive at highway speeds, the inside of the tailpipe should be a light grey in color. Black or soot on the insides indicates an overly rich mixture.

27. Check the fuel pump pressure. The fuel pump may be supplying more fuel than the engine needs.

28. Use the proper grade of gasoline for your engine. Don't try to compensate for knocking or "pinging" by advancing the ignition timing. This practice will only increase plug temperature and the chances of detonation or pre-ignition with relatively little performance gain.

Increasing ignition timing past the specified setting results in a drastic increase in spark plug temperature with increased chance of detonation or preignition. Performance increase is considerably less. (Photo courtesy Champion Spark Plug Co.)

that form in the engine should be flushed out to allow the engine to operate at peak efficiency.

35. Clean the radiator of debris that can decrease cooling efficiency.

36. Install a flex-type or electric cooling fan, if you don't have a clutch type fan. Flex fans use curved plastic blades to push more air at low speeds when more cooling is needed; at high speeds the blades flatten out for less resistance. Electric fans only run when the engine temperature reaches a predetermined level.

37. Check the radiator cap for a worn or cracked gasket. If the cap does not seal properly, the cooling system will not function properly.

42. Be sure the front end is correctly aligned. A misaligned front end actually has wheels going in differed directions. The increased drag can reduce fuel economy by .3 mpg.

43. Correctly adjust the wheel bearings. Wheel bearings that are adjusted too tight increase rolling resistance.

Check tire pressures regularly with a reliable pocket type gauge. Be sure to check the pressure on a cold tire.

GENERAL MAINTENANCE

Check the fluid levels (particularly engine oil) on a regular basis. Be sure to check the oil for grit, water or other contamination.

A vacuum gauge is another excellent indicator of internal engine condition and can also be installed in the dash as a mileage indicator.

44. Periodically check the fluid levels in the engine, power steering pump, master cylinder, automatic transmission and drive axle.

45. Change the oil at the recommended interval and change the filter at every oil change. Dirty oil is thick and causes extra friction between moving parts, cutting efficiency and increasing wear. A worn engine requires more frequent tune-ups and gets progressively worse fuel economy. In general, use the lightest viscosity oil for the driving conditions you will encounter.

46. Use the recommended viscosity fluids in the transmission and axle.

47. Be sure the battery is fully charged for fast starts. A slow starting engine wastes fuel.

48. Be sure battery terminals are clean and tight.

49. Check the battery electrolyte level and add distilled water if necessary.

50. Check the exhaust system for crushed pipes, blockages and leaks.

51. Adjust the brakes. Dragging brakes or brakes that are not releasing create increased drag on the engine.

52. Install a vacuum gauge or miles-per-gallon gauge. These gauges visually indicate engine vacuum in the intake manifold. High vacuum = good mileage and low vacuum = poorer mileage. The gauge can also be an excellent indicator of internal engine conditions.

53. Be sure the clutch is properly adjusted. A slipping clutch wastes fuel.

54. Check and periodically lubricate the heat control valve in the exhaust manifold. A sticking or inoperative valve prevents engine warm-up and wastes gas.

55. Keep accurate records to check fuel economy over a period of time. A sudden drop in fuel economy may signal a need for tune-up or other maintenance.

Year	Model	Trans.	Carburetor								
1982–83	E15 (Federal)		DCR 306-132 ①	117	125	60	80	45	50	N.A.	38
			DCR 306-133 ②	115	125	60	80	45	50	N.A.	38
	E15 (California)		DCR 306-142 ①	115	125	80	80	45	50	N.A.	38
			DCR 306-143 ②	114	125	80	80	45	50	N.A.	35
	E15 (Canada)		DCR 306-152 ①	100	130	70	60	43	80	N.A.	40
			DCR 306-153 ②	100	130	70	60	43	80	N.A.	40
	E15 (MPG)		DFP 306-2	98	135	60	80	43	55	N.A.	—
1984	E16 (Federal)	Man. Trans.	DFE2832-1	90	105	80	70	43	65	0.47	—
		Auto. Trans.	DFE2832-2	82	105	110	70	45	65	0.47	—
	(Calif.)	all		91	130	110	60	43	65	0.47	—
	(Canada)	all		100	135	110	60	180	100	0.47	35
1985	E16 (Federal)	Man. Trans.	DFE2832-5	90	105	80	70	43	65	0.47	—
		Auto. Trans.	DFE2832-6	82	105	110	70	45	65	0.47	—
	(Calif.)	all		91	130	110	60	43	65	0.47	—
	(Canada)	all		100	135	110	60	43	65	0.47	35

NOTE: FU models are 5-speed Hatchbacks sold in the United States except California.
① Manual transmission
② Automatic transmission
③ Slow jet air bleed: Primary #215, Secondary #100
④ Slow jet air bleed: Primary #240, Secondary #100
⑤ 1982 Canada carburetors same specs and models as 1981

Spring for the pump diaphragm

Major Repair Kits:

All jets and gaskets

All diaphragms

Float needle valve

Volume control screw

Pump ball valve

Main jet carrier

Float

Gasket Kits:

All gaskets

After cleaning and checking all components, reassemble the carburetor, using new parts and referring to the exploded view. When reassembling, make sure that all screws and jets are tight in their seats, but do not overtighten as the tips will be distorted. Tighten all screws gradually in rotation. Do not tighten needle valves into their seats; uneven jetting will result. Always use new gaskets. Be sure to adjust the float level when reassembling.

DIESEL FUEL SYSTEM

Injection Pump

REMOVAL AND INSTALLATION

1. Disconnect the battery ground.
2. Drain the coolant.
3. Disconnect and tag the wires and hoses attached to the pump or in the way of pump removal.
4. Remove the pump drive belt.
5. Remove the pump pulley.
6. Disconnect the injection lines at the pump.
7. Unbolt and remove the pump.
8. Installation is the reverse of removal. Observe the following points:

    a. Make sure that the engine is at TDC of #1 piston's compression stroke.

    b. Adjust the injection timing.

    c. Connect the injection lines in a 4–3–2–1 order.

    d. Bleed the fuel system.

Removing injection pump pulley using puller

9. Torque the injection pump nut to 9–13 ft.lb.; the pump-to-rear bracket bolts to 23–17 ft.lb.; the injection line nuts to 16–18 ft.lb.

Injector Nozzles

REMOVAL AND INSTALLATION

1. Remove the lines on the nozzle side and loosen them on the pump side.
2. Remove the spill tube.
3. Unscrew the injector from the engine.
4. Installation is the reverse of removal. Observe the following:

    a. Always use a new injector gasket.

    b. Torque the injectors to 43–51 ft.lb.

    c. Torque the lines to 16–18 ft.lb.

    d. Torque the spill tube to 29–36 ft.lb.

Injection Timing

ADJUSTMENT

NOTE: *Timing adjustment is necessary only if the injection pump or timing belt have been removed.*

1. Remove the air cleaner and duct.
2. Make sure that the #1 piston is at TDC of the compression stroke.
3. If the timing belt is still in position, remove it by freeing the tensioner.
4. If the injection pump was off the engine, install it at this time.
5. Clean the timing belt thoroughly and in-

Move the belt tensioner to the free position

Mark the timing belt before removal

spect it for cracks or wear. If any sign of wear exists, replace it.

6. On the outside of the belt, make a paint mark directly over one of the cogs. Count to your right, 23 cogs from the one with the paint mark, and place another paint mark directly over the 23rd cog.

7. If the engine is at TDC of #1 compression, the timing mark on the camshaft pulley should be roughly at the 1 o'clock position. Turn the injection pump pulley so that its timing mark is in roughly the same position. Install the timing belt so that the paint marks align with the timing marks on the pulleys. Some turning of the pulleys might be required.

8. When the timing marks are aligned, tighten the tensioner. Turn the engine over by hand, two complete revolutions in the normal direction of rotation and make sure that the timing marks are still aligned.

FUEL TANK

REMOVAL AND INSTALLATION

1200

1. Disconnect the battery. Remove the drain plug from the tank bottom and completely drain the tank into a suitable container.

2. Remove the fuel lines.
3. Remove the trunk finishing panel.
4. Remove the four bolts retaining the tank.
5. Disconnect the hose clamp and gauge wire.
6. Remove the fuel tank.

B210 Sedan

1. Disconnect the battery ground cable.
2. Remove the front trunk panel.
3. Remove the spare tire and the plug from the spare housing.
4. Place a pan under the drain plug, remove the plug and drain the gas.
5. Disconnect the filler hose, ventilation lines, and fuel line from the tank.
6. Disconnect the fuel gauge wires from the tank.
7. Remove the rear seat cushion and back. Remove the front mounting bolts.
8. Remove the other two retaining bolts, and lift out the tank.
9. Installation is the reverse of removal.

B210 Coupe

1. Disconnect the battery ground cable.
2. Remove the finish panel from the right side of the trunk.
3. Place a pan under the drain plug, remove the plug, and drain the gas.

1. Fuel tank
2. Drain plug
3. Filler hose
4. Ventilation tube
5. Evaporation tube
6. Fuel outlet hose
7. Fuel tank unit gauge
8. Fuel strainer

B210 fuel tank and lines

1. Fuel tank
2. Drain plug
3. Filler hose
4. Ventilation hose
5. Breather hose
6. Fuel tank gauge unit
7. Fuel return tube
8. Fuel outlet tube
9. Evaporative tube
10. Fuel tank protector
11. Fuel filter
12. Carbon canister

210 fuel tank and lines. Sentra similar

Removing fuel tank gauge unit and harness connection

4. Disconnect the filler hose, ventilation lines, and fuel line from the tank.

5. Disconnect the evaporative lines from the reservoir tank.

6. Remove the spare tire and then the inspection plate from the rear floor.

7. Disconnect the sending unit wires.

8. Remove the fuel tank mounting bolts and lift the tank out of the car.

9. Installation is the reverse of removal.

1979 and later 210 Sedan

NOTE: *Install fuel filler hose after fuel tank has been mounted in place. Failure to follow*

this rule could result in leakage from around the hose connections. Do not twist or smash vent hoses when they are routed. Be sure to retain them securely with clips.

1. Disconnect the battery ground cable.

2. Drain the fuel from the fuel tank, then disconnect the fuel hose.

3. Remove the filler hose protector and inspection cover in the luggage compartment.

4. Disconnect the fuel filler hose, vent hoses and the fuel tank gauge unit wire connector.

5. Remove the fuel tank protector.

6. Remove the fuel tank.

7. Installation is the reverse of removal.

1979 and later 210 Hatchback and Station Wagon

1. Disconnect the battery ground cable.

2. Drain the fuel from the fuel tank, then disconnect the fuel hose.

3. Remove the luggage carpet, luggage board, inspection cover and side finisher.

4. Disconnect the fuel filler hose, vent hoses and the fuel tank gauge unit wire connector.

5. Remove the fuel tank protector.

6. Remove the fuel tank.

7. Installation is the reverse of removal.

1982 and Later Sentra

1. Drain fuel.

2. Remove inspection cover and disconnect fuel tank gauge unit harness connector.

3. Disconnect fuel filler and ventilation tubes.

NOTE: *Plug hose and pipe openings to prevent entry of dust and dirt.*

4. Disconnect fuel outlet, return and evaporation hoses.

5. Remove six bolts attaching fuel tank and then take out fuel tank.

6. Install in the reverse order of removal.

Chassis Electrical

5

UNDERSTANDING AND TROUBLESHOOTING ELECTRICAL SYSTEMS

For any electrical system to operate, it must make a complete circuit. this simply means that the power flow from the battery must make a complete circle. When an electrical component is operating, power flows from the battery to the component, passes through the component causing it to perform its function (lighting a light bulb, for example) and then returns to the battery through the ground of the circuit. This ground is usually (but not always) the metal part of the car on which the electrical component is mounted.

Perhaps the easiest way to visualize this is to think of connecting a light bulb with two wires attached to it to your car battery. The battery in your car has two posts (negative and positive). If one of the two wires attached to the light bulb was attached to the negative post of the battery and the other wire was attached to the positive post of the battery, you would have a complete circuit. Current from the battery would flow out one post, through the wire attached to it and then to the light bulb, causing it to light. It would then leave the light bulb, travel through the other wire, and return to the other post of the battery.

The normal automotive circuit differs from this simple example in two ways. First, instead of having a return wire from the bulb to the battery, the light bulb returns the current to the battery through the chassis of the vehicle. Since the negative battery cable is attached to the chassis and the chassis is made of electrically conductive metal, the chassis of the vehicle can serve as a ground wire to complete the circuit. Secondly, most automotive circuits contain switches to turn components on and off as required.

There are many types of switches, but the most common simply serves to prevent the passage of current when it is turned off. Since the switch is a part of the circle necessary for a complete circuit, it operates to leave an opening in the circuit, and thus an incomplete or open circuit, when it is turned off.

Some electrical components which require a large amount of current to operate also have a relay in their circuit. Since these circuits carry a large amount of current, the thickness of the wire (gauge size) in the circuit is also greater. If this large wire were connected from the component to the control switch on the instrument panel, and then back to the component, a voltage drop would occur in the circuit. To prevent this potential drop in voltage, and electromagnetic switch (relay) is used. the large wires in the circuit are connected from the car battery t one side of the relay, and from the opposite side of the relay to the component. The relay is normally open, preventing current from passing through the circuit. An additional, smaller, wire is connected from the relay to the control switch for the circuit. When the control switch is turned on, it grounds the smaller wire from the relay and completes the circuit. This closes the relay and allows current to flow from the battery to the component. The horn, headlight, and starter circuits are three which use relays.

You have probably notices how the car's instrument panel lights get brighter the faster you rev the engine. This happens because your alternator (which supplies the battery) puts out more current at speeds above idle. This is normal. However, it is possible for larger surges of current to pass through the electrical system of your car. If this surge of current were to reach an electrical component, it could burn the component out. To prevent this from happening, fuses reconnected into the current supply wires of most of the major electrical systems of your car. The fuse serves to head off the surge at the pass. When an electrical current of excessive power passes through the component's fuse, the fuse blows out and breaks the circuit, saving it from destruction.

The fuse also protects the component from damage if the power supply wire to the component is grounded before the current reaches the component.

There is another important rule to the complete circle circuit. Every complete circuit from a power source must include a component which is using the power from the power source. If you were to disconnect the light bulb (from the previous example of a light bulb being connected to the battery by two wires together (take our word for it-don't try it) the result would literally be shocking. A similar thing happens (on a smaller scale) when the power supply wire to a component or the electrical component itself becomes grounded before the normal ground connection for the circuit. To prevent damage to the system, the fuse for the circuit blows to interrupt the circuit-protecting the components from damage. Because grounding a wire from a power source makes a complete circuit, less the required component to use the power, this phenominon is called a short circuit. The most common cause of short circuits are: the rubber insulation on a wire breaking or rubbing through to expose the current carrying core of the wire to a metal part of the car, or a short switch.

Some electrical systems on the car are protected by a circuit breaker which is, basically, a self-re-pairing fuse. When either of the above-described events takes place in a system which is protected by a circuit breaker, the circuit breaker opens the circuit the same way a fuse does. However, when either the short is removed from the circuit or the surge subsides, the circuit breaker resets itself and does not have to be replaced as a fuse does.

The final protective device in the chassis electrical system is a fuse link. A fuse link is a wire that acts as a fuse. It is connected between the starter relay and the main wiring harness for the car. This connection is under the hood, very near a similar fuse link which protects all the chassis electrical components. It is the probable cause of trouble when none of the electrical components function, unless the battery is disconnected or dead.

Electrical problems generally fall into one of three areas:

1. The component that is not functioning is not receiving current.
2. The component itself is not functioning.
3. The component is not properly grounded.

Problems that fall into the first category are by far the most complicated. It is the current supply system to the component which contains all the switches, relays, fuses, etc.

The electrical system can be checked with a test light and a jumper wire. A test light is a device that looks like a pointed screwdriver with a wire attached to it. It has a light bulb in its handle. A jumper wire is a piece of insulated wire with an alligator clip attached to each end.

If a light bulb is not working, you must follow a systematic plan to determine which of the three causes is the villain.

1. Turn on the switch that controls the inoperable bulb.
2. Disconnect the power supply wire from the bulb.
3. Attach the ground wire on the test light to a good metal ground.
4. Touch the probe end of the test light to the end of the power supply wire that was disconnected from the bulb. If the bulb is receiving current, the test light will go on.

NOTE: *If the bulb is one which works only when the engine key is turned on (turn signal), make sure the key is turned on.*

If the test light does not go on, then the problem is in the circuit between the battery and the bulb. As mentioned before, this includes all the switches, fuses, and relays in the system. The problem is an open circuit between the battery and the bulb. If the fuse is blown and, when replaced, immediately blows again, there is a short circuit in the system which must be located and repaired. If there is a switch in the system, bypass it with a jumper wire. This is done by connecting one end of the jumper wire to the power supply into the switch, and the other end of the jumper wire to the wire coming out of the switch. If the test light lights with the jumper wire installed, the switch or whatever was bypassed is defective.

NOTE: *Never substitute the jumper wire for the bulb, as the bulb is the component required to use the power from the power source.*

5. If the bulb in the test light goes on, then the current is getting to the bulb that is not working in the car. This eliminates the first of the three possible causes. Connect the power supply wire and connect a jumper wire from the bulb to a good metal ground. Do this with the switch which controls the bulb turned on, and also the ignition switch turned on if it is required for the light to work. If the bulb works with the jumper wire installed, then it has a bad ground. This is usually caused by the metal area on which the bulb mounts to the car being coated with some type of foreign matter or rust.

6. If neither test located the source of the

trouble, then the light bulb itself is defective.

The above test procedure can be applied to any of the components of the chassis electrical system by substituting the component that is not working for the light bulb. Remember that for any electrical system to work, all connections must be clean and tight.

HEATER

Heater Assembly
REMOVAL AND INSTALLATION
1973 1200

1. Remove the package tray and ashtray.
2. Drain the coolant. Disconnect the two hoses between the heater and engine.

CAUTION: *When draining the coolant, keep in mind that cats and dogs are attracted by the ethylene glycol antifreeze, and are quite likely to drink any that is left in an uncovered container or in puddles on the ground. This will prove fatal in sufficient quantity. Always drain the coolant into a sealable container. Coolant should be reused unless it is contaminated or several years old.*

3. Disconnect the cables from the heater unit and heater controls. Disconnect the wiring.
4. Disconnect the two control wires from the water cock and interior valve, and the control rod from the shut valve. Set the heater control upper lever to DEF and lower lever to OFF.

5. Pull off the right and left defroster hoses.
6. Remove the four screws holding the heater unit to the firewall. Remove the control knob and remove the screws holding the control unit to the instrument panel. Remove the heater unit.
7. Reverse the procedure for installation.

B210

1. Remove the package tray and ashtray.
2. Drain the coolant. Disconnect the two hoses between the heater and engine.

CAUTION: *When draining the coolant, keep in mind that cats and dogs are attracted by the ethylene glycol antifreeze, and are quite likely to drink any that is left in an uncovered container or in puddles on the ground. This will prove fatal in sufficient quantity. Always drain the coolant into a sealable container. Coolant should be reused unless it is contaminated or several years old.*

3. Disconnect the cables from the heater unit and heater controls. Disconnect the wiring.
4. Disconnect the two control wires from the water cock and interior valve, and the control rod from the shut valve. Set the heater control upper lever to DEF and lower lever to OFF.
5. Pull off the right and left defroster hoses.
6. Remove the four screws holding the heater unit to the firewall. Remove the control knob and remove the screws holding the con-

A: Defroster
B: Side defroster
C: Ventilation
D: Floor

Ghosted view of dash showing heater location and air flow

1. Defroster nozzle
2. Defroster hose
3. Air intake box
4. Heater box (L.H.)
5. Clip
6. Heater core
7. Ventilator valve
8. Resistor
9. Heater box (R.H.)
10. Fan and fan motor
11. Heater cock
12. Heater control
13. Center ventilator
14. Knob
15. Heat valve

B210 heater

1. Center ventilation duct
2. Side defroster duct
3. Defroster nozzle
4. Defroster duct
5. Heater unit
6. Heater control
7. Water cock
8. Water inlet hose
9. Water outlet hose
10. Air cond. duct

210 heater assembly. Others similar

trol unit to the instrument panel. Remove the heater unit.

7. Reverse the procedure for installation.

B210

1. Disconnect the battery ground cable.
2. Drain all the coolant from the radiator. CAUTION: *When draining the coolant, keep in mind that cats and dogs are attracted by the ethylene glycol antifreeze, and are quite likely to drink any that is left in an uncovered container or in puddles on the ground. This will prove fatal in sufficient quantity. Always drain the coolant into a sealable container. Coolant should be reused unless it is contaminated or several years old.*
3. Disconnect the coolant inlet and outlet hoses.
4. Remove the heater duct hoses from both sides of the heater unit. Remove the defroster hose or hoses.
5. Disconnect the electrical wires of the heater unit (and air conditioner, if so equipped) at their connections.
6. Disconnect and remove the heater control cables.
7. Remove one attaching bolt from each side and one bolt from the top center of the heater unit (all B210 models).
8. Remove the heater unit.
9. Installation is the reverse of removal. Run the engine for a few minutes (don't forget to top up the radiator with coolant) with the heater on to make sure the system is filled with coolant.

1978 and later 210

1. Disconnect the ground cable at the battery. Drain the coolant. CAUTION: *When draining the coolant, keep in mind that cats and dogs are attracted by the ethylene glycol antifreeze, and are quite likely to drink any that is left in an uncovered container or in puddles on the ground. This will prove fatal in sufficient quantity. Always drain the coolant into a sealable container. Coolant should be reused unless it is contaminated or several years old.*
2. Remove the package tray on the 210, if so equipped.
3. Remove the driver's side of the instrument panel. See the section below for instructions.
4. Remove the heater control assembly: remove the defroster ducts, vent door cables at the doors, harness connector and the control assembly.
5. Remove the radio.
6. On air conditioned models, disconnect the cooler ducts at heater unit side.
7. Disconnect the heater ducts, side defrosters and the center vent duct.
8. Remove the screws attaching the defroster nozzle to the unit. Disconnect the blower wiring harness and the heater hoses.
9. Remove the retaining bolts and the heater unit.
10. Installation is the reverse of removal.

1982 and later Sentra

1. Set "TEMP" lever to maximum "HOT" position and drain engine coolant. CAUTION: *When draining the coolant, keep in mind that cats and dogs are attracted by the ethylene glycol antifreeze, and are quite likely to drink any that is left in an uncovered container or in puddles on the ground. This will prove fatal in sufficient quantity. Always drain the coolant into a sealable container. Coolant should be reused unless it is contaminated or several years old.*

Typical heater unit showing blower assembly

2. Disconnect the heater hoses at the engine compartment.

3. Remove the instrument assembly.

4. Remove the heater control assembly.

5. Remove the heater unit assembly. Installation is the reverse of removal.

Heater Blower

REMOVAL AND INSTALLATION

210

1. Disconnect the battery ground cable.

2. Disconnect the heater blower harness connector.

3. Remove the three outer bolts holding the blower motor assembly in place and remove the motor with the fan attached.

NOTE: *Make sure you remove the outer bolts and not the bolts holding the motor to the backing plate.*

4. Installation is the reverse of removal.

Sentra

1. Remove the instrument panel lower cover.

2. Disconnect the blower motor harness connector.

3. Remove the lower casing attaching screws and drop the casing.

4. Remove the blower motor after removing the retaining screws. Install in the reverse order of removal.

Heater Core

REMOVAL AND INSTALLATION

1200, B210

1. Remove the heater from the car.

2. Remove the clip and slide the hose from the heater core cock.

3. Remove the clips and separate the left and right sides of the heater case.

4. Lift out the heater core.

1978 and Later 210 and Sentra

1. Remove the heater unit as outlined earlier.

2. Loosen the hose clamps and disconnect the inlet and outlet hoses.

3. Remove the clips securing the case halves and separate the cases.

4. Remove the heater core.

5. Installation is in the reverse order of removal.

RADIO

REMOVAL AND INSTALLATION

1200, B210

1. Remove the instrument cluster (procedure follows).

2. Detach all electrical connections attaching the radio to the car.

3. Remove the radio knobs and their retaining nuts.

4. Remove the rear support bracket.

5. Remove the radio.

6. Reverse the procedure for installation

210

NOTE: *The dashboard must be first removed on the 210 to gain access to the radio.*

1. Disconnect the battery ground cable.

2. Remove the steering column cover.

3. Remove the lighting control knob assembly.

4. Pull out the heater control knob and remove the heater control panel facing.

5. Remove the screws attaching the heater control assembly to the dash panel, or cluster lid "A" (see illustration).

6. Pull out the ash tray and remove the screws holding the ash tray holder in place.

8. Disconnect the harness connector and the antenna feeder cable.

9. Remove the eight screws holding the dashboard in place: three along the bottom, one on the driver's door side and four along the windshield. Remove the dashboard.

10. Remove the radio bracket by loosening the retaining screws.

11. Remove the radio.

12. Installation is the reverse of removal.

Radio removal, B210, 210

Sentra radio mounting screws under ash tray

Sentra

1. Remove the ash tray and ash tray bracket.

2. Remove the radio mounting bolts.

3. Remove the radio mask (front cover) after removing the tuning knobs.

4. Remove the radio unit. Installation is the reverse of removal.

Removing radio mask (cover) for radio access, Sentra

WINDSHIELD WIPER

Motor and Linkage

REMOVAL AND INSTALLATION

All Models

The wiper motor is on the firewall under the hood. The operating linkage is on the firewall inside the car.

1. Detach the motor wiring plug.

2. Inside the car, remove the nut connecting the linkage to the wiper shaft.

3. Unbolt and remove the wiper motor from the firewall.

4. Reverse the procedure for installation.

1200 dashboard removal

INSTRUMENT PANEL

Cluster

REMOVAL AND INSTALLATION

1200

1. Disconnect the battery negative lead.

2. Depress the wiper, light switch, and choke knobs, turning them counterclockwise to remove.

3. From the rear, disconnect the lighter wire. Turn and remove the lighter outer case.

4. Remove the radio and heater knobs.

5. Remove the shell cover from the steering column.

6. Remove the screws which hold the instrument cluster to the instrument panel. Pull out the cluster.

7. Disconnect the wiring connector. Disconnect the speedometer cable by unscrewing the nut at the back of the speedometer.

8. Individual instruments may be removed from the rear of the cluster.

B210

1. Disconnect the battery ground cable.

2. Remove the four screws and the steering column cover.

Wiper linkage and motor, 210. Others similar

A. Cluster cover
B. Instrument pad
C. Instrument panel
1. Light switch knob
2. Light control knob
3. Rear window defogger switch

4. Escutcheon
5. Wiper switch knob
6. Radio knob
7. Cigarette lighter
8. Gauges

9. Light switch
10. Tachometer
11. Wiper switch
12. Radio
13. Clock

B210 instrument cluster removal

1. Lock and striker
2. Lid finisher
3. Lid stopper
4. Cluster lid B compartment
5. Side vent grille

6. Instrument panel assembly
7. Cluster lid A
8. Radio mask
9. Center vent grille
10. Instrument lower assist cover

11. Instrument lower center cover
12. Heater control finisher
13. Illumination lamp
14. Ash tray
15. Heater control lever bracket

1980 210 instrument panel. Other 210 similar

210 instrument panel left side attaching points

Right side attaching points, 210 instrument panel

COMBINATION METER

CLUSTER LID A

HEATER CONTROL

GLOVE BOX

WHEN REMOVING,
PULL OUT.

CLUSTER LID C

BE SURE TO REMOVE THE FOLLOWING PARTS.
• CHOKE CONTROL CABLE
• HARNESS CONNECTORS
• HOOD LOCK CONTROL CABLE
• SPEEDOMETER CABLE

Sentra instrument panel and dash removal

3. Remove the screws which attach the cluster face. Two are just above the steering column, and there is one inside each of the outer instrument recesses.

4. Pull the cluster lid forward.

5. Disconnect the multiple connector.

6. Disconnect the speedometer cable.

7. Disconnect any other wiring.

8. Remove the cluster face.

9. Remove the odometer knob if the vehicle has one.

10. Remove the six screws and the cluster.

NOTE: *To make removal of the cluster easier, remove the steering wheel and turn signal switch.*

11. Instruments may now be readily replaced.

12. Reverse the procedure for installation.

210

See 210 Radio Removal and Installation for instrument cluster removal and installation procedure.

Speedometer Cable

REPLACEMENT

NOTE: *Cable routing varies slightly among the 1200, B210, 210 and Sentra models. Cable replacement procedures for all models are basically the same. On some models it may be easier to remove the instrument cluster to gain access to the cable.*

1. Remove any lower dash covers that may be in the way and disconnect the speedometer cable from the back of the speedometer.

2. Pull the cable from the cable housing. If the cable is broken, the other half of the cable will have to be removed from the transmission end. Unscrew the retaining knob at the transmission and remove the cable from the transmission on extension housing.

3. Lubricate the cable with graphite powder (sold as speedometer cable lubricant) and feed the cable into the housing. It is best to start at the speedometer end and feed the cable down towards the transmission. It is also usually necessary to unscrew the transmission connection and install the cable end to the gear, then reconnect the housing to the transmission. Slip the cable into the speedometer and reconnect the cable housing.

Ignition Switch

Ignition switch removal and installation procedures are covered in Chapter 7, Suspension and Steering.

SEATBELT SYSTEM

Warning Buzzer and Light

Since 1972, the federal government has required all cars to have a warning system designed to remind the driver to buckle his or her seat belt.

When the ignition switch is turned to the "ON" position, the warning lamp comes on and remains on for 4 to 8 seconds. At the same time, the chime (warning buzzer in 1980 and earlier models) sounds for 4 to 8 seconds intermittently if the driver's seat belt is not properly fastened. The chime or buzzer is also used as a theft warning alarm.

This warning system consists of an ignition switch, a timer unit, a warning lamp, a driver's seat belt switch and a buzzer or chime. The dash board seat belt lights and the buzzer or chime is controlled by pressure-sensitive switches hidden in the front bench or bucket seats. A switch in each of the front seat belt retractors turns off the warning system only when the belt or belts are pulled a specified distance out of their retractors.

Two different types of switches are used to control the system, depending upon the type of transmission used:

On manual transmission equipped cars, the transmission neutral switch is used to activate the seat belt warning circuit.

Sentra speedometer connection to speedometer. 210 similar

Seat belt warning buzzer unit, 210 (B210 similar). Sentra seat belt timer is under radio

Automatic transmissions use the inhibitor switch to activate the seat belt warning circuit.

When removing the seats, be sure to unplug the pressure-sensitive switches at their connections.

SEAT BELT SWITCH DISCONNECTION

1. Disconnect the battery ground cable.
2. Slide the seat all the way forward.
3. Disconnect the harness connector.
4. Remove the inner seat belt by removing the security bolt.
5. Install the inner seat belt in the reverse order of removal.

Seat belt warning switch

Seat Belt/Starter Interlock System

As required by law, all 1974 and most 1975 Datsun passenger cars cannot be started until the front seat occupants are seated and have fastened their seat belts. If the proper sequence is not followed, e.g., the occupants fasten the seat belts and then sit on them, the engine cannot be started.

The shoulder harness and lap belt are permanently fastened together, so that they both must be worn. The shoulder harness uses an inertia-lock reel to allow freedom of movement under normal driving conditions.

NOTE: *This type of reel locks up when the car decelerates rapidly, as during a crash.*

The switches for the interlock system have been removed from the lap belt retractors and placed in the belt buckles. The seat sensors remain the same as those used in 1973.

For ease of service, the car may be started from outside, by reaching in and turning the key, but without depressing the seat sensors. In case of system failure, an override switch is located under the hod. This is a "one start" switch and it must be reset each time it is used. This system is discontinued after 1975.

LIGHTING

Headlights

REMOVAL AND INSTALLATION

NOTE: *The 1200 and B210 Datsun have radiator grilles which are unit-constructed to also serve as headlight frames. For these models it will be necessary to remove the grille to gain access to the headlights.*

1. Remove the grille, if necessary.
2. Remove the headlight retaining ring (frame) screws. These are the three or four short screws in the assembly; there are also two longer screws at the top and side of the headlight which are used to aim the headlight. Do not tamper with these or the headlights will have to be re-aimed.
3. Remove the ring around the round (pre-'81) headlights by turning it clockwise. The square headlamp assemblies should pull straight out without having to turn them.
4. Pull the headlight bulb from its socket and disconnect the electrical socket.
5. Connect the plug to the new bulb.
6. Position the new headlight in the shell.

1. Retaining ring
2. Beam
3. Mounting ring

Exploded view of standard headlight. Square headlights similar

1. Vertical adjustment   2. Horizontal adjustment

210 headlight adjustment. Others similar except Sentra vertical adjustment screw is on bottom of unit

Most fusible links are found beside the battery

TO JUNCTION BLOCK

CONNECTOR COVERING

FUSIBLE LINK BEFORE SHORT CIRCUIT

CUT WIRE HERE

FUSIBLE LINK AFTER SHORT CIRCUIT

Fusible links before and after a short circuit

Make sure the word "TOP" is, indeed, at the top and that the knobs in the headlight lens engage the slots in the mounting shell.

7. Place the retaining ring over the bulb and install the screws.

8. Install the grille, if removed.

FUSIBLE LINK

CONNECTOR

THOROUGHLY TAPE ALL EXPOSED WIRES

CONNECTOR CRIMPED AND SOLDERED

New fusible links are spliced to the wire

CIRCUIT PROTECTION

Fusible Links

A fusible link is a protective device used in an electrical circuit. When current increases beyond a certain amperage, the fusible metal wire of the link melts, thus breaking the electrical circuit (like a fuse) and preventing further damage to the other components and wiring. Whenever a fusible link is melted because

Fusible Links

Year	Model	Number	Color/Products	Location
1973	1200	1	Green/Charging system	At positive battery terminal
1974–78	B210	1	Green/Fuse block, electrical systems	At positive battery terminal
1979–82	210	2	Green/Starting, ignition, charging, headlights	At positive battery terminal
1982–86	Sentra	2	Green/Starting, ignition, charging, headlights	At positive battery terminal

Fuse Box and Flasher Location

Year	Model	Fuse Box Location	Flasher Location
1973	1200	Under instrument panel, right of steering wheel	Under dash
1974–78	B210	Below hood release knob	Turn signal: Behind radio Hazard: Under driver's side of dashboard
1979–82	210	Below hood release knob	Under driver's side dashboard ①
1982–86	Sentra	Below hood release knob	Under driver's side dashboard ①

NOTE: The original turn signal flasher unit is pink, and larger than the original hazard flasher unit, which is gold.
① Both the turn signal and the hazard flashers are side by side.

of a short circuit, correct the cause before installing a new link.

Use the following chart to locate the fusible link(s) on your Datsun.

All Datsun fusible links are the plug in kind. To replace them, simply unplug the bad link and insert the new one.

CAUTION: *Never wrap vinyl tape around a fusible link. Extreme care should be taken with this link to ensure that it does not come into contact with any other wiring harness, vinyl, or rubber parts.*

WIRING DIAGRAMS

Wiring diagrams have been left out of this book. As cares have become more complex, and as more and more options have been available on them, wiring diagrams have also grown in size and complexity. It has become impossible to reproduce wiring diagrams that are readable yet do not take up an unreasonable number of pages. Contact your Datsun dealer if you are in need of a wiring diagram.

MANUAL TRANSMISSION

Various four speed manual transmissions are standard equipment on all 1200, B210 and 210 models covered in this guide, except for the 1981 and later 210 MPG, which is equipped with a five speed transmission as standard. The front wheel drive Nissan Sentra uses either a four or five speed manual transaxle, which is actually a combination transmission and differential. All models feature integral shift linkage, which requires no adjustment.

The 1973 1200, 1974 B210 and 1980 210s use the F4W56 four speed transmission, which is constructed in two sections: a combined clutch and transmission housing, and an extension housing. There is a cast iron adaptor plate between the housings, and no case cover plates. The 1981 and later 210s use the F4W56 four speed.

The 1977–78 B210 uses the model FS5W63A five speed transmission. The 1979 210 has a FS5W60L five speed transmission, while the 1980 and later use the FS5W60A five speed transmissions.

Front wheel drive Sentra models use either the RS5F30A five speed, or the RN4F30A four speed transaxle.

REMOVAL AND INSTALLATION

All 1200, B210 and 210 Models

1. Jack up the car and safely support it with jackstands. Disconnect the battery cables. Disconnect the backup light switch, neutral switch, Top gear, overdrive, and any other switches on the transmission after marking their positions with tape for later assembly.

2. On all models (1200, B210 and 210) disconnect the exhaust pipe from the exhaust manifold and bracket. Disconnect the speedometer cable from the speedometer cable drive on the transmission.

3. Scribe or paint matchmarks on the driveshaft flange and transmission flange so the driveshaft can be reinstalled with both flanges in the exact same relationship. Unbolt the driveshaft at the rear of the transmission. Quickly plug the end of the transmission extension housing to prevent leakage of transmission oil (which will begin immediately when the driveshaft is unbolted).

4. Remove the shift lever.

5. Remove the clutch operating cylinder from the clutch housing.

6. Support the engine by placing a jack under the oil pan with a wooden block used between the oil pan and the jack.

CAUTION: *Do not place the jack under the oil pan drain plug.*

7. Support the transmission, preferably with a jack, and unbolt the transmission from the crossmember. Remove the crossmember.

8. Lower the rear of the engine slightly to allow a little clearance.

9. Remove the starter from the engine.

10. Remove the bolts securing the transmission to the engine and gusset.

11. With the engine and transmission still supported, lower the jack supporting the transmission (with the transmission on it) to the rear and away from the engine. Remove the transmission from underneath the car.

NOTE: *When removing the transmission, take care not to strike any adjacent parts, especially the main drive gear and spline.*

12. Before installing, clean all mating surfaces of the engine rear plate and transmission case. Clean the transmission rear flange and front driveshaft flange. Make sure the matchmarks on both flanges are lined up during assembly.

13. Before installing, lightly apply a multi-purpose grease to the spline parts of the clutch disc and main drive gear. Also, apply the same

1200, B210 and 210 shift lever removal

1200 and B210—disconnect the back-up light switch (1), speedometer cable (2), clutch slave cylinder (3), rear engine mount bolts (4), crossmember bolts (5). 210 similar

Disconnect speedometer and back-up light switch

Remove the clutch slave cylinder

grease to the moving surfaces of the gear control lever and striking rod.

14. Remove the transmission filler plug and fill the transmission with a gearbox lubricant rated API GL-5 to the level of the filler plug hole.

15. Check the clutch linkage adjustment after installing the transmission.

Sentra Front Wheel Drive Models

1. Remove battery and battery holding plate.

2. Jack up front of car and safely support with jackstands.

3. Remove the radiator reservoir tank.

4. Drain transmission gear oil.

5. Draw out the drive halfshafts from the transaxle.

NOTE: *When removing halfshafts, use care not to damage the lip of the oil seal. After shafts are removed, insert a steel bar or wooden dowel of suitable diameter to prevent the side gears from rotating and falling into the differential case.*

6. Remove the wheel house protector.

7. Separate the control rod and support rod from the transaxle.

8. Remove the engine gusset securing bolt and the engine mounting.

9. Remove the clutch control cable from the withdrawal lever.

10. Disconnect speedometer cable from the transaxle.

11. Disconnect the wires from the reverse (back-up) and neutral switches.

12. Support the engine by placing a jack under the oil pan, with a wooden block placed between the jack and pan for protection.

13. Support the transaxle with a hydraulic floor jack.

14. Remove the engine mounting securing bolts.

15. Remove the bolts attaching the transaxle to the engine.

16. Using the hydraulic floor jack as a carrier, carefully lower the transaxle down and away from the car.

CAUTION: *Be careful not to strike any adjacent parts or input shaft (the shaft protruding from the transaxle which fits into the clutch assembly) when removing the transaxle from the car.*

17. Installation of the Sentra transaxle is in the reverse order of removal, but pay attention to the following points:

a. Before installing, clean the mating surfaces on the engine rear plate and clutch housing.

b. Apply a light coat of a lithium-based

Temporarily insert a bar or dowel into the trans-axle after halfshaft is removed

Separating control rod and support rod from Sentra transaxle

Removing Sentra wheel house protector

Sentra engine mount and gusset securing bolts

Sentra engine mounting bolts

grease (which includes molybdenum-disulfide) to the spline parts of the clutch disc and the transaxle input shaft.

c. Remove the filler plug and fill the transaxle with 4 ⅞ U.S. pints (four speed) and 5 ¾ U.S. pints (five speed) of a quality API GL-4 rating. Fill to the level of the plug hole.

d. Apply a thread sealant to the threads of the filler plug and install the plug in the transaxle case. Tighten the bolts securing the transaxle to the engine to 12–15 ft.lb.

CLUTCH

The purpose of the clutch is to disconnect and connect engine power from the transmission. A car at rest requires a lot of engine torque to get all that weight moving. An internal combustion engine does not develop a high starting torque (unlike steam engines for example), so it must be allowed to operate without any load until it builds up enough torque to move the car. Torque increases with engine rpm. The clutch allows the engine to build up torque by physically disconnecting the engine from the transmission, relieving the engine of any load or resistance. The transfer of engine power to the transmission (the load) must be smooth and gradual; if it isn't, driveline components would wear out or break quickly. This gradual power transfer is made possible by gradually releasing the clutch pedal. The clutch disc and pressure plate are the connecting link between the engine and transmission. When the clutch pedal is released, the disc and plate contact each other (clutch engagement), physically joining the engine and transmission. When the pedal is pushed in, the disc and plate separate (the clutch is disengaged), disconnecting the engine from the transmission.

The clutch used in all 1200, B210 and 210 Datsun models covered in this guide is a hydraulic, single dry-disc, diaphragm spring type clutch. The Sentra clutch is conventional (non-hydraulic) singleplate, diaphragm spring type clutch. The major clutch components consist of the flywheel, the clutch disc, the pressure plate, diaphragm springs, the throwout (release) bearing fork, the clutch master cylinder, slave cylinder and connecting line, and the pedal. The flywheel and the clutch pressure plate (driving members) are connected to the engine crankshaft and rotate with it. The clutch disc is located between the flywheel and pressure plate, and is splined to the transmission shaft. A driving member is one that is attached to the engine and transfers engine power to a driven member (clutch disc) on the transmission shaft. A driving member (pressure plate) rotates (drives) a driven member (clutch disc) on contact, and in so doing, turns the transmission shaft. There is a circular diaphragm spring within the pressure plate cover (transmission side). In a relaxed state (when the clutch pedal is fully released), this spring is convex, that is, it is dished outward toward the transmission. Pushing in the clutch pedal actuates the slave cylinder (only on hydraulic clutches), which is the smaller of the two hydraulic cylinders and the one that actually operates the clutch mechanism.

Connected to the other end of the slave cylinder rod is the throwout bearing fork, which is also found on the non-hydraulic Sentra clutch. When the clutch pedal is depressed, the slave cylinder (or the clutch cable on Sentra) pushes the fork and bearing forward to contact the diaphragm spring of the pressure plate. The outer edges of the spring are secured to the pressure plate and are pivoted on rings so that when the center of the spring is compressed by the throwout bearing, the outer edges bow outward, and, by so doing, pull the pressure plate in the same direction--away from the clutch disc. This action separates the disc from the plate, disengaging the clutch from the transmission and allowing the transmission to be shifted into another gear. Releasing the pedal allows the throwout bearing to pull away from the diaphragm spring resulting in a reversal of spring position. As bearing pressure is gradually released from the spring center, the outer edges of the spring bow inward, pushing the pressure plate into closer contact with the clutch disc. As the disc and plate move closer together, friction between the two increases and slippage is reduced until, when full spring pressure is applied (by fully releasing the pedal), the speed of the disc and plate are the same. This stops all slipping, creating a direction connection between the plate and disc which results in the transfer of power from the engine to the transmission. The clutch disc is

1. Clutch master cylinder
2. Clutch disc assembly
3. Clutch cover assembly
4. Release bearing and sleeve assembly
5. Return spring
6. Clutch line
7. Clutch pedal
8. Operating cylinder
9. Withdrawal lever
10. Withdrawal lever ball pin

1200 and B210 clutch control system. 210 similar

Sentra clutch control layout

now rotating with the pressure plate at the engine speed and, because it is splined to the transmission shaft, the shaft now turns at the same engine speed.

ADJUSTMENT

Refer to the Clutch Specifications Chart for clutch pedal height above floor and pedal free play.

Since all 1200, B210 and 210 models have a hydraulically operated clutch, pedal height is usually adjusted with a stopper limiting the upward travel of the pedal. Pedal free play is adjusted at the master cylinder pushrod. The Sentra clutch is adjusted with a pedal stopper and adjusting locknut.

1. Adjust pedal height on all models ("H" in illustration) with pedal stopper. Then tighten locknut (see illustration).

2. Adjust 1200, B210 and 210 pedal free

1. Adjust pedal height here
2. Adjust pedal free-play here
MG. Lubricate with multipurpose grease here
H. is pedal height
h. is free-play

Clutch adjusting points

play with master cylinder pushrod. Then tighten locknut.

3. Adjust Sentra withdrawal lever at the lever tip end (on side of transaxle) with adjusting nut. Play in lever is 0.08–0.16 in.

4. Depress and release clutch pedal (on all models) over its entire stroke to ensure that the clutch linkage operates smoothly without squeak, noise, and interference, or binding.

REMOVAL AND INSTALLATION

1200, B210, 210 Hydraulic Clutch

CAUTION: *The clutch driven disc contains asbestos, which has been determined to be a cancer causing agent. Never clean the clutch surfaces with compressed air! Avoid inhaling any dust from any cltuch surface! When cleaning clutch surfaces, use a commercially available brake cleaning fluid.*

1. Remove the transmission from the engine.

2. Loosen the bolts in sequence, a turn at a time. Remove the bolts.

3. Remove the pressure plate and clutch disc.

4. Remove the release mechanism. Apply multi-purpose grease to the bearing sleeve inside groove, the contact point of the withdrawal lever and bearing sleeve, the contact surface of the lever ball pin and lever. Replace the release mechanism.

5. Inspect the pressure plate for wear, scoring, etc., and reface or replace as necessary. Inspect the release bearing and replace as necessary. Apply a small amount of grease to the transmission splines. Install the disc on the splines and slide back and forth a few times. Remove the disc and remove excess grease on hub. Be sure no grease contacts the disc or pressure plate.

6. Install the disc, aligning it with a splined dummy shaft.

7. Install the pressure plate and torque the bolts to 11–16 ft.lb.

8. Remove the dummy shaft.

9. Replace the transmission.

Sentra

CAUTION: *The clutch driven disc contains asbestos, which has been determined to be a cancer causing agent. Never clean the clutch surfaces with compressed air! Avoid inhaling any dust from any cltuch surface! When cleaning clutch surfaces, use a commercially available brake cleaning fluid.*

1. Remove transaxle from engine.

2. Insert Nissan clutch aligning tool or a similar splined clutch tool (must fit the

Sentra's clutch splines) into the clutch disc hub.

3. Loosen the bolts attaching the clutch cover to the flywheel, one turn each at a time, until the spring pressure is released.

NOTE: *Be sure to turn them out in a criss-cross pattern.*

4. Remove the clutch disc and cover assembly.

5. Inspect the pressure plate for scoring or roughness, and reface or replace as necessary (slight roughness can be smoothed with a fine emery cloth). Inspect the clutch disc for worn or oily facings, loose rivets and broken or loose springs, and replace. (You probably have the clutch out of the car to replace it anyway).

6. Apply a light coat of a molybdenum disulfide grease to the transaxle input shaft spline. Slide the clutch disc on the input shaft several times to distribute the grease. Remove the clutch disc and wipe off the excess lubricant pushed off by the disc hub.

CAUTION: *Take special care to prevent any*

Sentra withdrawal lever adjustment. Arrow shows locknut adjustment

grease or oil from getting on the clutch facing. During assembly, keep all disc facings, flywheel and pressure plate clean and dry. Grease, oil or dirt on these parts will result in a slipping clutch when assembled.

7. Install the clutch cover assembly. Each bolt should be tightened one turn at a time in a crisscross pattern. Torque the bolts to 12–15 ft.lb.

8. Remove the clutch aligning tool.

9. Reinstall the transaxle.

Clutch Master Cylinder

REMOVAL AND INSTALLATION

Hydraulic Clutch Models

1. Remove snap pin from clevis pin, and pull out clevis pin.

2. Disconnect the clutch pedal arm from the pushrod.

3. Disconnect the clutch hydraulic line from the master cylinder.

NOTE: *Take precautions to keep brake fluid from coming in contact with any painted surfaces.*

4. Remove the nuts attaching the master cylinder and remove the master cylinder and pushrod toward the engine compartment side.

5. Install the master cylinder in the reverse order of removal and bleed the clutch hydraulic system.

OVERHAUL

1. Remove the master cylinder from the vehicle.

2. Drain the clutch fluid (same as brake fluid) from the master cylinder reservoir.

1. Reservoir cap
2. Reservoir
3. Reservoir band
4. Cylinder body
5. Supply valve stopper
6. Return spring
7. Spring seat
8. Valve spring
9. Supply valve rod
10. Supply valve
11. Primary cup
12. Piston
13. Secondary cup
14. Push rod
15. Stopper
16. Stopper ring
17. Dust cover
18. Lock nut

210 clutch master cylinder. 1200 and B210 similar

3. Remove the boot and circliup and remove the pushrod.

4. Remove the stopper, piston, cup and return spring.

5. Clean all of the parts in clean brake fluid.

6. Check the master cylinder and piston for wear, corrosion and scores and replace the parts as necessary. Light scoring and glaze can be removed with crocus cloth soaked in clean brake fluid.

7. The cup seal should be replaced each time the master cylinder is disassembled, if there is any evidence of wear, cracking, damage, or fatigue.

8. Check the clutch fluid reservoir, filler cap, dust cover and the pipe for distortion and damage and replace the parts as necessary.

9. Lubricate all new parts with clean brake fluid.

10. Reassemble the master cylinder arts in the reverse order of disassembly, taking note of the following:

 a. Reinstall the cup seal carefully to prevent damaging the lipped portions;

 b. Adjust the height of the clutch pedal after installing the master cylinder in position on the vehicle;

 c. Fill the master cylinder and clutch fluid reservoir and then bleed the clutch hydraulic system (see "Bleeding Clutch Hydraulic System").

Clutch Slave Cylinder

REMOVAL AND INSTALLATION

Hydraulic Clutch Models

1. Remove the slave cylinder attaching bolts and the pushrod from the shift fork.

2. Disconnect the flexible fluid hose from the slave cylinder and remove the unit from the vehicle.

1. Bleeder screw
2. Cylinder body
3. Piston cup
4. Piston
5. Dust cover
6. Push rod
7. Lock nut
8. Push nut

Typical hydraulic clutch slave cylinder

3. Install the slave cylinder in the reverse order of removal and bleed the clutch hydraulic system.

OVERHAUL

1. Remove the slave cylinder from the vehicle.

2. Remove the pushrod and boot.

3. Force out the piston by blowing compressed air into the slave cylinder at the hose connection.

NOTE: *Be careful not to apply excess air pressure to avoid possible injury.*

4. Clean all of the parts in clean brake fluid.

CAUTION: *Never use mineral solvents such as kerosene or gasoline to clean master cylinder and other brake parts. These solvents will ruin the rubber parts of the hydraulic system.*

5. Check and replace the slave cylinder bore and piston if wear or severe scoring exists. Light scoring and glaze can be removed with crocus cloth soaked in clean brake fluid.

6. Normally the piston cup should be replaced when the slave cylinder is disassembled. Check the piston cup and replace it if it is found to be worn, fatigued or scored.

7. Replace the rubber boot if it is cracked or broken.

8. Lubricate all of the new parts in clean brake fluid and reassemble in the reverse order of disassembly, taking note of the following:

 a. Use care when reassembling the piston cup to prevent damaging the lipped portion of the piston cup;

 b. Fill the master cylinder with brake fluid and bleed the clutch hydraulic system;

 c. Adjust the clearance between the pushrod and the shift fork to 5/64 in.

BLEEDING THE CLUTCH HYDRAULIC SYSTEM

1. Check and fill the clutch fluid reservoir to the specified level as necessary. During the bleeding process, continue to check and replenish the reservoir to prevent the fluid level from getting lower than $\frac{1}{2}$ the specified level.

2. Remove the dust cap from the bleeder screw on the clutch slave cylinder and connect a tube to the bleeder screw and insert the other end of the tube into a clean glass or metal container.

NOTE: *Take precautionary measures to prevent the brake fluid from getting on any painted surfaces.*

3. Pump the clutch pedal several times, hold it down and loosen the bleeder screw slowly.

4. Tighten the bleeder screw and release the clutch pedal gradually. Repeat this operation

until air bubbles disappear from the brake fluid being expelled out through the bleeder screw.

5. Repeat until all evidence of air bubbles completely disappears from the brake fluid being pumped out through the tube.

6. When the air is completely removed, securely tighten the bleeder screw and replace the dust cap.

7. Check and refill the master cylinder reservoir as necessary.

8. Depress the clutch pedal several times to check the operation of the clutch and check for leaks.

AUTOMATIC TRANSMISSION

All Datsun models covered in this guide are also available with a three-speed automatic transmission (Sentras have an automatic transaxle). Except for the various checks and maintenance procedures outlined here, it is recommended that major automatic transmission service be left to an automatic transmission specialist who has the expertise and special tools required to work on these units.

Fluid Pan

REMOVAL AND INSTALLATION

1. Jack up the front of the car and support it safely on stands.

2. Slide a drain pan under the transmission. Loosen the rear oil pan bolts first, to allow most of the fluid to drain off without making a mess on your garage floor.

3. Remove the oil pan guard on Sentra. Remove the remaining bolts and drop the pan.

4. Discard the old gasket, clean the pan, and reinstall the pan with a new gasket.

5. Tighten the retaining bolts in a crisscross pattern starting at the center.

CAUTION: *The transmission case is aluminum and easily stripped, so don't put too much torque on the bolts.*

6. Refill the transmission through the dipstick tube. Check the fluid level as described in Chapter 1.

SHIFT LINKAGE ADJUSTMENT

The adjustment of the manual linkage (control cable on Sentra) is an important adjustment of the automatic transmission. Move the shift lever from the "P" range into the "1" range. You should be able to feel the detents (stops) in each range.

If the detents cannot be felt or the pointer indicating the range is improperly aligned, the linkage (control cable) needs adjustment.

1200, B210 and 210

1. Place shift lever in "D" range.

2. Loosen locknuts (see illustration) and move shift lever until "D" is properly aligned and car is in "D" range.

3. Tighten locknuts when lever is in proper position.

4. Recheck "P" and range "1" positions. As a safety measure, be sure you can feel full detent when shift lever is placed in "P". If you are unable to make an adjustment, grommets may be badly worn or damaged and should be replaced.

Automatic transmission shift linkage adjustment, 1200, B210 and 210

Automatic transmission pan removal

Adjusting neutral (inhibitor) switch using alignment pin

Sentra

1. Place gear lever in the "P" position.

2. Connect the control cable end to the manual lever in the transaxle unit, and tighten the control cable securing bolts.

3. Move the gear lever from the "P" position to the "1" position. Make sure that the gear lever can move smoothly and without any sliding noise.

4. Place the gear lever in the "P" range again. Make sure that the control lever locks at the "P" range.

5. Remove the control cable adjusting nut A and loosen nut B, then connect the control cable to the trunnion. Install nut A and B, then tighten them.

6. Move the gear lever from "P" to "1" position again. Make sure the lever moves smoothly without any sliding noise.

7. Apply a dab of grease to the spring washer.

8. After properly adjusting the control cable, check the spring pin to see if it is assembled as shown in the illustration. If not, adjust the spring pin.

A   B
TRUNNION

Sentra automatic transaxle cable adjustment

LOWER END OF   CONNECTING PORTION
CONTROL LEVER   OF MANUAL LEVER

FRONT   UPPER
DIRECTION   DIRECTION

Proper Sentra automatic transaxle spring pin position

DOWNSHIFT SOLENOID/KICKDOWN SWITCH CHECK AND ADJUSTMENT

1200, B210 and 210 Models

The kickdown switch is located at the upper post of the accelerator pedal, inside the car.

The downshift solenoid is screwed into the outside of the transmission case.

When the kickdown operation is not made properly or the speed changing point is too high, check the kickdown switch, downshift solenoid and the wiring connection between them.

1. Turn the ignition switch "ON" to the first position.

2. Push the accelerator pedal all the way down to actuate the downshift switch.

3. The downshift solenoid should click when actuated if working properly. If there is no click, loosen the locknut and extend the switch until the pedal lever makes contact with the switch and the switch clicks.

CAUTION: *Do not allow the switch to make contact too soon. This would cause the transmission to downshift on part throttle.*

4. If the switch can be heard clicking even if the transmission is not kicking down, check the electrical continuity of the switch with a continuity tester. Also check to see if current is reaching the switch.

INHIBITOR SWITCH (NEUTRAL SAFETY AND BACKUP LIGHT) ADJUSTMENT

The switch unit is bolted to the left side of the transmission case, behind the transmission shift lever. The switch prevents the engine from being started in any transmission position except Park or Neutral. It also controls the backup lights.

1200, B210 and 210 Models

1. Remove the transmission shift lever retaining nut and the lever.

2. Remove the switch.

3. Remove the machine screw in the case under the switch.

4. Align the switch to the case by inserting a 0.059 in. (1.5 mm) diameter pin through the hole in the switch into the screw hole. Mark the switch location.

5. Remove the pin, replace the machine screw, install the switch as marked, and replace the transmission shift lever and retaining nut.

6. Make sure, while holding the brakes and parking brake on, that the engine will start only in Park or Neutral. Check that the backup lights go on only in Reverse.

Sentra

1. Loosen the inhibitor attaching screws (three Phillips head screws).

2. Set the select lever (manual shaft) at the "N" position.

3. Insert a 2.5mm (0.098 in.) diameter pin into the adjustment hoels in both the inhibitor

Sentra inhibitor switch adjustment

switch and the switch lever as near vertical as possible.

4. Tighten the screws.

5. Check the inhibitor switch for continuity at the "N", "P" and "R" ranges. With the gear lever in neutral position, turn the manual lever an equal amount in both directions to see if the current flow ranges are nearly the same.

Transmission

REMOVAL AND INSTALLATION

1. Disconnect the battery cable.

2. Remove the accelerator linkage.

3. Detach the shift linkage.

4. Disconnect the neutral safety switch and downshift solenoid wiring.

5. Remove the drain plug and drain the torque converter. If there is no converter drain plug, drain the transmission. If there is no transmission drain plug, remove the pan to drain. Replace the pan to keep out dirt.

6. Remove the front exhaust pipe.

7. Remove the vacuum tube and speedometer cable.

8. Disconnect the fluid cooler tubes.

9. Remove the driveshaft and starter.

10. Support the transmission with a jack and wood block under the oil pan and support the engine.

11. Remove the rear crossmember.

12. Mark the relationship between the

Disconnecting the torque converter bolts through access hole

torque converter and the drive plate with a scribe or grease pencil. Remove the four bolts holding the converter to the drive plate through the hole at the front, under the engine. Unbolt the transmission from the engine.

13. Reverse the procedure for installation. Make sure that the drive plate is warped no more than 0.020 in. Torque the drive plate-to-torque converter and converter housing-to-engine bolts to 29–36 ft.lb. Drive plate-to-crankshaft bolt torque is 101–116 ft.lb.

14. Refill the transmission and check the fluid level.

DRIVELINE

Driveshaft and Universal Joints

The driveshaft transfers power from the front-mounted engine and transmisison to the differential and rear axles and then to the rear wheels to drive the car. All 1200, B210 and 210 Datsun models covered in this guide utilize a conventional rear wheel drive system. The driveshafts in these models have two universal joints at each end, and a slip yoke at the front of the assembly which fits into the back of the transmisison. These "U-joints" permit the driveshaft to both connect transmission and differential, which are not mounted on the same plane and to follow the rear axle up and down with the rear suspension movement as it also spins on its axis.

On the front wheel drive Sentras, the entire drive train is bolted in unit with the engine up front. Since the Sentra engine is transversely mounted (across the chassis), its crankshaft is already spinning on the same plane as the front (drive) wheels. Compared to its Datsun cousins, the Sentra transaxle has an easy job-- instead of having to change the direction of the engine torque from a longitudinal plane to the transverse plane of the drive wheels, the Sentra transaxle merely has to connect the two. Instead of one long driveshaft and U-joints carrying the engine torque to the wheels, the Sentra transaxle drives the front wheels directly through two unequal length driveshafts, or "halfshafts". Each halfshaft has a U-joint type spider (called a Constant Velocity, or CV joint) on each end, making the wheels independent of one another.

REMOVAL AND INSTALLATION

1200, B210, 210

These driveshafts are all one-piece units with a U-joint and flange at the rear, and a U-joint and a splined sleeve yoke which fits into the

1. Sleeve yoke
2. Spider with four bearing journals
3. Bearing race snap-ring
4. Bearing race with needle rollers
5. Spider with four bearing journals
6. Flange yoke
7. Bearing race snap-ring
8. Bearing race with needle rollers
9. Bolt
10. Lockwasher
11. Nut

Exploded view of 1200, B210 and 210 driveshaft and U-joints

rear of the transmission, at the front. Early 1200 and some B210 models generally have U-joints with grease fittings. U-joints without grease fittings must be disassembled for lubrication, usually at 24,000 mile intervals. The splines are lubricated by transmission oil.

1. Jack up car and safely support it with jackstands. Matchmark both the driveshaft and rear flange so that the shaft can be reinstalled in the same position.

2. Be ready to catch oil coming from the rear of the transmission and to plug the extension housing.

3. Unbolt the rear flange (differential end).

4. Pull the driveshaft down and back.

5. Plug the transmission extension housing.

Sentra front drive train and suspension

Disconnecting the rear driveshaft flange

6. Reverse the procedure to install, oiling the splines. Flange bolt torque is 15–20 ft.lb. (1200), 17–24 ft.lb. (B210-210).

Sentra

1. Jack up the car and safely support it with jackstands.

2. Remove the wheel and tire assembly.

3. Remove the brake caliper assembly (refer to Chapter 8 Brakes for this procedure).

4. Pry off the cotter pin from the castellated nut on the wheel hub.

5. Loosen, but do not remove, the wheel hub nut from the halfshaft while holding the wheel hub with a suitable tool.

6. Remove the tie rod ball joint (see Chapter 8 "Suspension" for this procedure). Remove the lower ball joint. Do not reuse the nut once it has been removed; install a new nut during assembly.

7. Drain the gear oil from the transaxle.

8. Remove the bolts holding the halfshaft flange to the transaxle. Remove the halfshaft, along with the wheel hub and knuckle.

9. Insert a suitable bar, wooden dowel or similar tool into the transaxle to prevent the side gear from dropping inside (see Manual Transaxle Removal procedures for an illustration).

CAUTION: *When removing the transaxle, be very careful not to damage the grease seal on the transaxle side.*

10. Installation is the reverse of removal. Coat the transaxle end halfshaft spline with a molybdenum disulfide grease before insertion. Make sure the rubber gaiters on both ends of the halfshaft are in good shape; if not, replace them (use new metal bands to retain the gaiters).

U-JOINT OVERHAUL

All Rear Wheel Drive Models

DISASSEMBLY

1. Match mark the relationship of all components for reassembly.

2. Remove the snaprings. On early units, the snaprings are seated in the yokes. On later units, the snaring seat in the needle bearing races.

3. Tap the yoke with a rubber hammer to release one bearing cap. The needle rollers are lined up around the inside wall of the caps and may be loose if their grease packing has disappeared. Use care in disassembling the U-joint from this point, as the rollers are easily lost.

JOINT ASSEMBLY (WHEEL SIDE)
WHEEL SIDE
BOOT BAND (LARGE)
BOOT (WHEEL SIDE)
BOOT BAND (SMALL)
CIRCLIP
DRIVE SHAFT
SPIDER ASSEMBLY
SNAP RING
O-RING
BOOT BAND (SMALL)
BOOT (TRANSAXLE SIDE)
BOOT BAND (LARGE)
SLIDE JOINT COVER
SLIDE JOINT HOUSING
CIRCLIP

Sentra halfshaft, disassembled

4. Remove the other bearing caps. Remove the U-joint spiders from the yokes.

INSPECTION

1. Spline backlash should not exceed 0.0197 in. (0.5mm).
2. Driveshaft runout should not exceed 0.0015 in. (0.4mm).
3. On later models with snaprings seated in the needle bearing races, different thicknesses of snaprings are available for U-joint adjustment. Play should not exceed 0.0008 in. (0.02 mm).
4. U-joint spiders must be replaced if their bearing journals are worn more than 0.0059 in. (0.15mm) from their original diameter.

ASSEMBLY

1. Grease the inside diameter of the cap races with enough grease to hold the rollers in place. Line the rollers up tightly, side by side inside the races.
2. Put the spider into place in its yokes.
3. Replace all seals.
4. Tap the races into position and secure them with snaprings.

Sentra

The CV joints on the Sentra are a non-disassembling design. Special tools (a large press to remove the spider assembly from the shaft, for example) and experience are needed to disassemble and replace these joints. We recommend you take the halfshafts to a professional service facility for further repair.

Removing axle on 1200, B210 and 210 models using a slide hammer

REAR AXLE

All 1200, B210 and 210 Datsun models covered in this guide utilize a solid (non-independent) rear axle. On the 1200 and B210 models, the rear axle assembly is attached to the frame through semi-elliptical leaf springs and telescopic shock abosrbers. The rear axle of the 210 models is suspended through coil springs and links, and damped with telescopic shock absorbers.

Axle Shaft

REMOVAL AND INSTALLATION

NOTE: *Bearings must be pressed on and off the shaft with an arbor press. Unless you have access to one, it is inadvisable to attempt any repair work on the axle shaft and bearing assemblies.*

1. Remove the hub cap or wheel cover. Loosen the lug nuts.
2. Raise the rear of the car and support it safely on stands.
3. Remove the rear wheel. Remove the four brake backing plate retaining nuts. Detach the parking brake linkage from the brake backing plate.
4. Attach a slide hammer to the axle shaft and remove it. Use the slide hammer and a two pronged puller to remove the oil seal from the housing.

NOTE: *If a slide hammer is not available, the axle can sometimes be pried out using pry bars on opposing sides of the hub. If endplay is found to be excessive, the bearing should be replaced. Shimming the bearing is not recommended as this ignores endplay of the bearing itself and could result in improper seating of the bearing.*

5. Using a chisel, carefully nick the bearing retainer in three or four places. The retainer does not have to be cut, only collapsed enough to allow the bearing retainer to be slid off the shaft.
6. Pull or press the old bearing off and install the new one by pressing it into position.
7. Install the outer bearing retainer with its raised surface facing the wheel hub, and then install the bearing and the inner bearing retainer in that order on the axle shaft.
8. With the smaller chamfered side of the inner bearing retainer facing the bearing, press on the retainer. The edge of the retainer should fully touch the bearing.
9. Clean the oil seal seat in the rear axle housing. Apply a thin coat of chassis grease.
10. Using a seal installation tool, drive the oil seal into the rear axle housing. Wipe a thin coat of bearing grease on the lips of the seal.
11. Determine the number of retainer gaskets which will give the correct bearing-to-outer retainer clearance of 0.01 in.
12. Insert the axle shaft assembly into the axle housing, being careful not to damage the seal. Ensure that the shaft splines engage those of the differential pinion. Align the vent holes of the gasket and the outer bearing retainer. Install the retaining bolts.
13. Install the nuts on the bolts and tighten them evenly, and in a criss-cross pattern, to 20 ft.lb.

Differential

The rear axle on the 1200, B210 and 210 models must transmit power through a 90 degree bend. To accomplish this, straight cut bevel gears or spiral cut bevel gears were originally used. This type of gear drive is satisfactory for differential side gears, but since the centerline of the gears must intersect, they are not suitable for ring and pinion gears (main drive gears in all differentials). The lowering of the driveshaft brought about a variation of bevel gears called the hypoid gear. This type of gear does not require a meeting of the gear centerlines and can therefore be underslung, relative to the centerline of the ring gear.

NOTE: *All differential service should be performed by a professional mechanic, especially one well versed in differential repair. A great deal of experience and many special tools are required in servicing a differential; this is not an area the owner/mechanic should tackle without experience.*

OPERATION

The differential is an arrangement of gears which permits the rear wheels to turn at different speeds when cornering and divides the torque between the axle shafts. The differential gears are mounted on a pinion shaft and the gears are free to rotate on this shaft. The pinion shaft is fitted in a bore in the differential case and is at right angles to the axle shafts.

Power flow through the differential is as follows. The drive pinion, which is turned by the driveshaft, turns the ring gear. The ring gear, which is bolted to the differential case, rotates the case. The differential pinion forces the pinion gears against the side gears. In cases where both wheels have equal traction, the pinion gears do not rotate on the pinion shaft, because the input force of the pinion gear is divided equally between the two side gears. Consequently, the pinion gears revolve with the pinion shaft, although they do not rotate on the pinion shaft itself. The side gears, which are splined to the axle shafts, and meshed with the pinion gears, rotate the axle shafts.

When it becomes necessary to turn a corner, the differential becomes effective and allows the axle shafts to rotate at different speeds. As the inner wheel slows down, the side gear splined to the inner wheel axle shaft also slows down. The pinion gears act as balancing levers by maintianing equal tooth loads to both gears while allowing unequal speeds of rotation at the axle shafts. If the vehicle speed remains constant, and the inner wheel slows down to 90 percent of vehicle speed, the outer wheel will speed up to 110 percent.

Determining Gear Ratio

Determining the axle ratio of any given axle can be a very useful "tool" to the contemporary car owner. Axle ratios are a major factor in a vehicle's fuel mileage, so the car buyer of today should know both what he or she is looking for, and what the salesperson is talking about. Knowledge of axle ratios is also valuable to the owner/mechanic who is shopping through salvage yards for a used axle, who is repairing his

Bevel gears

Hypoid gears

Differential action during cornering

or her own rear axle, or who is changing rear axle ratios by changing rear axles.

The rear axle ratio is said to have a certain ratio, say 4.11. It is called a "4.11 rear" although the 4.11 actually means 4.11 to 1 (4.11:1). This means that the driveshaft will turn 4.11 times for every turn of the rear wheels. The number 4.11 is determined by dividing the number of teeth on the pinion gear into the number of teeth on the ring gear. In the case of a 4.11 rear, there could be 9 teeth on the pinion and 37 teeth on the ring gear (37 ÷ 9 = 4.11). This provides a sure way, although troublesome, of determining your rear axle's ratio. The axle must be drained and the rear cover removed to do this, and then the teeth counted.

A much easier method is to jack up the car and safely support it with jackstands, so BOTH rear wheels are off the ground. Block the front wheels, set the parking brake and put the transmission in Neutral. Make a calk mark on the rear wheel and the driveshaft. Turn the rear wheel one complete revolution and count the number of turns that the driveshaft makes (having an assistant here to count one or the other is helpful). The number of turns the driveshaft makes in one complete revolution of the rear wheel is an approximation of the rear axle ratio.

Suspension and Steering

FRONT SUSPENSION

All models covered in this book use MacPherson strut front suspension. In this type of suspension, each strut combines the function of coil spring and shock absorber. The spindle is mounted to the lower part of the strut through a single ball joint. No upper suspension arm is required in this design. The lower suspension arm is bolted to the front subframe assembly.

Springs and Shock Absorbers

TESTING SHOCK ABSORBER ACTION

Shock absorbers require replacement if the vehicle fails to recover quickly after a large bump is encountered, if there is a tendency for the vehicle to sway or nose dive excessively, or, sometimes, if the suspension is overly susceptible to vibration.

A good way to test the shocks is to intermittently apply downward pressure to one corner of the vehicle until it is moving up and down for almost the full suspension travel, then release it and watch the recovery. If the vehicle bounces slightly about one more time and then comes to rest, the shock absorbers are serviceable. If the vehicle goes on bouncing, the shocks require replacement.

Strut

REMOVAL AND INSTALLATION

1. Jack up the car and support it safely. Remove the wheel.
2. Disconnect and plug the brake hose. Remove the brake caliper as outlined in Chapter 8. Remove the disc and hub as described in this chapter. On some 1200 models and early B210s with drum front brakes, loosen the brake tube connecting nut, remove the brake hose locking spring, withdraw the plate, and remove the brake hose from the strut assembly bracket.

3. Disconnect the tension rod and stabilizer bar from the transverse link.
4. Unbolt the steering arm. Pry the control arm down to detach it from the strut.

Front top strut mounting bolts. All models similar

Brake caliper-to-strut mounting bolts

Disconnect brake hose before removing struts

Removing side rod ball joint using ball joint puller. Forked ball joint tool may also be used

1200 and B210 strut-to-control arm/steering knuckle bolts. 210 similar

Pry the control arm down to separate the strut from the knuckle

5. Place a jack under the bottom of the strut.
6. Open the hood and remove the nuts holding the top of the strut.
7. Lower the jack slowly and cautiously until the strut assembly can be removed.
8. Reverse the procedure to install. The self-locking nuts holding the top of the strut must be replaced. Bleed the brakes.

Coil Spring and Shock Abosrber
REMOVAL AND INSTALLATION

Coil springs on all models must be removed with the aid of a coil spring compressor. If you don't have one, don't try to improvise by using something else: you could risk injury. The Nissan coil spring compressor is Special Tool ST3565S001 or variations of that number. Basically, they are all the same tool. These are the recommended compressors, although they are probably not the only spring compressors which will work. Always follow manufacturer's instructions when operating a spring compressor. You can now buy cartridge type shock absorbers for many Nissans and Nissans: installation procedures are not the same as those given here. In the case of these aftermarket shocks, always follow the instructions that come with the shock absorbers.

CAUTION: *The coil springs are under considerable tension, and can exert pressure to cause serious injury. Disassemble the struts only if the proper tools are available, and use extreme caution.*

To remove the coil spring(s), you must first remove the strut assembly from the vehicle. See above for procedures and follow the caution.

1. Secure the strut assembly in a vise.
2. Attach the spring compressor to the spring, leaving the top few coils free.
3. Remove the dust cap from the top of the strut to expose the center nut, if a dust cap is provided.
4. Compress the spring just far enough to permit the strut insulator to be turned by hand. Remove the self-locking center nut.
5. Take out the strut insulator, strut bearing, oil seal, upper spring seat and bound bumper rubber from the top of the strut. Note their sequence of removal and be sure to assemble them in the same order.
6. Remove the spring with the spring compressor still attached.

NOTE: *If the replacement of any strut component parts is found to be necessary, make sure that parts are the same brand as those used in the strut assembly.*

7. Assembly is the reverse of disassembly. Observe the following. Make sure you assemble the unit with the shock absorber piston rod fully extended. When assembling, take care that the rubber spring seats, both top and bottom, and the spring are positioned in their grooves before releasing the spring.
8. To remove the shock abosrber: Remove the dust cap, if equipped, and push the piston rod down until it bottoms. With the piston in this position, loosen and remove the gland packing shock absorber retainer. This calls for Nissan Special Tool ST35500001, but you should be able to loosen it with a pipe wrench (very carefully) or by tapping it around with a drift.

1. Strut mounting insulator
2. Strut mounting bearing
3. Upper spring seat
4. Bumper rubber
5. Dust cover
6. Piston rod
7. Front spring
8. Strut assembly
9. Hub assembly
10. Spindle
11. Ball joint
12. Transverse link
13. Tension rod
14. Stabilizer
15. Suspension member

1200, B210 and 210 series front suspension

NOTE: *If the gland tube is dirty, clean it before removing it to prevent dirt from contaminating the fluid inside the strut tube.*

9. Remove the O-ring from the top of the piston rod guide and lift out the piston rod together with the cylinder. Drain all of the fluid from the strut and shock components into a suitable container. Clean all parts; do not use a mineral based solvent on any of the rubber parts.

10. Assembly is the reverse of disassembly, with the following notes to be closely observed:

a. After installing the cylinder and piston

1. Strut mounting insulator
2. Bearing
3. Spring upper seat and dust cover
4. Damper rubber
5. Coil spring
6. Strut assembly

Exploded view of 1200 and B210 strut, others similar

ST3565 1001

Datsun spring compressor correctly mounted on coil spring

rod assembly (the shock absorber kit) in the outer casing, remove the piston rod guide, if equipped, from the cylinder and pour the correct amount of fresh fluid into the cylinder and strut outer casing. Shock absorber kits list the correct amount of fluid to use, or check the following chart. Use only a high quality fluid made specifically for hydraulic struts (Nissan Strut Oil or equivalent).

NOTE: *When tightening the gland packing, extend the piston rod about 3 to 5 inches from the end of the outer casing to expel most of the air from the strut.*

b. After the kit is installed, bleed the air from the system in the following manner:

Removing the shock absorber from the gland tube

Filling the shock assembly with oil

Bleeding air from strut unit

hold the strut with its bottom end facing down. Pull the piston rod out as far as it will go. Turn the strut upside down and push the piston in as far as it will go. Repeat this procedure several times until an equal pressure is felt on both the pull out and the push in strokes of the piston rods. The remaining assembly is the reverse of disassembly.

Ball Joint
INSPECTION

The lower ball joint should be replaced when play becomes excessive. Nissan does not publish specifications on just what constitutes excessive play, relying instead on a method of determining the force (in inch pounds) required to keep the ball joint turning. This method is not very helpful to the owner mechanic since it involves removing the ball joint, which is what we are trying to avoid in the first place. An effective way to determine ball joint play is to jack up the car until the wheel is jsut a couple of inches off the ground and the ball joint is unloaded (meaning you can't jack directly underneath the ball joint). Place a long bar under the tire and move the wheel and tire assembly up and down. Keep one hand on top of the tire while you are doing this. If there is over ¼inch of play at the top of the tire, the ball joint is probably bad. This is assuming that the wheel bearings are in good shape and properly adjusted. As a double check on this, have someone watch the ball joint while you move the tire up and down with the bar. If you can see considerable play, besides feeling play at the top of the wheel, the ball joint needs replacing.

Cross section of a ball joint. Note plug at the bottom for grease nipple

REMOVAL AND INSTALLATION
All Models Except Sentra

The ball joint should be greased every 30,000 miles. There is a plugged hole in the bottom of the joint for the installation of grease fitting.

Shock Strut Refill Capacities

Year	Model	Shock Make	Capacity
1973	1200	AMPCO (ATSUGI)	280cc (17.1 cu. in.)
1974–78	B210	AMPCO (ATSUGI)	325cc (19.83 cu. in.)
1979 and later	210 (U.S.) 210 (1.2L Canadian)	ATSUGI ATSUGI TOKICO	325cc (19.83 cu. in.) 260cc (16 cu. in.) 230cc (14.5 cu. in.)

1. Raise and support the car so that the wheels hang freely. Remove the wheel.

2. Unbolt the tension rod and stabilizer bar from the transverse link.

3. Unbolt the strut from the steering arm.

4. Remove the cotter pin and ball joint stud nut. Separate the ball joint and steering arm.

5. Unbolt the ball joint from the transverse link.

6. Reverse the procedure to install a new ball joint. Grease the joint after installation, forcing grease in until the old grease begins to squeeze out of the joint.

Sentra

The Sentra lower ball joints can be unbolted from the lower control arm. The ball joint is attached to the arm by a plate with three bolts through it, from the top of the lower arm. The nuts screw up onto these bolts from underneath the joint.

1. Remove the driveshaft (refer to Driveshaft Removal for procedures).

2. Remove the lower ball joint by removing the three nuts and separating the ball joint form the steering knuckle using a ball joint removal tool.

3. Install the new ball joint in the reverse order of removal.

4. Lubricate the ball joint after assembly.

Lower Control Arm (Transverse Link) and Ball Joint

REMOVAL AND INSTALLATION

NOTE: *A ball joint removal tool of either the forked type or the puller type is needed.*

1. Jack up the vehicle and support it with jack stands; remove the wheel.

2. Remove the splash board, if so equipped.

3. Remove the cotter pin and castle nut from the side rod (steering arm) ball joint and separate the ball joint from the side rod.

4. Separate the steering knuckle arm from the MacPherson strut.

5. Remove the tension rod and stabilizer bar from the lower arm.

6. Remove the nuts and bolts connecting the lower control arm (transverse link) to the suspension crossmember on all models.

7. Remove the lower control arm (transverse link) with the suspension ball joint and knuckle arm still attached.

Removing bolt connecting control arm to crossmember—210

Separating ball joint from the knuckle using forked ball joint tool

Removing the ball joint

8. Installation is the reverse of removal, with the following notes:

9. Check all rubber parts, such as tension rod and stabilizer bar bushings), to be sure they are not deteriorated or cracked, and replace if necessary. Also examine tension rod and stabilizer bar for evidence of damage and replace if necessary.

10. Be sure the stabilizer bar is not closer to either side, but is located at the middle.

11. When installing the control arm, temporarily tighten the nuts and/or bolts securing the control arm to the suspension crossmember. Tighten them fully only after the car is sitting on its wheels.

12. Lubricate the ball joints after assembly.

Tie Rod Ends (Steering Side Rods)
REMOVAL AND INSTALLATION

NOTE: *You will need either type of ball joint remover for this operation.*

1. Jack up the front of the vehicle and support it on jack stands.

2. Locate the faulty tie rod end. It will have a lot of play in it and the dust cover will probably be ripped.

3. Remove the cotter key and nut from the tie rod stud. Note the position of the tie rod end in relation to the rest of the steering linkage.

4. Loosen the locknut holding the tie rod to the rest of the steering linkage.

5. Free the tie rod ball joint from either the relay rod or steering knuckle by using the ball joint remover.

6. Unscrew and remove the tie rod end, counting the number of turns it takes to completely free it.

7. Install the new tie rod end, turning in exactly as far as you screwed out the old one. Make sure it is correctly positioned in relation to the rest of the steering linkage.

8. Fit the ball joint and nut, tighten them and install a new cotter pin.

9. Before finally tightening the tie rod lock nut or clamp, adjust the toe-in of the vehicle.

Front End Alignment

The major front end adjustments for the Nissan are given here: caster/ camber, toe, and steering angle. However, we recommend that a professional shop, specializing in front end alignment handle the work. Shops such as this are fully equipped for these procedures, and get the alignment correct the first time, which is something the average owner/mechanic may not do (especially if you do not have access to a hydraulic lift). The usually modest cost of a professional front end alignment job is well worth it when compared to the prospect of an improperly aligned (and unsafe) front end.

CASTER AND CAMBER

Caster is the forward or rearward tilt of the upper end of the kingpin, or the upper ball joint,

1. Steering gear arm
2. Cross rod
3. Side rod
4. Side rod outer socket
5. Side rod inner socket
6. Idler arm assembly

Steering linkage—toe-in adjustment is made at the side rod (tie rod)

Wheel Alignment Specifications

Year	Model	Caster		Camber			Toe-In (in.)	Steering Axis Inclination (deg.)	Wheel Pivot Ratio (deg.)	
		Range (deg)	Preferred Setting (deg.)	Range (deg.)	Preferred Setting (deg.)				Inner Wheel	Outer Wheel
1973	1200	40'–1°40'	1°10'	35'–1°35'	1°05'	0.16–0.24	7°55'	42–44	35–37
1974	B210	1°15'–2°15'	1°45'	40'–1°40'	1°10'	0.079–0.157	7°47'–8°47'	37–39	31–33
1975–78	B210	1°00'–2°30'	1°45'	0°25'–1°55'	1°10'	0.08–0.16	7°32'–9°02'	37–39	31–33
1979–82	210 Sedan, Hatchback	1°40'–3°10'	2°25'	0'–1°30'	0°45'	0.04–0.12	7°50'–9°20'	38–42	31°30'–35°30'
	210 Station Wagon	1°55'–3°25'	2°40'	0'–1°30'	0°45'	0.04–0.12	7°50'–9°20'	38–42	31°30'–35°30'
1982–86	Sentra	45'–2°15'	1°30'	–35'–1°05' ①	0°15'	0.12–0.20	12°10'–13°40'	40–44	31–35

① 1984–86 (–25–1°05')

which results in a slight tilt of the steering axis forward or backward. Rearward tilt is referred to as a positive caster, while forward tilt is referred to as negative caster.

Camber is the inward or outward tilt from the vertical, measured in degrees, of the front wheels at the top. An outward tilt gives the wheel positive camber. Proper camber is critical to assure even tire wear.

Since caster and camber are adjusted traditionally by adding or subtracting shims behind the upper control arms, and the Nissans covered in this guide have replaced the upper control arm with the MacPherson strut, the only way to adjust caster and camber is to replace bent or worn parts of the front suspension.

TOE-IN

Toe is the amount, measured in a fraction of an inch, that the wheels are closer together at one end than the other. Toe-in means that the front wheels are closer together at the front than the rear; toe-out means the rears are closer than the front. Nissans are adjsuted to have a slight amount of toe-in. Toe-in is adjusted by turning the tie rod, which has a right hand thread on one end and a left hand thread on the other.

You can check your vehicle's toe-in yourself without special equipment is you make careful measurements. The wheels must be straight ahead.

1. Toe-in can be determined by measuring the distance between the center of the tire treads, at the front of the tire and at the rear. If the tread pattern of your car's tires makes this impossible, you can measure between the edges of the wheel rims, but make sure to move the car forward and measure in a couple of places to void errors caused by bent rims or wheel runout.

2. If the measurement is not within specifications, loosen the locknuts at both ends of the tie rod (the driver's side locknut is left hand threaded).

3. Turn the top of the tie rod toward the front of the car to reduce toe-in, or toward the rear to increase it. When the correct dimension is reached, tighten the locknuts and check the adjustment.

NOTE: *The length of the tie rods must always be equal to each other.*

STEERING ANGLE ADJUSTMENT

The maximum steering angle is adjusted by stopper bolts on the steering arms. Loosen the locknut on the stopper bolt, turn the stopped bolt in or out as required to obtain the proper maximum steering angle and retighten the locknut.

SUSPENSION HEIGHT

Suspension height is adjusted by replacing the springs. Various springs are available for adjustment.

REAR SUSPENSION

There are two basic rear suspension types used on the Nissans and Nissans covered in this guide. All 1200 and B210 models are equipped with solid (non-independent) rear axles sus-

1. Leaf spring
2. Front mounting
3. Shackle
4. Shock absorber
5. Axle housing
6. Differential carrier
7. Torque arrester
8. Handbrake cable
9. Brake hose
10. Bound bumper

1200 and B210 rear suspension

1. Rear axle case
2. Drain plug
3. Filler plug
4. Breather cap
5. Breather
6. Rear axle case end shim
7. Bearing collar
8. Oil seal
9. Rear axle bearing (wheel bearing)
10. Bearing spacer
11. Rear axle shaft
12. Shock absorber lower end bolt
13. Shock absorber assembly
14. Special washer
15. Shock absorber mounting bushing A
16. Shock absorber mounting bushing B
17. Bound bumper cover
18. Bound bumper rubber
19. Shock absorber mounting insulator
20. Coil spring
21. Upper link bushing bolt
22. Upper link bushing
23. Upper link
24. Lower link bushing bolt
25. Lower link bushing
26. Lower link
27. Torque arrester

Tightening torque (ft-lb)
Ⓐ (43–72)
Ⓑ (51–58)
Ⓒ (11–14)
Ⓓ (51–58)

210 rear axle and suspension

RUBBER SEAT*

COIL SPRING

SHOCK ABSORBER

BOUND BUMPER RUBBER*

LOWER ARM

RUBBER BUSHING*

LOWER ARM BUSHING*

*RUBBER PARTS: EXERCISE CARE TO ALLOW OIL OR GREASE TO COME INTO CONTACT WITH RUBBER PARTS.

Sentra rear suspension

pended by leaf springs and telescopic shock absorbers. The 1979 and later 210s including wagons, are equipped with four-link type solid rear axles suspended by coil springs and telescopic shock absorbers. The 1982 and later Nissan Sentras utilize an independent rear suspension: one lower control arm on each side, damped by a telescopic shock absorber and coil spring.

CAUTION: *Before doing any rear suspension work, block both front wheels of the car to insure that it won't move or shift while you are under it. Always support the rear of the car with jackstands, NOT a jack. Also, remember you are dealing with spring steel that has enough force when compressed to injure you (when released) if you don't follow the removal and installation procedures exactly.*

Springs
REMOVAL AND INSTALLATION
Leaf Type Spring
1200 and B210

1. Raise the rear axle until the wheels hang free. Support the car on stands. Support the rear axle with a hydraulic jack.
2. Unbolt the bottom end of shock absorber.
3. Unbolt the axle from the spring leaves. Unbolt and remove the front spring bracket. Lower the front of the spring to the floor.

1200 and B210 front spring bracket

1200 and B210 rear spring shackle

4. Unbolt and remove the spring rear shackle.
5. Before reinstallation, coat the front bracket pin, bushing, shackle pin, and shackle bushing with a soap and water solution to serve as a lubricant.
6. Reverse the procedure to install. The front pin nut and the shock absorber mounting should be tightened before the vehicle is lowered to the floor.

Coil Spring Type
210 AND SENTRA

1. Block the front wheels.
2. Jack up the rear of the car high enough to permit working underneath, and place jackstands securely underneath the body members on both sides.
3. Place a floor jack under the center of the differential carrier (not necessary on Sentra).
4. Remove the rear wheels.
5. Remove the bolts securing the shock absorber lower ends on each side.
6. Lower the jack slowly and remove the coil springs on each side after they are fully extended.
7. Inspect the springs for yield, deformation or cracks.
8. Install the springs in the reverse order of removal. The bottom of the coil springs must sit squarely on each spring seat.

Shock Absorber
INSPECTION AND TESTING

Inspect and test the rear shock absorbers in the same manner as outlined for the front shock absorbers. Shocks should always be replaced in pairs.

REMOVAL AND INSTALLATION
Leaf Spring Type
1200 AND B210

1. Jack up the rear of the car and support the rear axle on two stands.
2. Disconnect the lower shock mounting bolt at the spring plate (plenty of penetrating oil is often useful here).
3. From inside the car, remove the rear seat back and disconnect the upper mounting nut.
4. Remove the shock absorber.
5. Install the replacement shock in the reverse of the removal procedure.

210 AND SENTRA

1. Open the trunk and remove the nuts securing the shock absorber upper end to the wheel house panel. Pry off the shock mount covers on the station wagon.

2. Remove the bolt securing the shock absorber lower end to the lower control arm and remove the shock absorber (using penetrating oil if necessary).

NOTE: *When removing the shock absorber lower end from the bracket, squeeze the shock absorber and lift it out to accommodate the embossment inside bracket.*

3. Test the shock absorber action by slowly pulling the piston rod out to full extension. Check for a steady pull with plenty of resistance and no sticking. Now begin to push the rod back, with a steady motion until the shock is fully compressed. The feel of the damping should not be grabby, weak or loose. There should be no evidence of the shock leaking either air or oil (or both). Check the piston rod for straightness, and all rubber parts (including mount bushings) for wear, cracks, damage

Removing the lower shock absorber nut

Detach lower shock absorber mount (1) and spring U-bolts (2)—1200 and B210 coupe shown

Detach lower shock absorber mount (1) and spring U-bolts (2)—1200 and B210 sedan shown

Remove the spring shackle

Upper shock absorber retaining bolts

or deformation. Replace entire shock unit if necessary (usually replaced in pairs).

4. Install the shock absorbers in the reverse order of removal.

NOTE: *Tighten shock absorber upper end nut to 11–14 ft.lb. until it is fully tightened to thread end of piston rod. Then securely tighten lock nut. Tighten lower shock mounting nut to 51–58 ft.lb.*

STEERING

Steering Wheel

REMOVAL AND INSTALLATION

1. Position the wheels in the straight-ahead direction. The steering wheel should be right-side up and level.

Rear shock absorber top mounting (sedans)

Removing horn pad—210

Using puller to remove the steering wheel

2. Disconnect the battery ground cable.

3. Look at the back of your steering wheel. If there are countersunk screws in the back of the spokes, remove the screws and pull off the horn pad. Some models have a horn wire running from the pad to the steering wheel. Disconnect it. On the 3-spoke "sport" steering wheel on some 210s and the Sentra wheel, the central horn pad simply pulls off.

4. Remove the rest of the horn switching mechanism, noting the relative location of the parts. Remove the mechanism only if it hinders subsequent wheel removal procedures.

5. Matchmark the top of the steering column shaft and the steering wheel flange.

6. Remove the attaching nut and remove the steering wheel with a puller.

CAUTION: *Do not strike the shaft with a hammer, which may cause the column to collapse.*

7. Install the steering wheel in the reverse order of removal, aligning the punch marks. Do not drive or hammer the wheel into place, or you may cause the collapsible steering columns to collapse; in which case you'll have to buy a whole new steering column unit.

8. Tighten the steering wheel nut to 22–25 ft.lb. on the 1200 and B210, and to 27–38 ft.lb.

9. Reinstall the horn pad and button.

Turn Signal Switch
REMOVAL AND INSTALLATION

On the 1979 and later 210s, and 1982 and later Sentra, the turn signal switch is part of a combination switch (which includes lights, wipers, etc.). The entire unit is removed together. The turn signal switch on the B210 and 1200 models does not include any other functions (other than the high beam).

Combination Switch
210 AND SENTRA

1. Disconnect the battery ground cable.
2. Remove the steering wheel as previously

outlined. Observe the caution on the collapsible steering column.

3. Remove the steering column covers.

4. Disconnect the electrical plugs from the switch.

5. Remove the retaining screws and remove the switch.

6. Installation is the reverse of removal. Some turn signal switches have a tab which must fit into a hole in the steering shafts in order for the system to return the switch to the neutral position after the turn has been made. Be sure to align the tab and the hole when installing.

Turn Signal Switch
1200 AND B210 MODELS

1. Disconnect the battery ground cable.

2. Remove the steering wheel.

3. Remove the four screws securing the upper and lower shell covers to each other. Shell covers can then be taken out easily.

4. Disconnect the lead wires of the turn signal switch at the two connectors.

5. Loosen the two screws holding the switch assembly to the steering column jacket. The switch assembly can now be easily taken out.

6. Installation is the reverse of removal. Make sure that the location tab of the switch fits in the hole of the steering column jacket.

Steering Lock
REMOVAL AND INSTALLATION

The steering lock/ignition switch/warning buzzer assembly is attached to the steering column by special screws whose heads shear off when installed at the factory (so the lock cannot be removed easily). The screws must be drilled out to remove the assembly. The ignition switch or warning switch can be replaced without removing the assembly. The ignition switch is on the back of the assembly, and the warning switch on the side. The warning buzzer, which sounds when the driver's door is opened with the steering unlocked, is located behind the instrument panel.

Brakes

BRAKE SYSTEM

Adjustment

Front disc brakes are used on all models covered in this guide except some early 1200 models. All 1200, B210 and 210 Datsuns and Nissan Sentras are equipped with independent front and rear hydraulic systems with a warning light to indicate loss of pressure in either system. All models have rear hydraulic drum brakes.

The 1973 1200 is the only model covered here that does not have a power booster system to lessen the required brake pressure. The parking brake on all models operates the rear brakes through a cable system.

NOTE: *All front disc brakes covered in this guide are self-adjusting, needing no external adjustment. The drum brakes on the 1200 and B210 models require adjustment; 210 model drum brakes are automatically adjusted when the parking brake is applied (parking brake adjustment is also covered here).*

To adjust the brakes, jack up the car, remove the wheels, and safely support the rear with jackstands. Disconnect the parking brake linkage from the rear wheels, apply the brakes hard a few times to center the drums, and proceed as follows:

FRONT DRUM BRAKES

1. With the brake drum installed, insert the brake adjusting spoon through the backing plate. Tighten the cam adjusting stud clockwise until the brake shoes contact the brake drum (you will be unable to turn the drum freely).

2. Now turn the cam adjusting stud counterclockwise until the brake shoes separate slightly from the drums. The drums should turn freely.

3. Turn the brake drum, and if the brake shoe interferes (drags) on the drum, readjust

1200 front drum brake. All rear drums similar except utilize one wheel cylinder

the clearance. Depress the brake pedal and make sure the brake operates correctly.

REAR BRAKES

1200

1. Remove the rubber grommets from the backing plate, and insert a brake adjusting spoon through the backing plate. Tighten the brake adjuster wedge clockwise, moving the brake shoes against the brake drum. You should now be unable to turn the brake drum.

2. Back off the adjuster just enough that the brake drum will turn freely without dragging. Depress the brake pedal to make sure the brake operates effectively.

B210, 210 and Sentra

1. Make sure the hand brake lever assembly returns properly to its original position (down all the way).

2. Remove the rubber grommets from the adjuster holes in the backing plates.

3. Using a brake adjusting spoon or conventional screwdriver, turn the toothed adjusting nut to expand the brake shoes. Stop turning the adjusting nut when the shoes have made contact with the drum (drum won't turn).

4. Back off the adjusting nut several notches until the brake shoes are slightly away from the drum, with no drag. Test the brakes and make sure the operation is effective.

Rear brake adjustment. Brake adjusting spoon is recommended

PARKING BRAKE

All Models

1. Adjust the rear brake shoe-to-drum clearance before adjusting hand brake.

2. Turn the adjusting nut on the front (short) end of the turnbuckle so that the operating stroke is 78.5 mm (3.091 in.), pulled by a force of 24 to 33 lbs. This corresponds to the sixth notch from the completely released lever position.

3. After the above adjustment is made, operate the lever twice at a force of 55 to 66 lbs. so as to seal it properly.

1. Hand brake lever
2. Cable
3. Clip
4. Lock plate
5. Turn-buckle (Hand brake adjuster)
6. Cable
7. Cable
8. Hanger strap
9. Return spring
10. Cable shank
11. Hand brake lever cover

Parking brake adjustment turnbuckle

4. Adjust again as described above in number 2.

5. Tighten the locknut securely (see illustration).

6. If the adjustment is no longer effective on its threaded end, replace the front cable.

BRAKE PEDAL ADJUSTMENT

Before making this adjustment, make sure that the wheel brakes are properly adjusted. Adjust the pedal free play by means of the ped-

Free play
Free height
Depressed height

Brake pedal adjustment all models. "B" shows locknut

1200 and B210 parking brake assembly. 210 and Sentra similar

Brake Pedal Adjustments

	1200	B210	210	Sentra
Pedal free play (in.)	0.20–0.50	0.04–0.20	0.04–0.20	0.40–0.20
Pedal height (in.) ①	5.65–5.87	6.18	5.65–5.87	②
				③
Depressed height (in.)	1.00	2.76	2.76	④

① Pedal height measured from floorboard to pedal pad
② Manual transaxle—1982 (7.53–7.76), 1983–86 (7.64–8.03)
③ Automatic transaxle—1982 (7.60–7.83), 1983–86 (7.76–8.15)
④ Gasoline engine—3.35 or more, Diesel engine—3.15 or more

al pushrod locknut (on the floor side of the pedal). Adjust the pedal height by adjusting the brake lamp switch locknut (and operating rod if equipped with a brake booster).

HYDRAULIC SYSTEM

Master Cylinder

REMOVAL AND INSTALLATION

Clean the outside of the cylinder thoroughly, particularly around the cap and fluid lines. Disconnect the fluid lines and cap them to exclude dirt. (Be careful not to allow any dirt into the system). Remove the clevis pin connecting the pushrod to the brake pedal arm inside the car. This pin need not be removed with the vacuum booster, if equipped. Unbolt the master cylinder from the firewall and remove. The adjustable pushrod is used to adjust brake pedal

free-play (see Brake Pedal Adjustment above). After installation (which is the reverse of removal), bleed the system and check the pedal free-play.

NOTE: *Ordinary brake fluid will boil and cause brake failure under high temperatures developed in disc brake systems. Use only DOT 3 or 4 fluid developed for disc brake systems.*

OVERHAUL

The master cylinder can be disassembled using the illustrations as a guide. Clean all parts in clean brake fluid. Replace the cylinder or piston as necessary if clearance between the two exceeds 0.006 in. Lubricate all parts in clean brake fluid on assembly. Master cylinder rebuilding kits, containing all the necessary parts, are available to simplify and cheapen the expense of overhaul.

CAUTION: *Master cylinders are supplied to*

1. Reservoir cap
2. Filter
3. Stopper ring
4. Stopper screw
5. Stopper
6. Primary-piston assembly
7. Primary piston return spring
8. Secondary piston assembly
9. Secondary piston return spring
10. Plug
11. Check valve
12. Reservoir

Exploded view of 1200, B210 and 210 master cylinder. Sentra similar

Datsun by two manufacturers: Nabco and Tokico. Parts between these two manufacturers are not interchangeable. Be sure you obtain the correct rebuilding kit for your master cylinder.

Brake Proportioning Valve

All Datsuns covered in this guide are equipped with brake proportioning valves of several different types. The valves all do the same job, which is to separate the front and rear brake lines, allowing them to function independently, and preventing the rear brakes from locking before the front brakes. Damage, such as brake line leakage, in either the front or rear brake system will not affect the normal operation of the unaffected system. If, in the event of a panic stop, the rear brakes lock up before the front brakes, it could mean the proportioning valve is defective. In that case, replace the entire proportioning valve.

System Bleeding

Bleeding the brake system is required whenever air gets into the hydraulic fluid, causing a spongy feeling at the pedal and slow brake response. Air may find its way into the system through a worn master cylinder, worn wheel cylinders, a loose or broken brake line, or if any brake system component is removed from the system for repair.

NOTE: *The brake system must always be bled if a component is removed or the system disconnected in any way.*

1. Top up the master cylinder reservoir with the proper brake fluid. Make sure the fluid you use is approved for disc brakes (unless your car is a 1200 model with front drum brakes). All brake systems should use DOT 3 or 4 brake fluid.

2. Jack up the rear of the car and safely support it with jackstands.

3. Begin with the wheel farthest from the master cylinder. Clean all dirt off of the bleeder nipple. Fit a rubber hose over the bleeder nipple on the inside (facing underneath the car) of the brake backing plate. Submerge the other end of the hose in clean brake fluid in a clear glass jar.

NOTE: *Do not reuse any brake fluid that has been bled from the system.*

4. Have an assistant pump the brake pedal three or four times. On the bottom of the fourth stroke (pedal all the way down), loosen the bleeder screw behind the nipple (while your assistant keeps the pedal depressed) and allow the air bubbles to escape in the fluid. Quickly tighten the bleeder screw.

NOTE: *Continue to check the fluid level in*

FOR REAR WHEELS
FOR FRONT WHEELS
REFILL WHEN THERE IS A SMALL AMOUNT OF FLUID.
SLOWLY
AIR BLEED VALVE
REFILL UNTIL NEW FLUID APPEARS

Bleeding the brakes

the master cylinder during the bleeding procedure. Refill as necessary.

6. Proceed to the other rear wheel and perform the same operation. When this wheel is bled, take the car down off of the jackstands, jack up the front end and support it with the stands. Bleed the front wheel farthest from the master cylinder then the wheel closest.

7. After bleeding all four wheels, check that the brake pedal is now firm. If not, repeat the bleeding operation.

FRONT DISC BRAKES

CAUTION: *Brake shoes contain asbestos, which has been determined to be a cancer causing agent. Never clean the brake surfaces with compressed air! Avoid inhaling any dust from any brake surface! When cleaning brake surfaces, use a commercially available brake cleaning fluid.*

Disc Brake Pads
INSPECTION

You should be able to check the pad lining thickness without removing the pads. Check the Brake Specifications Chart at the end of this chapter to find the manufacturer's pad wear limit. However, this measurement may disagree with your state inspection laws. When replacing pads, always check the surface of the rotors for scoring or wear. The rotors should be removed for resurfacing if badly scored.

REMOVAL AND INSTALLATION

CAUTION: *Brake shoes contain asbestos, which has been determined to be a cancer causing agent. Never clean the brake surfaces with compressed air! Avoid inhaling any dust from any brake surface! When cleaning brake surfaces, use a commercially available brake cleaning fluid.*

NOTE: *All four front brake pads must always be replaced as a set.*

Annette Type

1. Raise and support the front of the car with jackstands. Remove the wheels.

2. Remove the clip, pull out the pins, and remove the pad springs.

3. Remove the pads by pulling them out with pliers.

4. To install, first lightly coat the yoke groove and end surface of the piston with grease. Do not allow grease to contact the pads or rotor.

5. Open the bleeder screw slightly and push the outer piston into the cylinder until its end

Pushing the inner piston in to install new brake pads, 1200, B210 and 210 calipers

aligns with the end of the boot retaining ring. Do not push too far; if you do, the caliper will have to be disassembled. Install the inner pad.

6. Pull the yoke toward the outside of the car to push the inner piston into place. Install the outer pad.

7. Apply the brakes a few times to seat the pads. Check the master cylinder and add fluid if necessary. Bleed the brakes if necessary.

Sentra Pad

1. Jack up the front of the car and safely support it with jack stands.

1. Retaining ring	6. Cylinder body	11. Clip
2. Boot	7. Piston B (outer piston)	12. Clevis pin
3. Bias ring	8. Hanger spring	13. Buffle plate
4. Piston A (inner piston)	9. Spring	14. Yoke
5. Piston seal	10. Pad	15. Yoke spring

Typical Annette-type disc brake

Make sure you don't push the piston in too far

Swing the Sentra cylinder body up for pad access

PAD
RETAINER

Sentra brake pad retainer location

2. Remove the caliper lock pin.

3. The caliper cylinder body swings upward for pad replacement. Remove the pad retainers and pads.

CAUTION: *When the cylinder body is in the "up" position, DO NOT depress the brake pedal, or the piston will jump out.*

4. Before installation, clean the piston end and the pin bolts.

5. Apply a coat of PBC grease or equivalent to the pad-to-torque member clearance.

NOTE: *DO NOT get any grease on the pads or brake rotor (disc).*

6. Install the inner pad. Swing the cylinder body down and to the other side.

7. Install the outer pad, then the pad retainers. Install the lock pin.

Calipers

NOTE: *Use the Brake Identification Chart in this section to find the brake system your car uses. This information will be useful in buying replacement brake parts.*

OVERHAUL

CAUTION: *Brake shoes contain asbestos, which has been determined to be a cancer causing agent. Never clean the brake surfaces with compressed air! Avoid inhaling any dust from any brake surface! When cleaning brake surfaces, use a commercially available brake cleaning fluid.*

Annette Type

1. Remove the pads.

2. Disconnect the brake tube.

3. Remove the two bottom strut assembly installation botls to provide clearance.

4. Remove the caliper assembly mounting bolts.

5. Loosen the bleeder screw and press the pistons into their bores.

6. Clamp the yoke in a vise and tap the yoke head with a hammer to loosen the cylinder. Be careful that primary piston does not fall out.

7. Remove the bias ring from primary piston. Remove the retaining rings and boots from both pistons. Depress and remove the pistons from the cylinder. Remove the piston seal from the cylinder carefully with the fingers so as not to mar the cylinder wall.

8. Remove the yoke springs from the yoke.

9. Wash all parts with clean brake fluid (do not use gasoline, kerosene, thinners or any other mineral solvent).

10. If the piston or cylinder is badly worn or scored, replace both. The piston surface is plated and must not be polished with emery paper. Replace all seals. The rotor can be removed and machined if scored, but final thickness must be at least 0.331 in. Runout must not exceed 0.001 in.

11. Lubricate the cylinder bore with clean brake fluid and install the piston seal.

12. Insert the bias ring into primary piston so that the rounded ring portion comes to the bottom of the piston. Primary piston has a small depression inside, while secondary does not.

13. Lubricate the pistons with clean brake fluid and insert into the cylinder. Install the boot and retaining ring. The yoke groove of the bias ring of primary piston must align with the yoke groove of the cylinder.

14. Install the yoke springs to the yoke so the projecting portion faces to the disc (rotor).

15. Lubricate the sliding portion of the cylin-

1. Bias spring
2. Yoke
3. Bleeder
4. Piston seal
5. Piston B
6. Boot
7. Retaining ring
8. Clip
9. Yoke spring
10. Bias ring
11. Piston A
12. Cylinder body
13. Pad spring
14. Pad
15. Pin
16. Shim

210 type Annette caliper

PG : PBC GREASE POINT
RG : RUBBER GREASE POINT

Sentra disc brake caliper exploded view—gasoline engine

PISTON A
(INNER PISTON)

PISTON B
(OUTER PISTON)

Piston comparison (inner and outer)

Tapping the yoke head with a hammer

Caliper removal

Assembling the yoke and cylinder (Annette type)

PISTON SEAL (RG)

PISTON

DUST SEAL (RG)

RETAINING RING

CYLINDER BODY

TORQUE MEMBER

GUIDE PIN BOOT

GUIDE PIN
(RG) TO SLIDING PORTION
23–30 FT. LBS.

TORQUE MEMBER FIXING BOLT
40–47 FT. LBS.

(PG) TO PAD CONTACT AREA

LOCK PIN
(RG) TO SLIDING PORTION
23–30 FT. LBS.

LOCK PIN BOOT

PAD WEAR INDICATOR

INNER SHIM

INNER SHIM

OUTER SHIM

PAD
MINIMUM THICKNESS
2.0 MM (0.079 IN)

PAD RETAINER

(PG) PBC GREASE POINT

(RG) RUBBER GREASE POINT

Sentra disc brake caliper exploded view—diesel engine

der and yoke. Assemble the cylinder and yoke by tapping the yoke lightly.

16. Replace the caliper assembly and pads. Torque the mounting bolts to 33–41 ft.lb Rotor bolt torque is 20–27 ft.lb Strut bolt torque is 33–44 ft.lb Bleed the system of air.

Sentra Type

1. Separate cylinder body of caliper from the torque member by unbolting the two, swinging the cylinder body up (as in pad replacement) and sliding the pin out of the hole.

2. Remove the brake hose. Press out the piston with the dust seal and retainer ring.

3. Remove the piston seal.

4. Remove the guide pin, lock pin, guide pin boot and lock pin boot.

5. Clean and check all parts. Clean parts with clean brake fluid only (never use solvents). Check the inside surface of the cylinder for rust, ear, damage or foreign material. Minor rust damage may be removed with crocus cloth soaked in clean brake fluid. Check the torque member for wear, cracks or damage.

Check the piston for scoring, rust, wear or damage. Replace if any fault is detected.

CAUTION: *The piston sliding surface is plated. Do not attempt to polish the surface with even crocus cloth or fine emery cloth.*

6. Replace the piston seal and dust seal during assembly.

7. Check the guide pin for wear, cracks or damage.

8. Install the piston seal, applying rubber grease or brake fluid to the seal groove and seal.

9. Apply rubber grease or brake fluid to the sliding portions and the inside of the dust seal.

10. With the dust seal fitted to the piston, insert the dust seal into the groove on the cylinder body and install the piston.

11. Install the retainer ring and properly secure the dust seal.

12. Apply a coat of rubber grease to the guide pin and lock pin sliding surfaces. Install the lock pin boot, guide pin boot, lock pin and guide pin.

13. Attach the torque member to the cylinder body, and connect the brake hose.

(MG) : MULTI-PURPOSE GREASE POINT

Sentra front disc and hub assembly

Disc Brake Rotor
REMOVAL AND INSTALLATION

CAUTION: *Brake shoes contain asbestos, which has been determined to be a cancer causing agent. Never clean the brake surfaces with compressed air! Avoid inhaling any dust from any brake surface! When cleaning brake surfaces, use a commercially available brake cleaning fluid.*

1200, B210 and 210

1. Block rear wheels with chocks, and firmly apply parking brake.
2. Jack up front of car and safely support it with jackstands.
3. Remove wheel and tire assembly.
4. Remove brake hose, brake caliper assembly.
5. Work off the small hub cap from the hub using thin screwdrivers or pry bars. If necessary, tap around it with a soft hammer while removing cap.
NOTE: *Use care while removing the cap, as there is an O-ring underneath that must not be damaged.*
6. Remove the cotter pin from the castellated nut and discard it (assemble the hub with a new cotter pin). Take out the adjusting cap and the wheel bearing locknut.
7. Remove the wheel hub with the disc brake rotor from the spindle with the bearing installed. Be careful not to drop the outer bearing cone out of the hub when removing the knuckle from the knuckle spindle.
8. Remove the outer bearing cone.
9. Loosen the four bolts securing the brake disc; remove the brake disc rotor from the wheel hub assembly.
10. Install in the reverse order of removal, making sure wheel bearings are properly greased and that a new cotter pin is used. Install a new hub grease seal. Torque rotor bolts to 20–38 ft.lb, and adjust wheel bearings by following the procedure outlined in this chapter.

Sentra

1. Remove the front hub and halfshaft as a unit, as described in Chapter 6 Drive Train.
2. Remove the hub nut and then separate the halfshaft from the hub assembly.
3. Separate the wheel hub from the steering knuckle using a sliding hammer.
4. Remove the bolts securing the wheel hub to the disc rotor and remove the rotor.
5. Installation is the reverse of removal. Grease the end of the halfshaft before installing it into the front hub. Install a new hub grease seal. The rotor bolts should be torqued

to 18–25 ft.lb, and the halfshaft to hub bolt is torqued to 87–145 ft.lb

FRONT DRUM BRAKES

CAUTION: *Brake shoes contain asbestos, which has been determined to be a cancer causing agent. Never clean the brake surfaces with compressed air! Avoid inhaling any dust from any brake surface! When cleaning brake surfaces, use a commercially available brake cleaning fluid.*

Brake Drums
REMOVAL AND INSTALLATION

1. Jack up the front of the vehicle so that the wheel which is to be serviced is off the ground. be sure to loosen the lug nuts before the wheel comes off the ground.
2. Remove the wheel and tire assembly.
3. Pull the brake drum off the hub. If the drum cannot be easily removed, back off on the brake adjustment.
NOTE: *Never depress the brake pedal while the brake drum is removed.*
4. Install the brake drum in the reverse order of removal and adjust the brakes.

Brake Shoes
REMOVAL AND INSTALLATION

CAUTION: *Brake shoes contain asbestos, which has been determined to be a cancer causing agent. Never clean the brake surfaces with compressed air! Avoid inhaling any dust from any brake surface! When cleaning brake surfaces, use a commercially available brake cleaning fluid.*

1. Jack up the vehicle until the wheel which is to be serviced if off the ground two or three inches. Remove the wheel and brake drum.
NOTE: *It is not absolutely essential to remove the hub assembly from the spindle, but it makes the job much easier. If you can work with the hub in place, skip down to Step 7.*
2. Remove the hub dust cap.
3. Straighten the cotter pin and remove it from the spindle.
4. Unscrew the spindle nut and remove the adjusting cap, spindle nut, and spindle washer.
5. Wiggle the hub assembly until the outer bearing comes unseated and can be removed from the hub. Remove the outer bearing.
6. Pull the hub assembly off the spindle.
7. Unhook the return springs on the brake shoes and remove the shoes.
8. Apply brake grease to the adjuster assemblies and back the adjusters off the whole way

using the bolts on the backing plate. Apply brake grease to the areas on the brake backing plate where the brake shoes make contact.

9. Install the brake shoes in the reverse order of removal.

10. Install the hub, brake drum and wheel in the reverse order of removal. Adjust the wheel bearings.

Wheel Cylinders

REMOVAL AND INSTALLATION

CAUTION: *Brake shoes contain asbestos, which has been determined to be a cancer causing agent. Never clean the brake surfaces with compressed air! Avoid inhaling any dust from any brake surface! When cleaning brake surfaces, use a commercially available brake cleaning fluid.*

1. Jack up the wheel to be serviced.

2. Remove the wheel, brake drum, hub assembly, and brake shoes.

3. Disconnect the brake hose from the wheel cylinder.

4. Unscrew the wheel cylinder securing nut and remove the wheel cylinder from the brake backing plate.

5. Install the wheel cylinder in the reverse order of removal, assemble the remaining components, and bleed the brake hydraulic system.

1. Dust cover
2. Piston
3. Piston cup
4. Wheel cylinder body
5. Spring
6. Bleeder
7. Bleeder cap

Typical wheel cylinder

OVERHAUL

NOTE: *Datsun obtains parts from two manufacturers: Nabco and Tokico. Parts are not interchangeable. The name of the manufacturer is usually on the wheel cylinder. Replacement wheel cylinder parts and complete rebuilt wheel cylinders are available from most auto parts stores under other names. Those parts must be replacements for the Tokico and Nabco originals, however.*

1. Remove the wheel cylinder form the backing plate.

2. Remove the dust boot and take out the piston. Discard the piston cup. The dust boot can be reused, if necessary, but it is better to replace it.

3. Wash all of the components in clean brake fluid.

4. Insepct the piston and piston bore. Replace any components which are severely corroded, scored, or worn. The piston and piston bore can be polished lightly with crocus cloth. Move the crocus cloth around the piston bore; not in and out of the piston bore.

5. Wash the wheel cylinder and piston thoroughly in clean brake fluid, allowing them to remain lubricated for assembly.

6. Coat all of the new components to be installed in the wheel cylinder with clean brake fluid prior to assembly.

7. Assemble the wheel cylinder and install it in the reverse order of removal. Assemble the remaining components and bleed the brake hydraulic system.

Front Wheel Bearings

ADJUSTMENT

1200, B210 210

NOTE: *The Sentra, a front wheel drive vehicle, has pressed bearings which are not adjustable on the front wheels. The factory procedures for wheel bearing adjustment is of little use to the owner/mechanic, since it involves the use of a spring scale, an inchpound torque wrench, and a foot-pound torque wrench. For the following procedure, you will only need a foot-pound torque wrench.*

1. Jack up the car and safely support it with jackstands.

2. Remove the bearing dust cap and the cotter pin. Discard the cotter pin, as you will be replacing it with a new one.

3. Torque the spindle nut to 16–18 ft.lb on the 1200; 18–22 ft.lb on the B210, and 22–25 ft.lb on the 210 sedan and wagon.

4. Spin the wheel hub a few times to seat the bearing, then check the torque on the nut again.

5. Loosen the nut about 60 degrees on all models except the 210. Loosen the 210 nut about 90 degrees.

6. Install the adjusting cap and a new cotter pin. You may have to loosen the nut a bit to allow the cotter pin holes to align, but do not loosen the nut beyond 15 degrees.

7. Reinstall the tire and wheel, and rotate the entire assembly. There should be no roughness or binding. Grasp the top of the tire and move it in and out. The play should be negligible. If there is excessive play, the wheel bear-

Tightening the hub nut with a torque wrench during wheel bearing adjustment

Split and spread the cotter pin

ings must be retightened. If roughness persists, check the condition of the wheel bearings for nicks, pitting and damage.

8. Install the cap and lower the car from the stands.

WHEEL BEARING PACKING AND REPLACEMENT

It is important to remember that wheel bearings, although basically very durable, are subject to many elements that can quickly destroy them. Grit, misalignment, and improper preload are especially brutal to any roller bearing assembly. And like any bearing (ball, roller, needle, etc.), lubrication is extremely important.

1. Loosen the lug nuts on the wheel you intend to fix. Jack up the car and safely support it with jackstands.

2. Remove the wheel and tire. Remove the brake drum or brake caliper, following the procedure(s) in this chapter.

3. It is not necessary to remove the drum or disc from the hub. The outer wheel bearing will come off with the hub. Simply pull the hub and disc or drum assembly toward you and off the spindle. (Follow hub removal procedures for Sentra). Be sure to catch the bearing before it falls to the ground.

4. From the inner side of the hub, remove the inner grease seal, and lift the inner bearing from the hub. Discard the grease seal, as you will be replacing it with a new one.

5. Clean the bearings carefully in solvent, and allow them to air dry (or blow them out with compressed air, if available). You risk leaving bits of lint in the races if you dry them with a rag. Clean the grease caps, nuts, spindle, and the races in the hub thoroughly, and allow the parts to dry.

6. Inspect the bearings carefully. If they show any signs of wear (pitting, cracks, scoring, brinelling, burns, etc.), replace them along with the bearing cups in which they run in the hub. Do not mix old and new parts; you won't regret replacing everything if the parts look marginal.

7. If the cups are worn at all, remove them from the hub, using a brass rod as a drift. Use care not to damage the cup seats with the drift.

8. If the old cups were removed, install the new inner and outer cups into the hub, using either a tool made for the purpose, or a socket or piece of pipe of a large enough diameter to press on the outside rim of the cup only.

CAUTION: *Be careful not to cock the bearings in the hub. If they are not fully seated, the bearings will be impossible to adjust properly.*

9. Pack the inside of the hub and cups with grease. Pack the inside of the grease cap while you're at it, but do not install the cap into the hub.

10. Pack the inner bearing with grease. Place a large glob of grease into the palm of one hand and push the inner bearing through it with a sliding motion. The grease must be

Sentra wheel bearing spacer size number

Packing wheel bearing with grease

forced through the side of the bearing and in between each roller. Continue until the grease begins to ooze out the other side through the gaps between the rollers; the bearing must be completely packed with grease. Install the inner bearing into its cup in the hub, then press a new grease seal into place over it.

11. Install the hub and rotor or drum assembly onto the spindle. Pack the outer bearing with grease in the same manner as the inner bearing, then install the outer bearing into place in the hub.

12. Apply a thin coat of grease to the washer and the threaded portion of the spindle, then loosely install the washer and adjusting nut. Go on to the bearing preload adjustment.

Sentra

The Sentra front wheel bearings are fitted using spacers, which fit between the bearing race in the steering knuckle and the outer wheel bearing. The spacers are available from Nissan dealers and parts stores, and are numbered as to their size. New spacers must be installed whenever the knuckle is replaced, or when the bearings and/or their races are worn to an extent that end play is noticeable at the front wheel. When new grease seals or bearings are installed, new spacers should be installed. Make sure they have the same mark as the spacers you have removed. If there is not much wear in your bearings, etc., and you are just repacking bearings, the old spacer can be reused.

1. With the front hub and halfshaft disassembled, install the outside grease seal and bearing into the wheel hub with a suitable drift.

2. Pack the seal lip with a quality multipurpose wheel bearing grease. Be sure that the grease seal is facing in the proper direction.

Press the bearing into the inner race to install. Do not force the bearing.

3. Install the spacer. Spacer numbering ranges from number 05 to number 22, with each succeeding spacer being 0.0023 in. thicker.

4. Tighten the bolts securing the hub to the disc rotor.

5. Assemble the halfshaft into the knuckle and wheel hub. Install the rotor and hub assembly.

6. Tighten the hub nut to 87–145 ft.lb

7. Spin the wheel several times in both directions.

8. Measure wheel bearing preload. The rotation starting torque of the wheel bearings is $1/2$ to 2 lbs. Measured at the wheel hub bolt, you should obtain a reading of 3.1 to 10.8 lbs. on a pull scale.

9. If the bearing preload does not accord the specifications, reselect the spacer. When any axial endplay is present in the wheel bearing, replace the spacer with a smaller one. If bearing preload is greater and endplay is present, replace spacer with a larger one.

REAR DRUM BRAKES

CAUTION: *Brake shoes contain asbestos, which has been determined to be a cancer causing agent. Never clean the brake surfaces with compressed air! Avoid inhaling any dust from any brake surface! When cleaning brake surfaces, use a commercially available brake cleaning fluid.*

Brake Drums

REMOVAL AND INSTALLATION

1. Raise the rear of the vehicle and support it on jackstands.

1. Brake disc
2. Bleeder
3. Wheel cylinder
4. Shoe assembly
5. Return spring

Rear drum brake assembly—1200 series

1. Brake disc
2. Wheel cylinder assembly
3. Brake shoe assembly
4. Return spring
5. Adjuster assembly
6. Stopper
7. Stopper pin
8. Anti-rattle pin
9. Spring seat
10. Anti-rattle spring
11. Retainer

Direction of rotation

Front of car

Exploded view of drum brake assembly—210 series

2. Remove the wheels.

3. Release the parking brake.

4. Pull off the brake drums. On some models there are two threaded service holes in each brake drum. If the drum will not come off, fit two correct size bolts in the service holes and screw them in: this will force the drum away from the axle.

5. If the drum cannot be easily removed, back off the brake adjustment.

Exploded view of drum brake assembly—Sentra

NOTE: *Never depress the brake pedal while the brake drum is removed.*

6. Installation is the reverse of removal.

INSPECTION

1. After removing the brake drum, wipe out the accumulated dust with a damp cloth.

CAUTION: *Brake shoes contain asbestos, which has been determined to be a cancer causing agent. Never clean the brake surfaces with compressed air! Avoid inhaling any dust from any brake surface! When cleaning brake surfaces, use a commercially available brake cleaning fluid.*

2. Inspect the drum for cracks, deep grooves, roughness, scoring, or out-of- roundness. Replace any brake drum which is cracked.

3. Smooth any slight scores by polishing the friction surface with the fine emery cloth. Heavy or extensive scoring will cause excessive brake lining wear and should be removed from the brake drum through resurfacing (most auto repair shops and machine shops provide this service).

Brake Shoes
REMOVAL AND INSTALLATION

CAUTION: *Brake shoes contain asbestos, which has been determined to be a cancer causing agent. Never clean the brake surfaces with compressed air! Avoid inhaling any dust from any brake surface! When cleaning brake surfaces, use a commercially available brake cleaning fluid.*

All models

1. Jack up the rear of the car and safely support it with jackstands.

2. Loosen the handbrake cable, remove the clevis pin from the wheel cylinder lever, disconnect the handbrake cable, and remove the return pull spring.

3. Remove the brake drum, shoe retainers, return springs, and brake shoes. Loosen the brake adjusters if the drums are difficult to remove. Place a heavy rubber band around the cylinder to prevent the piston from coming out.

4. Clean the backing plate and check the wheel cylinder for leaks. To remove the wheel cylinder, remove the brake line, dust cover, se-

Brake Identification Chart

Match the numbers on the chart with those below to identify your brake system

Model	1973	1974	1975	1976	1977	1978	1979	1980	1981	1982	1983	1984	1985
1200	①②⑤												
B210		①②		①②		①②		①③		①③			
210								①④		①④		①④	①④
Sentra										⑥④		⑥④	⑥④	⑥④

① Annette Type front disc brakes
② Rear drum brakes with bolt-type adjuster
③ Rear drum brakes with internal, toothed adjusting nut
④ Rear drum brakes with automatic adjustment
⑤ Front drum brakes with top and bottom bolt-type adjusters
⑥ CL18B front disc brakes—Gasoline engine, AD20V front disc brakes—Diesel engine

Brake Specifications

All measurements given are in inches unless noted

Model	Year	Lug Nut Torque (ft. lbs.)	Master Cylinder Bore	Brake Disc		Drum		Minimum Lining Thickness	
				Minimum Thickness	Maximum Run-Out	Diameter	Max. Wear Limit	Front	Rear
1200	1973	58–65	0.6875	0.3307	0.0012	8.000	8.051	0.0630 (disc) 0.0591 (drum)	0.0591
B210	1974–78	58–65	0.750	0.331	0.0047	8.000	8.051	0.063	0.059
210	1979–82	58–72	0.8125	0.331	0.0047	8.000	8.050	0.063	0.059
Sentra	1982–84	58–72	0.750	0.433 ①	0.0047 ②	7.09	7.13	0.079	0.059

NOTE: Minimum lining thickness is as recommended by the manufacturer. Due to variation in state inspection regulations, the minimum allowable thickness may be different than recommended by the manufacturer.
① 0.394 in. (1983–86)
② 0.0028 in. (1983–86)

curing nuts or plates and adjusting shims. Clearance between cylinder and piston should not exceed 0.006 in.

5. The drums must be machined if scored or out-of-round more than 0.008 in. The drum inside diameter must not be machined beyond 8.04 in. Minimum safe lining thickness is 0.059 in. (0.039 in.-F10).

6. Follow Steps 6–9 for 510, 610, 710, and 810.

Wheel Cylinder

See correct section under "Brake Shoes Removal and Installation" for wheel cylinder removal and installation procedures. See the "Front Drum Brake Wheel Cylinder Overhaul" for overhaul procedures for the rear drum brake cylinders. Observe the "NOTE" about different manufacturers of wheel cylinder components.

Body and Trim 9

EXTERIOR

Doors

REMOVAL AND INSTALLATION

Front

1. Remove the windshield wiper blades and cowl top grille.
2. Remove the front fender.
3. With the door in the full open position, place a garage jack or stand under the door to support its weight. Place a rag on top of the jack to protect the paint.
4. Loosen the bolts attaching the door hinge to the body and remove the front door from the car.
5. Installation is the reverse of removal.

Adjusting door lock striker

Rear

1. Open the front door and keep it open.
2. Open the rear door to the full open position, and place a support under it. Protect the paint with a rag between the support and the door.
3. Loosen the bolts attaching the rear door hinges to the center pillar and remove the rear door from the body.
4. Installation is the reverse of removal.

ADJUSTMENT

Front and Rear

Proper door alignment can be obtained by adjusting the door hinge and door lock striker. The door hinge and striker can be moved up and down fore and aft in enlarged holes by loosening the attaching bolts.

NOTE: *The door should be adjusted for an even and parallel fit for the door opening and surrounding body panels.*

Door Locks

REMOVAL AND INSTALLATION

1. Remove the door finisher and sealing screen.
2. Remove the lock cylinder from the rod by turning the resin clip.
3. Loosen the nuts attaching the outside door handle and remove the outside door handle.
4. Remove the screws retaining the iside door handle and door lock, and remove the door lock assembly from the hole in the inside of the door.
5. Remove the lock cylinder by removing the retaining clip.
6. Installation is the reverse of removal.

1. Door lock cylinder
2. Retaining clip
3. Resin clip
4. Lock cylinder rod

Removing the lock cylinder rod

SBF552A

Install regulator handle as shown below, using set pins. Door should be closed

Regulator handle and set pin removal and installation

Hood

REMOVAL AND INSTALLATION

1. Open the hood and protect the body with covers to protect the painted surfaces.
2. Mark the hood hinge locations on the hood for proper reinstallation.
3. Holding both sides of the hood, unscrew the bolts securing the hinge to the hood. This operation requires a helper.
4. Installation is the reverse of removal.

ALIGNMENT

The hood can be adjusted with bolts attaching the hood to the hood hinges, hood lock mechanism and hood bumpers. Adjust the hood for an even fit between the front fenders.

1. Adjust the hood fore and aft by loosening the bolts attaching the hood to the hinge and repositioning hood.
2. Loosen the hood bumper lock nuts and lower bumpers until they do not contact the front of the hood when the hood is closed.
3. Set the striker at the center of the hood lock, and tighten the hood lock securing bolts temporarily.
4. Raise the two hood bumpers until the hood is flush with the fenders.
5. Tighten the hood lock securing bolts after the proper adjustment has been obtained.

Trunklid

REMOVAL AND INSTALLATION

1. Open the trunk lid and position a cloth or cushion to protect the painted areas.

2. Mark the trunk lid hinge locations or trunk lid for proper reinstallation.
3. Support the trunk lid by hand and remove the bolts attaching the trunk lid to the hinge. Then remove the trunk lid.
4. Installation is the reverse of removal.

ALIGNMENT

1. Loosen the trunk lid hinge attaching bolts until they are just loose enough to move the trunk lid.
2. Move the trunk lid for and aft to obtain a flush fit between the trunk lid and the rear fender.
3. To obtain a snug fit between the trunk lid and weatherstrip, loosen the trunk lid lock striker attaching bolts enough to move the lid, working the striker up and down and from side to side as required.
4. After the adjustment is made tighten the striker bolts securely.

Hatchback or Tailgate Lid

REMOVAL AND INSTALLATION

1. Open the lid and disconnect the rear defogger harness if so equipped.
2. Mark the hinge locations on the lid for proper relocation.
3. Position rags between the roof and the upper end of the lid to prevent scratching the paint.
4. Support the lid and remove the support bolts the the hinge retaining bolts and remove the lid.
5. Installation is the reverse of removal.
CAUTION: *Be careful not to scratch the lift support rods. A scratched rod may cause oil or gas leakaged*

ALIGNMENT

1. Open the hatchback lid.
2. Loosen the lid hinge to body attaching bolts until they are just loose enough to move the lid.
3. Move the lid up and down to obtain a flush fit between the lid and the roof.
4. After adjustment is completed tighten the hinge attaching bolts securely.

Windshield Glass

REMOVAL

1. Place a protective cover over the hood, front fenders, instrument panel and front seats.
2. Remove the windshield wiper arm assemblies.
3. Remove the windshield moldings.

1. Trunk lid
2. Trunk lid hinge
3. Striker
4. Torsion bar
5. Trunk lid lock
6. Lock cylinder

Trunk lid assembly—210 series, typical

When installing weatherstrip, align the portion painted white with the center of vehicle body.

SBF750A

ADJUSTMENT
HINGE

STRIKER

Trunk lid assembly—Sentra series, typical

1. Back door hinge
2. Side stopper striker
3. Back door
4. Striker
5. Back door stay
6. Side stopper
7. Lock cylinder
8. Back door lock

Hatchback door assembly—210 series typical

4. On the inside of the body, loosen the lip of the weatherstrip from the body flange along the top and the sides of the windshield opening. Use an appropriate tool and carefully put the weatherstrip over the body flange.

5. After the windshield weatherstrip is free from the body flange, with the aid of a helper, carefully lift the windshield from the opening. There are special suction cup tools available especially made for this purpose.

6.1–7.4 FT. LBS.

6.1–7.4 FT. LBS.

REMOVE AT BODY SIDE

12–15 FT. LBS.

ADJUSTMENT
HINGE

BODY SIDE

BACK DOOR LOCK AND
LOCK CYLINDER

INSTALLATION
REFER TO TRUNK LID

Hatchback door assembly—Sentra series

1. Lock
2. Bumper rubber
3. Tailgate
4. Tailgate stay
5. Lock cylinder
6. Retaining clip
7. Striker catcher
8. Shim
9. Striker
10. Wedge bumper
11. Back door hinge

Tailgate assembly—210 series

SUCTION TOOL

Removing windshield glass with the aid of special suction tools

INSTALLATION

1. Check the windshield weatherstrip for irregularities.

2. Clean off the old sealer around the winshield opening and check the entire body opening flange for irregularities.

3. With the aid of a helper carefully position the replacement glass on the windshield opening.

CAUTION: *Be careful not to chip the edge of the glass during installation. Edge chips can lead to future breaks.*

4. With the windshield glass supported and centered in the body opening, check the rela-

tionship of the glass to the body opening around the entire perimeter of the glass.

a. The inside surface of the glass should completely lap to body flange.

b. The curvature of the glass should be uniform to that of the body opening.

5. Mark any sections of the body to be reformed. Remove the glass, and reform the opening as required.

6. Clean out the old sealer in the glass cavity of the windshield weatherstrip and around the base of the weatherstrip.

7. Install the weatherstrip to the glass.

8. Insert a strong cord in the groove of the weatherstrip where the body flange fits. Apply soapy water to it, so it will fit into the weatherstrip groove easily. Tie the ends of the cord and tape to the inside surface of the glass at the bottom center of the glass.

9. With the aid of a helper, carefully position and center the windshield assembly in the body opening.

NOTE: *Do not tap or hammer on the glass at any time.*

10. When the glass and weatherstrip are properly positioned in the opening, slowly pull the ends of the cord, starting at the lower center of the windshield to seat the lip of the

HARNESS

PULL OUT HARNESS

WEATHERSTRIP

ADJUSTMENT
BACK DOOR

STRIKER

Tailgate assembly—Sentra series

weatherstrip over the body flange. The cord should be pulled first across the bottom of the windshield, then up each side and finally across the windshield top.

11. Using a pressure type applicator, seal the inner and outer lips of the weatherstrip to the glass with an approved weatherstrip adhesive. Seal completely around the weatherstrip.

CAUTION: *The car should not be driven on rough roads or surfaces until the sealant has properly vulcanized. Also it is a good idea to leave one window open slightly for a few days to reduce the chance of pressure induced leaks before the seal has completelty vulcanized.*

NOTE: *The rear glass on most sedan models is removed and installed in the manner as as the windshield glass. Most rear glass on*

hatchbacks and and wagons are replaced as an assembly only. Check with the manufacturer.

INTERIOR

Door Panel, Glass and Regulator
REMOVAL AND INSTALLATION
Front and Rear

1. Remove the regulator handle by pushing the set pin spring.

2. Remove the arm rest, door inside handle escutcheon and door lock.

3. Remove the door finisher and sealing screen.

1. Door glass
2. Inside door handle
3. Front lower sash
4. Regulator handle
5. Regulator assembly
6. Glass lower guide
7. Guide channel B
8. Door lock assembly
9. Door lock cylinder
10. Outside door handle
11. Guide channel A
12. Door lock knob

Front door assembly—4 dr. models—210 series

1. Door glass
2. Guide channel A
3. Inside door handle
4. Front lower sash
5. Regulator handle
6. Regulator assembly
7. Guide channel B
8. Glass lower guide
9. Door lock assembly
10. Door lock cylinder
11. Outside door handle
12. Inside door lock knob

Front door assembly—2 dr. models—210 series

1. Door glass
2. Inside door lock knob
3. Inside door handle
4. Guide channel A
5. Regulator handle
6. Regulator assembly
7. Lower sash
8. Center sash
9. Door lock assembly
10. Outside door handle

Rear door assembly—210 series

DOOR LOCK ADJUSTMENT

DOOR GLASS ADJUSTMENT

Ⓖ : LUBRICATION POINT

OUTSIDE MOLDING

DOOR GLASS ADJUSTMENT

CHECK LINK

HINGE

REGULATOR

GUIDE CHANNEL B

GUIDE CHANNEL A

DOOR GLASS ADJUSTMENT

DOOR LOCK

Front door assembly—Sentra series

DOOR GLASS ADJUSTMENT

SBF464B

Ⓖ : LUBRICATION POINT

CORNER GLASS

OUTSIDE MOLDING

HINGE

CHECK LINK

REGULATOR

DOOR LOCK

DOOR GLASS ADJUSTMENT

DOOR GLASS ADJUSTMENT

Rear door assembly—Sentra series

4. On some models it may be necessary to remove the outer door moulding.

5. Lower the door glass with the regulator handle until the regulator-to-glass attaching bolts appear at the access holes in the door inside panel.

6. Raise the door glass and draw it upwards.

7. Remove the regulator attaching bolts and remove the regulator assembly through the large access hole in ther door panel.

8. Installation is the reverse of removal.

Headliner
REMOVAL AND INSTALLATION

1. Remove the lamp, assist grip, coat hangers, inside rear view mirror and sun visors.

2. Remove the body side welts and remove the roof side garnishes and tail rail garnish.

3. Remove the rear side finishers.

4. Draw out the roof headlining from the windshield weatherstrip.

5. Installation is the reverse of removal.

Troubleshooting 10

This section is designed to aid in the quick, accurate diagnosis of automotive problems. While automotive repairs can be made by many people, accurate troubleshooting is a rare skill for the amateur and professional alike.

In its simplest state, troubleshooting is an exercise in logic. It is essential to realize that an automobile is really composed of a series of systems. Some of these systems are interrelated; others are not. Automobiles operate within a framework of logical rules and physical laws, and the key to troubleshooting is a good understanding of all the automotive systems.

This section breaks the car or truck down into its component systems, allowing the problem to be isolated. The charts and diagnostic road maps list the most common problems and the most probable causes of trouble. Obviously it would be impossible to list every possible problem that could happen along with every possible cause, but it will locate MOST problems and eliminate a lot of unnecessary guesswork. The systematic format will locate problems within a given system, but, because many automotive systems are interrelated, the solution to your particular problem may be found in a number of systems on the car or truck.

USING THE TROUBLESHOOTING CHARTS

This book contains all of the specific information that the average do-it-yourself mechanic needs to repair and maintain his or her car or truck. The troubleshooting charts are designed to be used in conjunction with the specific procedures and information in the text. For instance, troubleshooting a point-type ignition system is fairly standard for all models, but you may be directed to the text to find procedures for troubleshooting an individual type of electronic ignition. You will also have to refer to the specification charts throughout the book for specifications applicable to your car or truck.

TOOLS AND EQUIPMENT

The tools illustrated in Chapter 1 (plus two more diagnostic pieces) will be adequate to troubleshoot most problems. The two other tools needed are a voltmeter and an ohmmeter. These can be purchased separately or in combination, known as a VOM meter.

In the event that other tools are required, they will be noted in the procedures.

Tach-dwell hooked-up to distributor

Troubleshooting Engine Problems

See Chapters 2, 3, 4 for more information and service procedures.

Index to Systems

System	To Test	Group
Battery	Engine need not be running	1
Starting system	Engine need not be running	2
Primary electrical system	Engine need not be running	3
Secondary electrical system	Engine need not be running	4
Fuel system	Engine need not be running	5
Engine compression	Engine need not be running	6
Engine vacuum	Engine must be running	7
Secondary electrical system	Engine must be running	8
Valve train	Engine must be running	9
Exhaust system	Engine must be running	10
Cooling system	Engine must be running	11
Engine lubrication	Engine must be running	12

Index to Problems

Problem: Symptom	Begin at Specific Diagnosis, Number
Engine Won't Start:	
Starter doesn't turn	1.1, 2.1
Starter turns, engine doesn't	2.1
Starter turns engine very slowly	1.1, 2.4
Starter turns engine normally	3.1, 4.1
Starter turns engine very quickly	6.1
Engine fires intermittently	4.1
Engine fires consistently	5.1, 6.1
Engine Runs Poorly:	
Hard starting	3.1, 4.1, 5.1, 8.1
Rough idle	4.1, 5.1, 8.1
Stalling	3.1, 4.1, 5.1, 8.1
Engine dies at high speeds	4.1, 5.1
Hesitation (on acceleration from standing stop)	5.1, 8.1
Poor pickup	4.1, 5.1, 8.1
Lack of power	3.1, 4.1, 5.1, 8.1
Backfire through the carburetor	4.1, 8.1, 9.1
Backfire through the exhaust	4.1, 8.1, 9.1
Blue exhaust gases	6.1, 7.1
Black exhaust gases	5.1
Running on (after the ignition is shut off)	3.1, 8.1
Susceptible to moisture	4.1
Engine misfires under load	4.1, 7.1, 8.4, 9.1
Engine misfires at speed	4.1, 8.4
Engine misfires at idle	3.1, 4.1, 5.1, 7.1, 8.4

Sample Section

Test and Procedure	Results and Indications	Proceed to
4.1—Check for spark: Hold each spark plug wire approximately ¼″ from ground with gloves or a heavy, dry rag. Crank the engine and observe the spark.	→ If no spark is evident:	→ **4.2**
	→ If spark is good in some cases:	→ **4.3**
	→ If spark is good in all cases:	→ **4.6**

Specific Diagnosis

This section is arranged so that following each test, instructions are given to proceed to another, until a problem is diagnosed.

Section 1—Battery

Test and Procedure	Results and Indications	Proceed to
1.1—Inspect the battery visually for case condition (corrosion, cracks) and water level.	If case is cracked, replace battery:	**1.4**
	If the case is intact, remove corrosion with a solution of baking soda and water (**CAUTION:** *do not get the solution into the battery*), and fill with water:	**1.2**

DIRT ON TOP OF BATTERY
CORROSION
PLUGGED VENT
LOOSE CABLE OR POSTS
CRACKS
LOW WATER LEVEL

Inspect the battery case

Test and Procedure	Results and Indications	Proceed to
1.2—Check the battery cable connections: Insert a screwdriver between the battery post and the cable clamp. Turn the headlights on high beam, and observe them as the screwdriver is gently twisted to ensure good metal to metal contact.	If the lights brighten, remove and clean the clamp and post; coat the post with petroleum jelly, install and tighten the clamp:	**1.4**
	If no improvement is noted:	**1.3**

TESTING BATTERY CABLE CONNECTIONS USING A SCREWDRIVER

Test and Procedure	Results and Indications	Proceed to
1.3—Test the state of charge of the battery using an individual cell tester or hydrometer.	If indicated, charge the battery. **NOTE:** *If no obvious reason exists for the low state of charge (i.e., battery age, prolonged storage), proceed to:*	**1.4**

°F

ADD THIS NUMBER TO THE HYDROMETER READING TO OBTAIN THE CORRECTED SPECIFIC GRAVITY

SUBTRACT THIS NUMBER FROM THE HYDROMETER READING TO OBTAIN THE CORRECTED SPECIFIC GRAVITY

Specific Gravity (@ 80° F.)

Minimum		Battery Charge
1.260	....	100% Charged
1.230	....	75% Charged
1.200	....	50% Charged
1.170	....	25% Charged
1.140	....	Very Little Power Left
1.110	....	Completely Discharged

The effects of temperature on battery specific gravity (left) and amount of battery charge in relation to specific gravity (right)

Test and Procedure	Results and Indications	Proceed to
1.4—Visually inspect battery cables for cracking, bad connection to ground, or bad connection to starter.	If necessary, tighten connections or replace the cables:	**2.1**

Section 2—Starting System
See Chapter 3 for service procedures

Test and Procedure	Results and Indications	Proceed to
Note: Tests in Group 2 are performed with coil high tension lead disconnected to prevent accidental starting.		
2.1—Test the starter motor and solenoid: Connect a jumper from the battery post of the solenoid (or relay) to the starter post of the solenoid (or relay).	If starter turns the engine normally:	**2.2**
	If the starter buzzes, or turns the engine very slowly:	**2.4**
	If no response, replace the solenoid (or relay).	**3.1**
	If the starter turns, but the engine doesn't, ensure that the flywheel ring gear is intact. If the gear is undamaged, replace the starter drive.	**3.1**
2.2—Determine whether ignition override switches are functioning properly (clutch start switch, neutral safety switch), by connecting a jumper across the switch(es), and turning the ignition switch to "start".	If starter operates, adjust or replace switch:	**3.1**
	If the starter doesn't operate:	**2.3**
2.3—Check the ignition switch "start" position: Connect a 12V test lamp or voltmeter between the starter post of the solenoid (or relay) and ground. Turn the ignition switch to the "start" position, and jiggle the key.	If the lamp doesn't light or the meter needle doesn't move when the switch is turned, check the ignition switch for loose connections, cracked insulation, or broken wires. Repair or replace as necessary:	**3.1**
	If the lamp flickers or needle moves when the key is jiggled, replace the ignition switch.	**3.3**

Checking the ignition switch "start" position

STARTER RELAY
(IF EQUIPPED)

2.4—Remove and bench test the starter, according to specifications in the engine electrical section.	If the starter does not meet specifications, repair or replace as needed:	**3.1**
	If the starter is operating properly:	**2.5**
2.5—Determine whether the engine can turn freely: Remove the spark plugs, and check for water in the cylinders. Check for water on the dipstick, or oil in the radiator. Attempt to turn the engine using an 18″ flex drive and socket on the crankshaft pulley nut or bolt.	If the engine will turn freely only with the spark plugs out, and hydrostatic lock (water in the cylinders) is ruled out, check valve timing:	**9.2**
	If engine will not turn freely, and it is known that the clutch and transmission are free, the engine must be disassembled for further evaluation:	**Chapter 3**

Section 3—Primary Electrical System

Test and Procedure	Results and Indications	Proceed to
3.1—Check the ignition switch "on" position: Connect a jumper wire between the distributor side of the coil and ground, and a 12V test lamp between the switch side of the coil and ground. Remove the high tension lead from the coil. Turn the ignition switch on and jiggle the key.	If the lamp lights:	**3.2**
	If the lamp flickers when the key is jiggled, replace the ignition switch:	**3.3**
	If the lamp doesn't light, check for loose or open connections. If none are found, remove the ignition switch and check for continuity. If the switch is faulty, replace it:	**3.3**

Checking the ignition switch "on" position

3.2—Check the ballast resistor or resistance wire for an open circuit, using an ohmmeter. See Chapter 3 for specific tests.	Replace the resistor or resistance wire if the resistance is zero. **NOTE:** *Some ignition systems have no ballast resistor.*	**3.3**

RESISTOR
BLOCK

CALIBRATED
RESISTANCE
LEAD

Two types of resistors

3.3—On point-type ignition systems, visually inspect the breaker points for burning, pitting or excessive wear. Gray coloring of the point contact surfaces is normal. Rotate the crankshaft until the contact heel rests on a high point of the distributor cam and adjust the point gap to specifications. On electronic ignition models, remove the distributor cap and visually inspect the armature. Ensure that the armature pin is in place, and that the armature is on tight and rotates when the engine is cranked. Make sure there are no cracks, chips or rounded edges on the armature.	If the breaker points are intact, clean the contact surfaces with fine emery cloth, and adjust the point gap to specifications. If the points are worn, replace them. On electronic systems, replace any parts which appear defective. If condition persists:	**3.4**

Test and Procedure	Results and Indications	Proceed to
3.4—On point-type ignition systems, connect a dwell-meter between the distributor primary lead and ground. Crank the engine and observe the point dwell angle. On electronic ignition systems, conduct a stator (magnetic pickup assembly) test. See Chapter 3.	On point-type systems, adjust the dwell angle if necessary. **NOTE:** *Increasing the point gap decreases the dwell angle and vice-versa.*	**3.6**
	If the dwell meter shows little or no reading;	**3.5**
	On electronic ignition systems, if the stator is bad, replace the stator. If the stator is good, proceed to the other tests in Chapter 3.	

Dwell is a function of point gap

3.5—On the point-type ignition systems, check the condenser for short: connect an ohmeter across the condenser body and the pigtail lead.	If any reading other than infinite is noted, replace the condenser	**3.6**

Checking the condenser for short

3.6—Test the coil primary resistance: On point-type ignition systems, connect an ohmmeter across the coil primary terminals, and read the resistance on the low scale. Note whether an external ballast resistor or resistance wire is used. On electronic ignition systems, test the coil primary resistance as in Chapter 3.	Point-type ignition coils utilizing ballast resistors or resistance wires should have approximately 1.0 ohms resistance. Coils with internal resistors should have approximately 4.0 ohms resistance. If values far from the above are noted, replace the coil.	**4.1**

Check the coil primary resistance

Section 4—Secondary Electrical System
See Chapters 2–3 for service procedures

Test and Procedure	Results and Indications	Proceed to
4.1—Check for spark: Hold each spark plug wire approximately ¼″ from ground with gloves or a heavy, dry rag. Crank the engine, and observe the spark.	If no spark is evident:	**4.2**
	If spark is good in some cylinders:	**4.3**
	If spark is good in all cylinders:	**4.6**

Check for spark at the plugs

4.2—Check for spark at the coil high tension lead: Remove the coil high tension lead from the distributor and position it approximately ¼″ from ground. Crank the engine and observe spark. **CAUTION:** *This test should not be performed on engines equipped with electronic ignition.*	If the spark is good and consistent:	**4.3**
	If the spark is good but intermittent, test the primary electrical system starting at 3.3:	**3.3**
	If the spark is weak or non-existent, replace the coil high tension lead, clean and tighten all connections and retest. If no improvement is noted:	**4.4**
4.3—Visually inspect the distributor cap and rotor for burned or corroded contacts, cracks, carbon tracks, or moisture. Also check the fit of the rotor on the distributor shaft (where applicable).	If moisture is present, dry thoroughly, and retest per 4.1:	**4.1**
	If burned or excessively corroded contacts, cracks, or carbon tracks are noted, replace the defective part(s) and retest per 4.1:	**4.1**
	If the rotor and cap appear intact, or are only slightly corroded, clean the contacts thoroughly (including the cap towers and spark plug wire ends) and retest per 4.1:	
	If the spark is good in all cases:	**4.6**
	If the spark is poor in all cases:	**4.5**

CORRODED OR LOOSE WIRE

EXCESSIVE WEAR OF BUTTON

HIGH RESISTANCE CARBON

ROTOR TIP BURNED AWAY

Inspect the distributor cap and rotor

Test and Procedure	Results and Indications	Proceed to
4.4—Check the coil secondary resistance: On point-type systems connect an ohmmeter across the distributor side of the coil and the coil tower. Read the resistance on the high scale of the ohmmeter. On electronic ignition systems, see Chapter 3 for specific tests.	The resistance of a satisfactory coil should be between 4,000 and 10,000 ohms. If resistance is considerably higher (i.e., 40,000 ohms) replace the coil and retest per 4.1. **NOTE:** *This does not apply to high performance coils.*	

Testing the coil secondary resistance

4.5—Visually inspect the spark plug wires for cracking or brittleness. Ensure that no two wires are positioned so as to cause induction firing (adjacent and parallel). Remove each wire, one by one, and check resistance with an ohmmeter.	Replace any cracked or brittle wires. If any of the wires are defective, replace the entire set. Replace any wires with excessive resistance (over 8000 Ω per foot for suppression wire), and separate any wires that might cause induction firing.	**4.6**

Misfiring can be the result of spark plug leads to adjacent, consecutively firing cylinders running parallel and too close together

On point-type ignition systems, check the spark plug wires as shown. On electronic ignitions, do not remove the wire from the distributor cap terminal; instead, test through the cap

Spark plug wires can be checked visually by bending them in a loop over your finger. This will reveal any cracks, burned or broken insulation. Any wire with cracked insulation should be replaced

4.6—Remove the spark plugs, noting the cylinders from which they were removed, and evaluate according to the color photos in the middle of this book.	See following.	**See following.**

Test and Procedure	Results and Indications	Proceed to
4.7—Examine the location of all the plugs.	The following diagrams illustrate some of the conditions that the location of plugs will reveal.	**4.8**

Two adjacent plugs are fouled in a 6-cylinder engine, 4-cylinder engine or either bank of a V-8. This is probably due to a blown head gasket between the two cylinders

The two center plugs in a 6-cylinder engine are fouled. Raw fuel may be "boiled" out of the carburetor into the intake manifold after the engine is shut-off. Stop-start driving can also foul the center plugs, due to overly rich mixture. Proper float level, a new float needle and seat or use of an insulating spacer may help this problem

An unbalanced carburetor is indicated. Following the fuel flow on this particular design shows that the cylinders fed by the right-hand barrel are fouled from overly rich mixture, while the cylinders fed by the left-hand barrel are normal

If the four rear plugs are overheated, a cooling system problem is suggested. A thorough cleaning of the cooling system may restore coolant circulation and cure the problem

Finding one plug overheated may indicate an intake manifold leak near the affected cylinder. If the overheated plug is the second of two adjacent, consecutively firing plugs, it could be the result of ignition cross-firing. Separating the leads to these two plugs will eliminate cross-fire

Occasionally, the two rear plugs in large, lightly used V-8's will become oil fouled. High oil consumption and smoky exhaust may also be noticed. It is probably due to plugged oil drain holes in the rear of the cylinder head, causing oil to be sucked in around the valve stems. This usually occurs in the rear cylinders first, because the engine slants that way

Test and Procedure	Results and Indications	Proceed to
4.8—Determine the static ignition timing. Using the crankshaft pulley timing marks as a guide, locate top dead center on the compression stroke of the number one cylinder.	The rotor should be pointing toward the No. 1 tower in the distributor cap, and, on electronic ignitions, the armature spoke for that cylinder should be lined up with the stator.	**4.8**
4.9—Check coil polarity: Connect a voltmeter negative lead to the coil high tension lead, and the positive lead to ground (**NOTE:** *Reverse the hook-up for positive ground systems*). Crank the engine momentarily. **Checking coil polarity**	If the voltmeter reads up-scale, the polarity is correct: If the voltmeter reads down-scale, reverse the coil polarity (switch the primary leads):	**5.1** **5.1**

Section 5—Fuel System
See Chapter 4 for service procedures

Test and Procedure	Results and Indications	Proceed to
5.1—Determine that the air filter is functioning efficiently: Hold paper elements up to a strong light, and attempt to see light through the filter.	Clean permanent air filters in solvent (or manufacturer's recommendation), and allow to dry. Replace paper elements through which light cannot be seen:	**5.2**
5.2—Determine whether a flooding condition exists: Flooding is identified by a strong gasoline odor, and excessive gasoline present in the throttle bore(s) of the carburetor. **If the engine floods repeatedly, check the choke butterfly flap**	If flooding is not evident: If flooding is evident, permit the gasoline to dry for a few moments and restart. If flooding doesn't recur: If flooding is persistent:	**5.3** **5.7** **5.5**
5.3—Check that fuel is reaching the carburetor: Detach the fuel line at the carburetor inlet. Hold the end of the line in a cup (not styrofoam), and crank the engine. **Check the fuel pump by disconnecting the output line (fuel pump-to-carburetor) at the carburetor and operating the starter briefly**	If fuel flows smoothly: If fuel doesn't flow (**NOTE:** *Make sure that there is fuel in the tank*), or flows erratically:	**5.7** **5.4**

Test and Procedure	Results and Indications	Proceed to
5.4—Test the fuel pump: Disconnect all fuel lines from the fuel pump. Hold a finger over the input fitting, crank the engine (with electric pump, turn the ignition or pump on); and feel for suction.	If suction is evident, blow out the fuel line to the tank with low pressure compressed air until bubbling is heard from the fuel filler neck. Also blow out the carburetor fuel line (both ends disconnected):	**5.7**
	If no suction is evident, replace or repair the fuel pump: NOTE: *Repeated oil fouling of the spark plugs, or a no-start condition, could be the result of a ruptured vacuum booster pump diaphragm, through which oil or gasoline is being drawn into the intake manifold (where applicable).*	**5.7**
5.5—Occasionally, small specks of dirt will clog the small jets and orifices in the carburetor. With the engine cold, hold a flat piece of wood or similar material over the carburetor, where possible, and crank the engine.	If the engine starts, but runs roughly the engine is probably not run enough. If the engine won't start:	**5.9**
5.6—Check the needle and seat: Tap the carburetor in the area of the needle and seat.	If flooding stops, a gasoline additive (e.g., Gumout) will often cure the problem:	**5.7**
	If flooding continues, check the fuel pump for excessive pressure at the carburetor (according to specifications). If the pressure is normal, the needle and seat must be removed and checked, and/or the float level adjusted:	**5.7**
5.7—Test the accelerator pump by looking into the throttle bores while operating the throttle.	If the accelerator pump appears to be operating normally:	**5.8**
	If the accelerator pump is not operating, the pump must be reconditioned. Where possible, service the pump with the carburetor(s) installed on the engine. If necessary, remove the carburetor. Prior to removal:	**5.8**

Check for gas at the carburetor by looking down the carburetor throat while someone moves the accelerator

Test and Procedure	Results and Indications	Proceed to
5.8—Determine whether the carburetor main fuel system is functioning: Spray a commercial starting fluid into the carburetor while attempting to start the engine.	If the engine starts, runs for a few seconds, and dies:	**5.9**
	If the engine doesn't start:	**6.1**

Test and Procedure	Results and Indications	Proceed to
5.9—Uncommon fuel system malfunctions: See below:	If the problem is solved:	**6.1**
	If the problem remains, remove and recondition the carburetor.	

Condition	Indication	Test	Prevailing Weather Conditions	Remedy
Vapor lock	Engine will not restart shortly after running.	Cool the components of the fuel system until the engine starts. Vapor lock can be cured faster by draping a wet cloth over a mechanical fuel pump.	Hot to very hot	Ensure that the exhaust manifold heat control valve is operating. Check with the vehicle manufacturer for the recommended solution to vapor lock on the model in question.
Carburetor icing	Engine will not idle, stalls at low speeds.	Visually inspect the throttle plate area of the throttle bores for frost.	High humidity, 32–40° F.	Ensure that the exhaust manifold heat control valve is operating, and that the intake manifold heat riser is not blocked.
Water in the fuel	Engine sputters and stalls; may not start.	Pump a small amount of fuel into a glass jar. Allow to stand, and inspect for droplets or a layer of water.	High humidity, extreme temperature changes.	For droplets, use one or two cans of commercial gas line anti-freeze. For a layer of water, the tank must be drained, and the fuel lines blown out with compressed air.

Section 6—Engine Compression

See Chapter 3 for service procedures

6.1—Test engine compression: Remove all spark plugs. Block the throttle wide open. Insert a compression gauge into a spark plug port, crank the engine to obtain the maximum reading, and record.	If compression is within limits on all cylinders:	**7.1**
	If gauge reading is extremely low on all cylinders:	**6.2**
	If gauge reading is low on one or two cylinders: (If gauge readings are identical and low on two or more adjacent cylinders, the head gasket must be replaced.)	**6.2**

Checking compression

6.2—Test engine compression (wet): Squirt approximately 30 cc. of engine oil into each cylinder, and retest per 6.1.	If the readings improve, worn or cracked rings or broken pistons are indicated:	**See Chapter 3**
	If the readings do not improve, burned or excessively carboned valves or a jumped timing chain are indicated:	**7.1**
	NOTE: *A jumped timing chain is often indicated by difficult cranking.*	

Section 7—Engine Vacuum
See Chapter 3 for service procedures

Test and Procedure	Results and Indications	Proceed to
7.1—Attach a vacuum gauge to the intake manifold beyond the throttle plate. Start the engine, and observe the action of the needle over the range of engine speeds.	See below.	**See below**

INDICATION: normal engine in good condition

Proceed to: 8.1

Normal engine
Gauge reading: steady, from 17–22 in./Hg.

INDICATION: sticking valves or ignition miss

Proceed to: 9.1, 8.3

Sticking valves
Gauge reading: intermittent fluctuation at idle

INDICATION: late ignition or valve timing, low compression, stuck throttle valve, leaking carburetor or manifold gasket

Proceed to: 6.1

Incorrect valve timing
Gauge reading: low (10–15 in./Hg) but steady

INDICATION: improper carburetor adjustment or minor intake leak.

Proceed to: 7.2

Carburetor requires adjustment
Gauge reading: drifting needle

INDICATION: ignition miss, blown cylinder head gasket, leaking valve or weak valve spring

Proceed to: 8.3, 6.1

Blown head gasket
Gauge reading: needle fluctuates as engine speed increases

INDICATION: burnt valve or faulty valve clearance. Needle will fall when defective valve operates

Proceed to: 9.1

Burnt or leaking valves
Gauge reading: steady needle, but drops regularly

INDICATION: choked muffler, excessive back pressure in system

Proceed to: 10.1

Clogged exhaust system
Gauge reading: gradual drop in reading at idle

INDICATION: worn valve guides

Proceed to: 9.1

Worn valve guides
Gauge reading: needle vibrates excessively at idle, but steadies as engine speed increases

White pointer = steady gauge hand   Black pointer = fluctuating gauge hand

Test and Procedure	Results and Indications	Proceed to
7.2—Attach a vacuum gauge per 7.1, and test for an intake manifold leak. Squirt a small amount of oil around the intake manifold gaskets, carburetor gaskets, plugs and fittings. Observe the action of the vacuum gauge.	If the reading improves, replace the indicated gasket, or seal the indicated fitting or plug: If the reading remains low:	**8.1** **7.3**
7.3—Test all vacuum hoses and accessories for leaks as described in 7.2. Also check the carburetor body (dashpots, automatic choke mechanism, throttle shafts) for leaks in the same manner.	If the reading improves, service or replace the offending part(s): If the reading remains low:	**8.1** **6.1**

Section 8—Secondary Electrical System
See Chapter 2 for service procedures

Test and Procedure	Results and Indications	Proceed to
8.1—Remove the distributor cap and check to make sure that the rotor turns when the engine is cranked. Visually inspect the distributor components.	Clean, tighten or replace any components which appear defective.	**8.2**
8.2—Connect a timing light (per manufacturer's recommendation) and check the dynamic ignition timing. Disconnect and plug the vacuum hose(s) to the distributor if specified, start the engine, and observe the timing marks at the specified engine speed.	If the timing is not correct, adjust to specifications by rotating the distributor in the engine: (Advance timing by rotating distributor opposite normal direction of rotor rotation, retard timing by rotating distributor in same direction as rotor rotation.)	**8.3**
8.3—Check the operation of the distributor advance mechanism(s): To test the mechanical advance, disconnect the vacuum lines from the distributor advance unit and observe the timing marks with a timing light as the engine speed is increased from idle. If the mark moves smoothly, without hesitation, it may be assumed that the mechanical advance is functioning properly. To test vacuum advance and/or retard systems, alternately crimp and release the vacuum line, and observe the timing mark for movement. If movement is noted, the system is operating.	If the systems are functioning: If the systems are not functioning, remove the distributor, and test on a distributor tester:	**8.4** **8.4**
8.4—Locate an ignition miss: With the engine running, remove each spark plug wire, one at a time, until one is found that doesn't cause the engine to roughen and slow down.	When the missing cylinder is identified:	**4.1**

Section 9—Valve Train
See Chapter 3 for service procedures

Test and Procedure	Results and Indications	Proceed to
9.1—Evaluate the valve train: Remove the valve cover, and ensure that the valves are adjusted to specifications. A mechanic's stethoscope may be used to aid in the diagnosis of the valve train. By pushing the probe on or near push rods or rockers, valve noise often can be isolated. A timing light also may be used to diagnose valve problems. Connect the light according to manufacturer's recommendations, and start the engine. Vary the firing moment of the light by increasing the engine speed (and therefore the ignition advance), and moving the trigger from cylinder to cylinder. Observe the movement of each valve.	Sticking valves or erratic valve train motion can be observed with the timing light. The cylinder head must be disassembled for repairs.	**See Chapter 3**
9.2—Check the valve timing: Locate top dead center of the No. 1 piston, and install a degree wheel or tape on the crankshaft pulley or damper with zero corresponding to an index mark on the engine. Rotate the crankshaft in its direction of rotation, and observe the opening of the No. 1 cylinder intake valve. The opening should correspond with the correct mark on the degree wheel according to specifications.	If the timing is not correct, the timing cover must be removed for further investigation.	**See Chapter 3**

Section 10—Exhaust System

Test and Procedure	Results and Indications	Proceed to
10.1—Determine whether the exhaust manifold heat control valve is operating: Operate the valve by hand to determine whether it is free to move. If the valve is free, run the engine to operating temperature and observe the action of the valve, to ensure that it is opening.	If the valve sticks, spray it with a suitable solvent, open and close the valve to free it, and retest. If the valve functions properly: If the valve does not free, or does not operate, replace the valve:	**10.2** **10.2**
10.2—Ensure that there are no exhaust restrictions: Visually inspect the exhaust system for kinks, dents, or crushing. Also note that gases are flowing freely from the tailpipe at all engine speeds, indicating no restriction in the muffler or resonator.	Replace any damaged portion of the system:	**11.1**

Section 11—Cooling System
See Chapter 3 for service procedures

Test and Procedure	Results and Indications	Proceed to
11.1—Visually inspect the fan belt for glazing, cracks, and fraying, and replace if necessary. Tighten the belt so that the longest span has approximately ½″ play at its mid-point under thumb pressure (see Chapter 1).	Replace or tighten the fan belt as necessary:	**11.2**

Checking belt tension

Test and Procedure	Results and Indications	Proceed to
11.2—Check the fluid level of the cooling system.	If full or slightly low, fill as necessary:	**11.5**
	If extremely low:	**11.3**
11.3—Visually inspect the external portions of the cooling system (radiator, radiator hoses, thermostat elbow, water pump seals, heater hoses, etc.) for leaks. If none are found, pressurize the cooling system to 14–15 psi.	If cooling system holds the pressure:	**11.5**
	If cooling system loses pressure rapidly, reinspect external parts of the system for leaks under pressure. If none are found, check dipstick for coolant in crankcase. If no coolant is present, but pressure loss continues:	**11.4**
	If coolant is evident in crankcase, remove cylinder head(s), and check gasket(s). If gaskets are intact, block and cylinder head(s) should be checked for cracks or holes.	
	If the gasket(s) is blown, replace, and purge the crankcase of coolant:	**12.6**
	NOTE: *Occasionally, due to atmospheric and driving conditions, condensation of water can occur in the crankcase. This causes the oil to appear milky white. To remedy, run the engine until hot, and change the oil and oil filter.*	
11.4—Check for combustion leaks into the cooling system: Pressurize the cooling system as above. Start the engine, and observe the pressure gauge. If the needle fluctuates, remove each spark plug wire, one at a time, noting which cylinder(s) reduce or eliminate the fluctuation.	Cylinders which reduce or eliminate the fluctuation, when the spark plug wire is removed, are leaking into the cooling system. Replace the head gasket on the affected cylinder bank(s).	

Pressurizing the cooling system

Test and Procedure	Results and Indications	Proceed to
11.5—Check the radiator pressure cap: Attach a radiator pressure tester to the radiator cap (wet the seal prior to installation). Quickly pump up the pressure, noting the point at which the cap releases.	If the cap releases within ± 1 psi of the specified rating, it is operating properly:	**11.6**
	If the cap releases at more than ± 1 psi of the specified rating, it should be replaced:	**11.6**

Checking radiator pressure cap

Test and Procedure	Results and Indications	Proceed to
11.6—Test the thermostat: Start the engine cold, remove the radiator cap, and insert a thermometer into the radiator. Allow the engine to idle. After a short while, there will be a sudden, rapid increase in coolant temperature. The temperature at which this sharp rise stops is the thermostat opening temperature.	If the thermostat opens at or about the specified temperature:	**11.7**
	If the temperature doesn't increase: (If the temperature increases slowly and gradually, replace the thermostat.)	**11.7**
11.7—Check the water pump: Remove the thermostat elbow and the thermostat, disconnect the coil high tension lead (to prevent starting), and crank the engine momentarily.	If coolant flows, replace the thermostat and retest per 11.6:	**11.6**
	If coolant doesn't flow, reverse flush the cooling system to alleviate any blockage that might exist. If system is not blocked, and coolant will not flow, replace the water pump.	

Section 12—Lubrication
See Chapter 3 for service procedures

Test and Procedure	Results and Indications	Proceed to
12.1—Check the oil pressure gauge or warning light: If the gauge shows low pressure, or the light is on for no obvious reason, remove the oil pressure sender. Install an accurate oil pressure gauge and run the engine momentarily.	If oil pressure builds normally, run engine for a few moments to determine that it is functioning normally, and replace the sender.	—
	If the pressure remains low:	**12.2**
	If the pressure surges:	**12.3**
	If the oil pressure is zero:	**12.3**
12.2—Visually inspect the oil: If the oil is watery or very thin, milky, or foamy, replace the oil and oil filter.	If the oil is normal:	**12.3**
	If after replacing oil the pressure remains low:	**12.3**
	If after replacing oil the pressure becomes normal:	—

Test and Procedure	Results and Indications	Proceed to
12.3—Inspect the oil pressure relief valve and spring, to ensure that it is not sticking or stuck. Remove and thoroughly clean the valve, spring, and the valve body.	If the oil pressure improves: If no improvement is noted:	— **12.4**
12.4—Check to ensure that the oil pump is not cavitating (sucking air instead of oil): See that the crankcase is neither over nor underfull, and that the pickup in the sump is in the proper position and free from sludge.	Fill or drain the crankcase to the proper capacity, and clean the pickup screen in solvent if necessary. If no improvement is noted:	**12.5**
12.5—Inspect the oil pump drive and the oil pump:	If the pump drive or the oil pump appear to be defective, service as necessary and retest per 12.1: If the pump drive and pump appear to be operating normally, the engine should be disassembled to determine where blockage exists:	**12.1** **See Chapter 3**
12.6—Purge the engine of ethylene glycol coolant: Completely drain the crankcase and the oil filter. Obtain a commercial butyl cellosolve base solvent, designated for this purpose, and follow the instructions precisely. Following this, install a new oil filter and refill the crankcase with the proper weight oil. The next oil and filter change should follow shortly thereafter (1000 miles).		

TROUBLESHOOTING EMISSION CONTROL SYSTEMS

See Chapter 4 for procedures applicable to individual emission control systems used on specific combinations of engine/transmission/model.

TROUBLESHOOTING THE CARBURETOR

See Chapter 4 for service procedures

Carburetor problems cannot be effectively isolated unless all other engine systems (particularly ignition and emission) are functioning properly and the engine is properly tuned.

Condition	Possible Cause
Engine cranks, but does not start	1. Improper starting procedure 2. No fuel in tank 3. Clogged fuel line or filter 4. Defective fuel pump 5. Choke valve not closing properly 6. Engine flooded 7. Choke valve not unloading 8. Throttle linkage not making full travel 9. Stuck needle or float 10. Leaking float needle or seat 11. Improper float adjustment
Engine stalls	1. Improperly adjusted idle speed or mixture **Engine hot** 2. Improperly adjusted dashpot 3. Defective or improperly adjusted solenoid 4. Incorrect fuel level in fuel bowl 5. Fuel pump pressure too high 6. Leaking float needle seat 7. Secondary throttle valve stuck open 8. Air or fuel leaks 9. Idle air bleeds plugged or missing 10. Idle passages plugged **Engine Cold** 11. Incorrectly adjusted choke 12. Improperly adjusted fast idle speed 13. Air leaks 14. Plugged idle or idle air passages 15. Stuck choke valve or binding linkage 16. Stuck secondary throttle valves 17. Engine flooding—high fuel level 18. Leaking or misaligned float
Engine hesitates on acceleration	1. Clogged fuel filter 2. Leaking fuel pump diaphragm 3. Low fuel pump pressure 4. Secondary throttle valves stuck, bent or misadjusted 5. Sticking or binding air valve 6. Defective accelerator pump 7. Vacuum leaks 8. Clogged air filter 9. Incorrect choke adjustment (engine cold)
Engine feels sluggish or flat on acceleration	1. Improperly adjusted idle speed or mixture 2. Clogged fuel filter 3. Defective accelerator pump 4. Dirty, plugged or incorrect main metering jets 5. Bent or sticking main metering rods 6. Sticking throttle valves 7. Stuck heat riser 8. Binding or stuck air valve 9. Dirty, plugged or incorrect secondary jets 10. Bent or sticking secondary metering rods. 11. Throttle body or manifold heat passages plugged 12. Improperly adjusted choke or choke vacuum break.
Carburetor floods	1. Defective fuel pump. Pressure too high. 2. Stuck choke valve 3. Dirty, worn or damaged float or needle valve/seat 4. Incorrect float/fuel level 5. Leaking float bowl

Condition	Possible Cause
Engine idles roughly and stalls	1. Incorrect idle speed 2. Clogged fuel filter 3. Dirt in fuel system or carburetor 4. Loose carburetor screws or attaching bolts 5. Broken carburetor gaskets 6. Air leaks 7. Dirty carburetor 8. Worn idle mixture needles 9. Throttle valves stuck open 10. Incorrectly adjusted float or fuel level 11. Clogged air filter
Engine runs unevenly or surges	1. Defective fuel pump 2. Dirty or clogged fuel filter 3. Plugged, loose or incorrect main metering jets or rods 4. Air leaks 5. Bent or sticking main metering rods 6. Stuck power piston 7. Incorrect float adjustment 8. Incorrect idle speed or mixture 9. Dirty or plugged idle system passages 10. Hard, brittle or broken gaskets 11. Loose attaching or mounting screws 12. Stuck or misaligned secondary throttle valves
Poor fuel economy	1. Poor driving habits 2. Stuck choke valve 3. Binding choke linkage 4. Stuck heat riser 5. Incorrect idle mixture 6. Defective accelerator pump 7. Air leaks 8. Plugged, loose or incorrect main metering jets 9. Improperly adjusted float or fuel level 10. Bent, misaligned or fuel-clogged float 11. Leaking float needle seat 12. Fuel leak 13. Accelerator pump discharge ball not seating properly 14. Incorrect main jets
Engine lacks high speed performance or power	1. Incorrect throttle linkage adjustment 2. Stuck or binding power piston 3. Defective accelerator pump 4. Air leaks 5. Incorrect float setting or fuel level 6. Dirty, plugged, worn or incorrect main metering jets or rods 7. Binding or sticking air valve 8. Brittle or cracked gaskets 9. Bent, incorrect or improperly adjusted secondary metering rods 10. Clogged fuel filter 11. Clogged air filter 12. Defective fuel pump

TROUBLESHOOTING FUEL INJECTION PROBLEMS

Each fuel injection system has its own unique components and test procedures, for which it is impossible to generalize. Refer to Chapter 4 of this Repair & Tune-Up Guide for specific test and repair procedures, if the vehicle is equipped with fuel injection.

TROUBLESHOOTING ELECTRICAL PROBLEMS

See Chapter 5 for service procedures

For any electrical system to operate, it must make a complete circuit. This simply means that the power flow from the battery must make a complete circle. When an electrical component is operating, power flows from the battery to the component, passes through the component causing it to perform its function (lighting a light bulb), and then returns to the battery through the ground of the circuit. This ground is usually (but not always) the metal part of the car or truck on which the electrical component is mounted.

Perhaps the easiest way to visualize this is to think of connecting a light bulb with two wires attached to it to the battery. If one of the two wires attached to the light bulb were attached to the negative post of the battery and the other were attached to the positive post of the battery, you would have a complete circuit. Current from the battery would flow to the light bulb, causing it to light, and return to the negative post of the battery.

The normal automotive circuit differs from this simple example in two ways. First, instead of having a return wire from the bulb to the battery, the light bulb returns the current to the battery through the chassis of the vehicle. Since the negative battery cable is attached to the chassis and the chassis is made of electrically conductive metal, the chassis of the vehicle can serve as a ground wire to complete the circuit. Secondly, most automotive circuits contain switches to turn components on and off as required.

Every complete circuit from a power source must include a component which is using the power from the power source. If you were to disconnect the light bulb from the wires and touch the two wires together (don't do this) the power supply wire to the component would be grounded before the normal ground connection for the circuit.

Because grounding a wire from a power source makes a complete circuit—less the required component to use the power—this phenomenon is called a short circuit. Common causes are: broken insulation (exposing the metal wire to a metal part of the car or truck), or a shorted switch.

Some electrical components which require a large amount of current to operate also have a relay in their circuit. Since these circuits carry a large amount of current, the thickness of the wire in the circuit (gauge size) is also greater. If this large wire were connected from the component to the control switch on the instrument panel, and then back to the component, a voltage drop would occur in the circuit. To prevent this potential drop in voltage, an electromagnetic switch (relay) is used. The large wires in the circuit are connected from the battery to one side of the relay, and from the opposite side of the relay to the component. The relay is normally open, preventing current from passing through the circuit. An additional, smaller, wire is connected from the relay to the control switch for the circuit. When the control switch is turned on, it grounds the smaller wire from the relay and completes the circuit. This closes the relay and allows current to flow from the battery to the component. The horn, headlight, and starter circuits are three which use relays.

It is possible for larger surges of current to pass through the electrical system of your car or truck. If this surge of current were to reach an electrical component, it could burn it out. To prevent this, fuses, circuit breakers or fusible links are connected into the current supply wires of most of the major electrical systems. When an electrical current of excessive power passes through the component's fuse, the fuse blows out and breaks the circuit, saving the component from destruction.

Typical automotive fuse

A circuit breaker is basically a self-repairing fuse. The circuit breaker opens the circuit the same way a fuse does. However, when either the short is removed from the circuit or the surge subsides, the circuit breaker resets itself and does not have to be replaced as a fuse does.

A fuse link is a wire that acts as a fuse. It is normally connected between the starter relay and the main wiring harness. This connection is usually under the hood. The fuse link (if installed) protects all the

Most fusible links show a charred, melted insulation when they burn out

The test light will show the presence of current when touched to a hot wire and grounded at the other end

chassis electrical components, and is the probable cause of trouble when none of the electrical components function, unless the battery is disconnected or dead.

Electrical problems generally fall into one of three areas:

1. The component that is not functioning is not receiving current.

2. The component itself is not functioning.

3. The component is not properly grounded.

The electrical system can be checked with a test light and a jumper wire. A test light is a device that looks like a pointed screwdriver with a wire attached to it and has a light bulb in its handle. A jumper wire is a piece of insulated wire with an alligator clip attached to each end.

If a component is not working, you must follow a systematic plan to determine which of the three causes is the villain.

1. Turn on the switch that controls the inoperable component.

2. Disconnect the power supply wire from the component.

3. Attach the ground wire on the test light to a good metal ground.

4. Touch the probe end of the test light to the end of the power supply wire that was disconnected from the component. If the component is receiving current, the test light will go on.

NOTE: *Some components work only when the ignition switch is turned on.*

If the test light does not go on, then the problem is in the circuit between the battery and the component. This includes all the switches, fuses, and relays in the system. Follow the wire that runs back to the battery. The problem is an open circuit between the

battery and the component. If the fuse is blown and, when replaced, immediately blows again, there is a short circuit in the system which must be located and repaired. If there is a switch in the system, bypass it with a jumper wire. This is done by connecting one end of the jumper wire to the power supply wire into the switch and the other end of the jumper wire to the wire coming out of the switch. If the test light lights with the jumper wire installed, the switch or whatever was bypassed is defective.

NOTE: *Never substitute the jumper wire for the component, since it is required to use the power from the power source.*

5. If the bulb in the test light goes on, then the current is getting to the component that is not working. This eliminates the first of the three possible causes. Connect the power supply wire and connect a jumper wire from the component to a good metal ground. Do this with the switch which controls the component turned on, and also the ignition switch turned on if it is required for the component to work. If the component works with the jumper wire installed, then it has a bad ground. This is usually caused by the metal area on which the component mounts to the chassis being coated with some type of foreign matter.

6. If neither test located the source of the trouble, then the component itself is defective. Remember that for any electrical system to work, all connections must be clean and tight.

Troubleshooting Basic Turn Signal and Flasher Problems
See Chapter 5 for service procedures

Most problems in the turn signals or flasher system can be reduced to defective flashers or bulbs, which are easily replaced. Occasionally, the turn signal switch will prove defective.

F = Front   R = Rear   ● = Lights off   ○ = Lights on

Condition		Possible Cause
Turn signals light, but do not flash		Defective flasher
No turn signals light on either side		Blown fuse. Replace if defective. Defective flasher. Check by substitution. Open circuit, short circuit or poor ground.
Both turn signals on one side don't work		Bad bulbs. Bad ground in both (or either) housings.
One turn signal light on one side doesn't work		Defective bulb. Corrosion in socket. Clean contacts. Poor ground at socket.
Turn signal flashes too fast or too slowly		Check any bulb on the side flashing too fast. A heavy-duty bulb is probably installed in place of a regular bulb. Check the bulb flashing too slowly. A standard bulb was probably installed in place of a heavy-duty bulb. Loose connections or corrosion at the bulb socket.
Indicator lights don't work in either direction		Check if the turn signals are working. Check the dash indicator lights. Check the flasher by substitution.
One indicator light doesn't light		On systems with one dash indicator: See if the lights work on the same side. Often the filaments have been reversed in systems combining stoplights with taillights and turn signals. Check the flasher by substitution. On systems with two indicators: Check the bulbs on the same side. Check the indicator light bulb. Check the flasher by substitution.

Troubleshooting Lighting Problems
See Chapter 5 for service procedures

Condition	Possible Cause
One or more lights don't work, but others do	1. Defective bulb(s) 2. Blown fuse(s) 3. Dirty fuse clips or light sockets 4. Poor ground circuit
Lights burn out quickly	1. Incorrect voltage regulator setting or defective regulator 2. Poor battery/alternator connections
Lights go dim	1. Low/discharged battery 2. Alternator not charging 3. Corroded sockets or connections 4. Low voltage output
Lights flicker	1. Loose connection 2. Poor ground. (Run ground wire from light housing to frame) 3. Circuit breaker operating (short circuit)
Lights "flare"—Some flare is normal on acceleration—If excessive, see "Lights Burn Out Quickly"	High voltage setting
Lights glare—approaching drivers are blinded	1. Lights adjusted too high 2. Rear springs or shocks sagging 3. Rear tires soft

Troubleshooting Dash Gauge Problems
Most problems can be traced to a defective sending unit or faulty wiring. Occasionally, the gauge itself is at fault. See Chapter 5 for service procedures.

Condition	Possible Cause
COOLANT TEMPERATURE GAUGE	
Gauge reads erratically or not at all	1. Loose or dirty connections 2. Defective sending unit. 3. Defective gauge. To test a bi-metal gauge, remove the wire from the sending unit. Ground the wire for an instant. If the gauge registers, replace the sending unit. To test a magnetic gauge, disconnect the wire at the sending unit. With ignition ON gauge should register COLD. Ground the wire; gauge should register HOT.
AMMETER GAUGE—TURN HEADLIGHTS ON (DO NOT START ENGINE). NOTE REACTION	
Ammeter shows charge Ammeter shows discharge Ammeter does not move	1. Connections reversed on gauge 2. Ammeter is OK 3. Loose connections or faulty wiring 4. Defective gauge

Condition	Possible Cause

OIL PRESSURE GAUGE

| Gauge does not register or is inaccurate | 1. On mechanical gauge, Bourdon tube may be bent or kinked.
2. Low oil pressure. Remove sending unit. Idle the engine briefly. If no oil flows from sending unit hole, problem is in engine.
3. Defective gauge. Remove the wire from the sending unit and ground it for an instant with the ignition ON. A good gauge will go to the top of the scale.
4. Defective wiring. Check the wiring to the gauge. If it's OK and the gauge doesn't register when grounded, replace the gauge.
5. Defective sending unit. |

ALL GAUGES

| All gauges do not operate

All gauges read low or erratically
All gauges pegged | 1. Blown fuse
2. Defective instrument regulator
3. Defective or dirty instrument voltage regulator
4. Loss of ground between instrument voltage regulator and frame
5. Defective instrument regulator |

WARNING LIGHTS

| Light(s) do not come on when ignition is ON, but engine is not started

Light comes on with engine running | 1. Defective bulb
2. Defective wire
3. Defective sending unit. Disconnect the wire from the sending unit and ground it. Replace the sending unit if the light comes on with the ignition ON.
4. Problem in individual system
5. Defective sending unit |

Troubleshooting Clutch Problems

It is false economy to replace individual clutch components. The pressure plate, clutch plate and throwout bearing should be replaced as a set, and the flywheel face inspected, whenever the clutch is overhauled. See Chapter 6 for service procedures.

Condition	Possible Cause
Clutch chatter	1. Grease on driven plate (disc) facing 2. Binding clutch linkage or cable 3. Loose, damaged facings on driven plate (disc) 4. Engine mounts loose 5. Incorrect height adjustment of pressure plate release levers 6. Clutch housing or housing to transmission adapter misalignment 7. Loose driven plate hub
Clutch grabbing	1. Oil, grease on driven plate (disc) facing 2. Broken pressure plate 3. Warped or binding driven plate. Driven plate binding on clutch shaft
Clutch slips	1. Lack of lubrication in clutch linkage or cable (linkage or cable binds, causes incomplete engagement) 2. Incorrect pedal, or linkage adjustment 3. Broken pressure plate springs 4. Weak pressure plate springs 5. Grease on driven plate facings (disc)

Troubleshooting Clutch Problems (cont.)

Condition	Possible Cause
Incomplete clutch release	1. Incorrect pedal or linkage adjustment or linkage or cable binding 2. Incorrect height adjustment on pressure plate release levers 3. Loose, broken facings on driven plate (disc) 4. Bent, dished, warped driven plate caused by overheating
Grinding, whirring grating noise when pedal is depressed	1. Worn or defective throwout bearing 2. Starter drive teeth contacting flywheel ring gear teeth. Look for milled or polished teeth on ring gear.
Squeal, howl, trumpeting noise when pedal is being released (occurs during first inch to inch and one-half of pedal travel)	Pilot bushing worn or lack of lubricant. If bushing appears OK, polish bushing with emery cloth, soak lube wick in oil, lube bushing with oil, apply film of chassis grease to clutch shaft pilot hub, reassemble. NOTE: Bushing wear may be due to misalignment of clutch housing or housing to transmission adapter
Vibration or clutch pedal pulsation with clutch disengaged (pedal fully depressed)	1. Worn or defective engine transmission mounts 2. Flywheel run out. (Flywheel run out at face not to exceed 0.005″) 3. Damaged or defective clutch components

Troubleshooting Manual Transmission Problems
See Chapter 6 for service procedures

Condition	Possible Cause
Transmission jumps out of gear	1. Misalignment of transmission case or clutch housing. 2. Worn pilot bearing in crankshaft. 3. Bent transmission shaft. 4. Worn high speed sliding gear. 5. Worn teeth or end-play in clutch shaft. 6. Insufficient spring tension on shifter rail plunger. 7. Bent or loose shifter fork. 8. Gears not engaging completely. 9. Loose or worn bearings on clutch shaft or mainshaft. 10. Worn gear teeth. 11. Worn or damaged detent balls.
Transmission sticks in gear	1. Clutch not releasing fully. 2. Burred or battered teeth on clutch shaft, or sliding sleeve. 3. Burred or battered transmission mainshaft. 4. Frozen synchronizing clutch. 5. Stuck shifter rail plunger. 6. Gearshift lever twisting and binding shifter rail. 7. Battered teeth on high speed sliding gear or on sleeve. 8. Improper lubrication, or lack of lubrication. 9. Corroded transmission parts. 10. Defective mainshaft pilot bearing. 11. Locked gear bearings will give same effect as stuck in gear.
Transmission gears will not synchronize	1. Binding pilot bearing on mainshaft, will synchronize in high gear only. 2. Clutch not releasing fully. 3. Detent spring weak or broken. 4. Weak or broken springs under balls in sliding gear sleeve. 5. Binding bearing on clutch shaft, or binding countershaft. 6. Binding pilot bearing in crankshaft. 7. Badly worn gear teeth. 8. Improper lubrication. 9. Constant mesh gear not turning freely on transmission mainshaft. Will synchronize in that gear only.

CHILTON'S
AUTO BODY
REPAIR TIPS

Tools and Materials • Step-by-Step Illustrated Procedures
How To Repair Dents, Scratches and Rust Holes
Spray Painting and Refinishing Tips

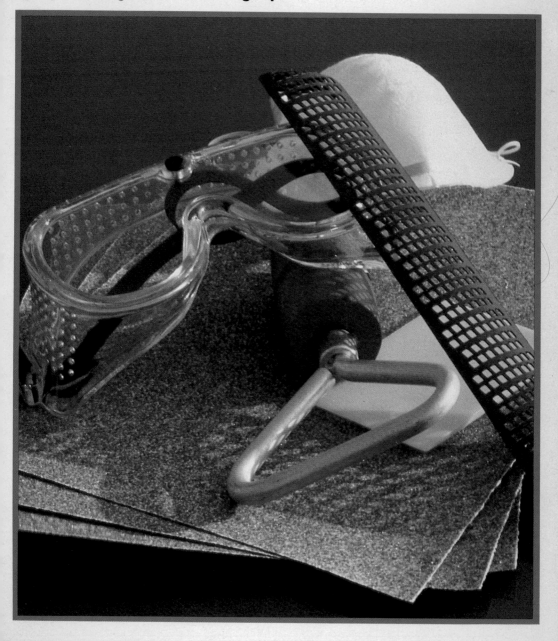

With a little practice, basic body repair procedures can be mastered by any do-it-yourself mechanic. The step-by-step repairs shown here can be applied to almost any type of auto body repair.

TOOLS & MATERIALS

You may already have basic tools, such as hammers and electric drills. Other tools unique to body repair — body hammers, grinding attachments, sanding blocks, dent puller, half-round plastic file and plastic spreaders — are relatively inexpensive and can be obtained wherever auto parts or auto body repair parts are sold. Portable air compressors and paint spray guns can be purchased or rented.

Auto Body Repair Kits

The best and most often used products are available to the do-it-yourselfer in kit form, from major manufacturers of auto body repair products. The same manufacturers also merchandise the individual products for use by pros.

Kits are available to make a wide variety of repairs, including holes, dents and scratches and fiberglass, and offer the advantage of buying the materials you'll need for the job. There is little waste or chance of materials going bad from not being used. Many kits may also contain basic body-working tools such as body files, sanding blocks and spreaders. Check the contents of the kit before buying your tools.

BODY REPAIR TIPS

Safety

Many of the products associated with auto body repair and refinishing contain toxic chemicals. Read all labels before opening containers and store them in a safe place and manner.

• Wear eye protection (safety goggles) when using power tools or when performing any operation that involves the removal of any type of material.

• Wear lung protection (disposable mask or respirator) when grinding, sanding or painting.

Sanding

1 Sand off paint before using a dent puller. When using a non-adhesive sanding disc, cover the back of the disc with an overlapping layer or two of masking tape and trim the edges. The disc will last considerably longer.

2 Use the circular motion of the sanding disc to grind *into* the edge of the repair. Grinding or sanding away from the jagged edge will only tear the sandpaper.

3 Use the palm of your hand flat on the panel to detect high and low spots. Do not use your fingertips. Slide your hand slowly back and forth.

WORKING WITH BODY FILLER

Mixing The Filler

Cleanliness and proper mixing and application are extremely important. Use a clean piece of plastic or glass or a disposable artist's palette to mix body filler.

1 Allow plenty of time and follow directions. No useful purpose will be served by adding more hardener to make it cure (set-up) faster. Less hardener means more curing time, but the mixture dries harder; more hardener means less curing time but a softer mixture.

2 Both the hardener and the filler should be thoroughly kneaded or stirred before mixing. Hardener should be a solid paste and dispense like thin toothpaste. Body filler should be smooth, and free of lumps or thick spots.

Getting the proper amount of hardener in the filler is the trickiest part of preparing the filler. Use the same amount of hardener in cold or warm weather. For contour filler (thick coats), a bead of hardener twice the diameter of the filler is about right. There's about a 15% margin on either side, but, if in doubt use less hardener.

3 Mix the body filler and hardener by wiping across the mixing surface, picking the mixture up and wiping it again. Colder weather requires longer mixing times. Do not mix in a circular motion; this will trap air bubbles which will become holes in the cured filler.

Applying The Filler

1 For best results, filler should not be applied over 1/4″ thick.

Apply the filler in several coats. Build it up to above the level of the repair surface so that it can be sanded or grated down.

The first coat of filler must be pressed on with a firm wiping motion.

Apply the filler in one direction only. Working the filler back and forth will either pull it off the metal or trap air bubbles.

REPAIRING DENTS

Before you start, take a few minutes to study the damaged area. Try to visualize the shape of the panel before it was damaged. If the damage is on the left fender, look at the right fender and use it as a guide. If there is access to the panel from behind, you can reshape it with a body hammer. If not, you'll have to use a dent puller. Go slowly and work the metal a little at a time. Get the panel as straight as possible before applying filler.

1 This dent is typical of one that can be pulled out or hammered out from behind. Remove the headlight cover, headlight assembly and turn signal housing.

2 Drill a series of holes ½ the size of the end of the dent puller along the stress line. Make some trial pulls and assess the results. If necessary, drill more holes and try again. Do not hurry.

3 If possible, use a body hammer and block to shape the metal back to its original contours. Get the metal back as close to its original shape as possible. Don't depend on body filler to fill dents.

4 Using an 80-grit grinding disc on an electric drill, grind the paint from the surrounding area down to bare metal. Use a new grinding pad to prevent heat buildup that will warp metal.

5 The area should look like this when you're finished grinding. Knock the drill holes in and tape over small openings to keep plastic filler out.

6 Mix the body filler (see Body Repair Tips). Spread the body filler evenly over the entire area (see Body Repair Tips). Be sure to cover the area completely.

7 Let the body filler dry until the surface can just be scratched with your fingernail. Knock the high spots from the body filler with a body file ("Cheesegrater"). Check frequently with the palm of your hand for high and low spots.

8 Check to be sure that trim pieces that will be installed later will fit exactly. Sand the area with 40-grit paper.

9 If you wind up with low spots, you may have to apply another layer of filler.

10 Knock the high spots off with 40-grit paper. When you are satisfied with the contours of the repair, apply a thin coat of filler to cover pin holes and scratches.

11 Block sand the area with 40-grit paper to a smooth finish. Pay particular attention to body lines and ridges that must be well-defined.

12 Sand the area with 400 paper and then finish with a scuff pad. The finished repair is ready for priming and painting (see Painting Tips).

Materials and photos courtesy of Ritt Jones Auto Body, Prospect Park, PA.

REPAIRING RUST HOLES

There are many ways to repair rust holes. The fiberglass cloth kit shown here is one of the most cost efficient for the owner because it provides a strong repair that resists cracking and moisture and is relatively easy to use. It can be used on large and small holes (with or without backing) and can be applied over contoured areas. Remember, however, that short of replacing an entire panel, no repair is a guarantee that the rust will not return.

1 Remove any trim that will be in the way. Clean away all loose debris. Cut away all the rusted metal. But be sure to leave enough metal to retain the contour or body shape.

2 Grind away all traces of rust with a 24-grit grinding disc. Be sure to grind back 3-4 inches from the edge of the hole down to bare metal and be sure all traces of paint, primer and rust are removed.

3 Block sand the area with 80 or 100 grit sandpaper to get a clear, shiny surface and feathered paint edge. Tap the edges of the hole inward with a ball peen hammer.

4 If you are going to use release film, cut a piece about 2-3″ larger than the area you have sanded. Place the film over the repair and mark the sanded area on the film. Avoid any unnecessary wrinkling of the film.

5 Cut 2 pieces of fiberglass matte to match the shape of the repair. One piece should be about 1″ smaller than the sanded area and the second piece should be 1″ smaller than the first. Mix enough filler and hardener to saturate the fiberglass material (see Body Repair Tips).

6 Lay the release sheet on a flat surface and spread an even layer of filler, large enough to cover the repair. Lay the smaller piece of fiberglass cloth in the center of the sheet and spread another layer of filler over the fiberglass cloth. Repeat the operation for the larger piece of cloth.

7 Place the repair material over the repair area, with the release film facing outward. Use a spreader and work from the center outward to smooth the material, following the body contours. Be sure to remove all air bubbles.

8 Wait until the repair has dried tack-free and peel off the release sheet. The ideal working temperature is 60°-90° F. Cooler or warmer temperatures or high humidity may require additional curing time. Wait longer, if in doubt.

9

9 Sand and feather-edge the entire area. The initial sanding can be done with a sanding disc on an electric drill if care is used. Finish the sanding with a block sander. Low spots can be filled with body filler; this may require several applications.

10

10 When the filler can just be scratched with a fingernail, knock the high spots down with a body file and smooth the entire area with 80-grit. Feather the filled areas into the surrounding areas.

11

11 When the area is sanded smooth, mix some topcoat and hardener and apply it directly with a spreader. This will give a smooth finish and prevent the glass matte from showing through the paint.

12

12 Block sand the topcoat smooth with finishing sandpaper (200 grit), and 400 grit. The repair is ready for masking, priming and painting (see Painting Tips).

Materials and photos courtesy Marson Corporation, Chelsea, Massachusetts

PAINTING TIPS

Preparation

1 SANDING — Use a 400 or 600 grit wet or dry sandpaper. Wet-sand the area with a ¼ sheet of sandpaper soaked in clean water. Keep the paper wet while sanding. Sand the area until the repaired area tapers into the original finish.

2 CLEANING — Wash the area to be painted thoroughly with water and a clean rag. Rinse it thoroughly and wipe the surface dry until you're sure it's completely free of dirt, dust, fingerprints, wax, detergent or other foreign matter.

3 MASKING — Protect any areas you don't want to overspray by covering them with masking tape and newspaper. Be careful not get fingerprints on the area to be painted.

4 PRIMING — All exposed metal should be primed before painting. Primer protects the metal and provides an excellent surface for paint adhesion. When the primer is dry, wet-sand the area again with 600 grit wet-sandpaper. Clean the area again after sanding.

4

Painting Techniques

P aint applied from either a spray gun or a spray can (for small areas) will provide good results. Experiment on an old piece of metal to get the right combination before you begin painting.

SPRAYING VISCOSITY (SPRAY GUN ONLY) — Paint should be thinned to spraying viscosity according to the directions on the can. Use only the recommended thinner or reducer and the same amount of reduction regardless of temperature.

AIR PRESSURE (SPRAY GUN ONLY) — This is extremely important. Be sure you are using the proper recommended pressure.

TEMPERATURE — The surface to be painted should be approximately the same temperature as the surrounding air. Applying warm paint to a cold surface, or vice versa, will completely upset the paint characteristics.

THICKNESS — Spray with smooth strokes. In general, the thicker the coat of paint, the longer the drying time. Apply several thin coats about 30 seconds apart. The paint should remain wet long enough to flow out and no longer; heavier coats will only produce sags or wrinkles. Spray a light (fog) coat, followed by heavier color coats.

DISTANCE — The ideal spraying distance is 8″-12″ from the gun or can to the surface. Shorter distances will produce ripples, while greater distances will result in orange peel, dry film and poor color match and loss of material due to overspray.

OVERLAPPING — The gun or can should be kept at right angles to the surface at all times. Work to a wet edge at an even speed, using a 50% overlap and direct the center of the spray at the lower or nearest edge of the previous stroke.

RUBBING OUT (BLENDING) FRESH PAINT — Let the paint dry thoroughly. Runs or imperfections can be sanded out, primed and repainted.

Don't be in too big a hurry to remove the masking. This only produces paint ridges. When the finish has dried for at least a week, apply a small amount of fine grade rubbing compound with a clean, wet cloth. Use lots of water and blend the new paint with the surrounding area.

WRONG   **CORRECT**   **WRONG**

Thin coat. Stroke too fast, not enough overlap, gun too far away.

Medium coat. Proper distance, good stroke, proper overlap.

Heavy coat. Stroke too slow, too much overlap, gun too close.

Condition	Possible Cause
Gears spinning when shifting into gear from neutral	1. Clutch not releasing fully. 2. In some cases an extremely light lubricant in transmission will cause gears to continue to spin for a short time after clutch is released. 3. Binding pilot bearing in crankshaft.
Transmission noisy in all gears	1. Insufficient lubricant, or improper lubricant. 2. Worn countergear bearings. 3. Worn or damaged main drive gear or countergear. 4. Damaged main drive gear or mainshaft bearings. 5. Worn or damaged countergear anti-lash plate.
Transmission noisy in neutral only	1. Damaged main drive gear bearing. 2. Damaged or loose mainshaft pilot bearing. 3. Worn or damaged countergear anti-lash plate. 4. Worn countergear bearings.
Transmission noisy in one gear only	1. Damaged or worn constant mesh gears. 2. Worn or damaged countergear bearings. 3. Damaged or worn synchronizer.
Transmission noisy in reverse only	1. Worn or damaged reverse idler gear or idler bushing. 2. Worn or damaged mainshaft reverse gear. 3. Worn or damaged reverse countergear. 4. Damaged shift mechanism.

TROUBLESHOOTING AUTOMATIC TRANSMISSION PROBLEMS

Keeping alert to changes in the operating characteristics of the transmission (changing shift points, noises, etc.) can prevent small problems from becoming large ones. If the problem cannot be traced to loose bolts, fluid level, misadjusted linkage, clogged filters or similar problems, you should probably seek professional service.

Transmission Fluid Indications

The appearance and odor of the transmission fluid can give valuable clues to the overall condition of the transmission. Always note the appearance of the fluid when you check the fluid level or change the fluid. Rub a small amount of fluid between your fingers to feel for grit and smell the fluid on the dipstick.

If the fluid appears:	It indicates:
Clear and red colored	Normal operation
Discolored (extremely dark red or brownish) or smells burned	Band or clutch pack failure, usually caused by an overheated transmission. Hauling very heavy loads with insufficient power or failure to change the fluid often result in overheating. Do not confuse this appearance with newer fluids that have a darker red color and a strong odor (though not a burned odor).
Foamy or aerated (light in color and full of bubbles)	1. The level is too high (gear train is churning oil) 2. An internal air leak (air is mixing with the fluid). Have the transmission checked professionally.
Solid residue in the fluid	Defective bands, clutch pack or bearings. Bits of band material or metal abrasives are clinging to the dipstick. Have the transmission checked professionally.
Varnish coating on the dipstick	The transmission fluid is overheating

TROUBLESHOOTING DRIVE AXLE PROBLEMS

First, determine when the noise is most noticeable.

Drive Noise: Produced under vehicle acceleration.

Coast Noise: Produced while coasting with a closed throttle.

Float Noise: Occurs while maintaining constant speed (just enough to keep speed constant) on a level road.

External Noise Elimination

It is advisable to make a thorough road test to determine whether the noise originates in the rear axle or whether it originates from the tires, engine, transmission, wheel bearings or road surface. Noise originating from other places cannot be corrected by servicing the rear axle.

ROAD NOISE

Brick or rough surfaced concrete roads produce noises that seem to come from the rear axle. Road noise is usually identical in Drive or Coast and driving on a different type of road will tell whether the road is the problem.

TIRE NOISE

Tire noise can be mistaken as rear axle noise, even though the tires on the front are at fault. Snow tread and mud tread tires or tires worn unevenly will frequently cause vibrations which seem to originate elsewhere; *temporarily, and for test purposes only,* inflate the tires to 40–50 lbs. This will significantly alter the noise produced by the tires, but will not alter noise from the rear axle. Noises from the rear axle will normally cease at speeds below 30 mph on coast, while tire noise will continue at lower tone as speed is decreased. The rear axle noise will usually change from drive conditions to coast conditions, while tire noise will not. Do not forget to lower the tire pressure to normal after the test is complete.

ENGINE/TRANSMISSION NOISE

Determine at what speed the noise is most pronounced, then stop in a quiet place. With the transmission in Neutral, run the engine through speeds corresponding to road speeds where the noise was noticed. Noises produced with the vehicle standing still are coming from the engine or transmission.

FRONT WHEEL BEARINGS

Front wheel bearing noises, sometimes confused with rear axle noises, will not change when comparing drive and coast conditions. While holding the speed steady, lightly apply the footbrake. This will often cause wheel bearing noise to lessen, as some of the weight is taken off the bearing. Front wheel bearings are easily checked by jacking up the wheels and spinning the wheels. Shaking the wheels will also determine if the wheel bearings are excessively loose.

REAR AXLE NOISES

Eliminating other possible sources can narrow the cause to the rear axle, which normally produces noise from worn gears or bearings. Gear noises tend to peak in a narrow speed range, while bearing noises will usually vary in pitch with engine speeds.

Noise Diagnosis

The Noise Is:	Most Probably Produced By:
1. Identical under Drive or Coast	Road surface, tires or front wheel bearings
2. Different depending on road surface	Road surface or tires
3. Lower as speed is lowered	Tires
4. Similar when standing or moving	Engine or transmission
5. A vibration	Unbalanced tires, rear wheel bearing, unbalanced driveshaft or worn U-joint
6. A knock or click about every two tire revolutions	Rear wheel bearing
7. Most pronounced on turns	Damaged differential gears
8. A steady low-pitched whirring or scraping, starting at low speeds	Damaged or worn pinion bearing
9. A chattering vibration on turns	Wrong differential lubricant or worn clutch plates (limited slip rear axle)
10. Noticed only in Drive, Coast or Float conditions	Worn ring gear and/or pinion gear

Troubleshooting Steering & Suspension Problems

Condition	Possible Cause
Hard steering (wheel is hard to turn)	1. Improper tire pressure 2. Loose or glazed pump drive belt 3. Low or incorrect fluid 4. Loose, bent or poorly lubricated front end parts 5. Improper front end alignment (excessive caster) 6. Bind in steering column or linkage 7. Kinked hydraulic hose 8. Air in hydraulic system 9. Low pump output or leaks in system 10. Obstruction in lines 11. Pump valves sticking or out of adjustment 12. Incorrect wheel alignment
Loose steering (too much play in steering wheel)	1. Loose wheel bearings 2. Faulty shocks 3. Worn linkage or suspension components 4. Loose steering gear mounting or linkage points 5. Steering mechanism worn or improperly adjusted 6. Valve spool improperly adjusted 7. Worn ball joints, tie-rod ends, etc.
Veers or wanders (pulls to one side with hands off steering wheel)	1. Improper tire pressure 2. Improper front end alignment 3. Dragging or improperly adjusted brakes 4. Bent frame 5. Improper rear end alignment 6. Faulty shocks or springs 7. Loose or bent front end components 8. Play in Pitman arm 9. Steering gear mountings loose 10. Loose wheel bearings 11. Binding Pitman arm 12. Spool valve sticking or improperly adjusted 13. Worn ball joints
Wheel oscillation or vibration transmitted through steering wheel	1. Low or uneven tire pressure 2. Loose wheel bearings 3. Improper front end alignment 4. Bent spindle 5. Worn, bent or broken front end components 6. Tires out of round or out of balance 7. Excessive lateral runout in disc brake rotor 8. Loose or bent shock absorber or strut
Noises (see also "Troubleshooting Drive Axle Problems")	1. Loose belts 2. Low fluid, air in system 3. Foreign matter in system 4. Improper lubrication 5. Interference or chafing in linkage 6. Steering gear mountings loose 7. Incorrect adjustment or wear in gear box 8. Faulty valves or wear in pump 9. Kinked hydraulic lines 10. Worn wheel bearings
Poor return of steering	1. Over-inflated tires 2. Improperly aligned front end (excessive caster) 3. Binding in steering column 4. No lubrication in front end 5. Steering gear adjusted too tight
Uneven tire wear (see "How To Read Tire Wear")	1. Incorrect tire pressure 2. Improperly aligned front end 3. Tires out-of-balance 4. Bent or worn suspension parts

HOW TO READ TIRE WEAR

The way your tires wear is a good indicator of other parts of the suspension. Abnormal wear patterns are often caused by the need for simple tire maintenance, or for front end alignment.

Excessive wear at the center of the tread indicates that the air pressure in the tire is consistently too high. The tire is riding on the center of the tread and wearing it prematurely. Occasionally, this wear pattern can result from outrageously wide tires on narrow rims. The cure for this is to replace either the tires or the wheels.

Over-inflation

Under-inflation

Feathering

One side wear

Cupping

Second-rib wear

This type of wear usually results from consistent under-inflation. When a tire is under-inflated, there is too much contact with the road by the outer treads, which wear prematurely. When this type of wear occurs, and the tire pressure is known to be consistently correct, a bent or worn steering component or the need for wheel alignment could be indicated.

Feathering is a condition when the edge of each tread rib develops a slightly rounded edge on one side and a sharp edge on the other. By running your hand over the tire, you can usually feel the sharper edges before you'll be able to see them. The most common causes of feathering are incorrect toe-in setting or deteriorated bushings in the front suspension.

When an inner or outer rib wears faster than the rest of the tire, the need for wheel alignment is indicated. There is excessive camber in the front suspension, causing the wheel to lean too much putting excessive load on one side of the tire. Misalignment could also be due to sagging springs, worn ball joints, or worn control arm bushings. Be sure the vehicle is loaded the way it's normally driven when you have the wheels aligned.

Cups or scalloped dips appearing around the edge of the tread almost always indicate worn (sometimes bent) suspension parts. Adjustment of wheel alignment alone will seldom cure the problem. Any worn component that connects the wheel to the suspension can cause this type of wear. Occasionally, wheels that are out of balance will wear like this, but wheel imbalance usually shows up as bald spots between the outside edges and center of the tread.

Second-rib wear is usually found only in radial tires, and appears where the steel belts end in relation to the tread. It can be kept to a minimum by paying careful attention to tire pressure and frequently rotating the tires. This is often considered normal wear but excessive amounts indicate that the tires are too wide for the wheels.

Troubleshooting Disc Brake Problems

Condition	Possible Cause
Noise—groan—brake noise emanating when slowly releasing brakes (creep-groan)	Not detrimental to function of disc brakes—no corrective action required. (This noise may be eliminated by slightly increasing or decreasing brake pedal efforts.)
Rattle—brake noise or rattle emanating at low speeds on rough roads, (front wheels only).	1. Shoe anti-rattle spring missing or not properly positioned. 2. Excessive clearance between shoe and caliper. 3. Soft or broken caliper seals. 4. Deformed or misaligned disc. 5. Loose caliper.
Scraping	1. Mounting bolts too long. 2. Loose wheel bearings. 3. Bent, loose, or misaligned splash shield.
Front brakes heat up during driving and fail to release	1. Operator riding brake pedal. 2. Stop light switch improperly adjusted. 3. Sticking pedal linkage. 4. Frozen or seized piston. 5. Residual pressure valve in master cylinder. 6. Power brake malfunction. 7. Proportioning valve malfunction.
Leaky brake caliper	1. Damaged or worn caliper piston seal. 2. Scores or corrosion on surface of cylinder bore.
Grabbing or uneven brake action—Brakes pull to one side	1. Causes listed under "Brakes Pull". 2. Power brake malfunction. 3. Low fluid level in master cylinder. 4. Air in hydraulic system. 5. Brake fluid, oil or grease on linings. 6. Unmatched linings. 7. Distorted brake pads. 8. Frozen or seized pistons. 9. Incorrect tire pressure. 10. Front end out of alignment. 11. Broken rear spring. 12. Brake caliper pistons sticking. 13. Restricted hose or line. 14. Caliper not in proper alignment to braking disc. 15. Stuck or malfunctioning metering valve. 16. Soft or broken caliper seals. 17. Loose caliper.
Brake pedal can be depressed without braking effect	1. Air in hydraulic system or improper bleeding procedure. 2. Leak past primary cup in master cylinder. 3. Leak in system. 4. Rear brakes out of adjustment. 5. Bleeder screw open.
Excessive pedal travel	1. Air, leak, or insufficient fluid in system or caliper. 2. Warped or excessively tapered shoe and lining assembly. 3. Excessive disc runout. 4. Rear brake adjustment required. 5. Loose wheel bearing adjustment. 6. Damaged caliper piston seal. 7. Improper brake fluid (boil). 8. Power brake malfunction. 9. Weak or soft hoses.

Troubleshooting Disc Brake Problems (cont.)

Condition	Possible Cause
Brake roughness or chatter (pedal pumping)	1. Excessive thickness variation of braking disc. 2. Excessive lateral runout of braking disc. 3. Rear brake drums out-of-round. 4. Excessive front bearing clearance.
Excessive pedal effort	1. Brake fluid, oil or grease on linings. 2. Incorrect lining. 3. Frozen or seized pistons. 4. Power brake malfunction. 5. Kinked or collapsed hose or line. 6. Stuck metering valve. 7. Scored caliper or master cylinder bore. 8. Seized caliper pistons.
Brake pedal fades (pedal travel increases with foot on brake)	1. Rough master cylinder or caliper bore. 2. Loose or broken hydraulic lines/connections. 3. Air in hydraulic system. 4. Fluid level low. 5. Weak or soft hoses. 6. Inferior quality brake shoes or fluid. 7. Worn master cylinder piston cups or seals.

Troubleshooting Drum Brakes

Condition	Possible Cause
Pedal goes to floor	1. Fluid low in reservoir. 2. Air in hydraulic system. 3. Improperly adjusted brake. 4. Leaking wheel cylinders. 5. Loose or broken brake lines. 6. Leaking or worn master cylinder. 7. Excessively worn brake lining.
Spongy brake pedal	1. Air in hydraulic system. 2. Improper brake fluid (low boiling point). 3. Excessively worn or cracked brake drums. 4. Broken pedal pivot bushing.
Brakes pulling	1. Contaminated lining. 2. Front end out of alignment. 3. Incorrect brake adjustment. 4. Unmatched brake lining. 5. Brake drums out of round. 6. Brake shoes distorted. 7. Restricted brake hose or line. 8. Broken rear spring. 9. Worn brake linings. 10. Uneven lining wear. 11. Glazed brake lining. 12. Excessive brake lining dust. 13. Heat spotted brake drums. 14. Weak brake return springs. 15. Faulty automatic adjusters. 16. Low or incorrect tire pressure.

Condition	Possible Cause
Squealing brakes	1. Glazed brake lining. 2. Saturated brake lining. 3. Weak or broken brake shoe retaining spring. 4. Broken or weak brake shoe return spring. 5. Incorrect brake lining. 6. Distorted brake shoes. 7. Bent support plate. 8. Dust in brakes or scored brake drums. 9. Linings worn below limit. 10. Uneven brake lining wear. 11. Heat spotted brake drums.
Chirping brakes	1. Out of round drum or eccentric axle flange pilot.
Dragging brakes	1. Incorrect wheel or parking brake adjustment. 2. Parking brakes engaged or improperly adjusted. 3. Weak or broken brake shoe return spring. 4. Brake pedal binding. 5. Master cylinder cup sticking. 6. Obstructed master cylinder relief port. 7. Saturated brake lining. 8. Bent or out of round brake drum. 9. Contaminated or improper brake fluid. 10. Sticking wheel cylinder pistons. 11. Driver riding brake pedal. 12. Defective proportioning valve. 13. Insufficient brake shoe lubricant.
Hard pedal	1. Brake booster inoperative. 2. Incorrect brake lining. 3. Restricted brake line or hose. 4. Frozen brake pedal linkage. 5. Stuck wheel cylinder. 6. Binding pedal linkage. 7. Faulty proportioning valve.
Wheel locks	1. Contaminated brake lining. 2. Loose or torn brake lining. 3. Wheel cylinder cups sticking. 4. Incorrect wheel bearing adjustment. 5. Faulty proportioning valve.
Brakes fade (high speed)	1. Incorrect lining. 2. Overheated brake drums. 3. Incorrect brake fluid (low boiling temperature). 4. Saturated brake lining. 5. Leak in hydraulic system. 6. Faulty automatic adjusters.
Pedal pulsates	1. Bent or out of round brake drum.
Brake chatter and shoe knock	1. Out of round brake drum. 2. Loose support plate. 3. Bent support plate. 4. Distorted brake shoes. 5. Machine grooves in contact face of brake drum (Shoe Knock). 6. Contaminated brake lining. 7. Missing or loose components. 8. Incorrect lining material. 9. Out-of-round brake drums. 10. Heat spotted or scored brake drums. 11. Out-of-balance wheels.

Troubleshooting Drum Brakes (cont.)

Condition	Possible Cause
Brakes do not self adjust	1. Adjuster screw frozen in thread. 2. Adjuster screw corroded at thrust washer. 3. Adjuster lever does not engage star wheel. 4. Adjuster installed on wrong wheel.
Brake light glows	1. Leak in the hydraulic system. 2. Air in the system. 3. Improperly adjusted master cylinder pushrod. 4. Uneven lining wear. 5. Failure to center combination valve or proportioning valve.

Mechanic's Data

General Conversion Table

Multiply By	To Convert	To	
LENGTH			
2.54	Inches	Centimeters	.3937
25.4	Inches	Millimeters	.03937
30.48	Feet	Centimeters	.0328
.304	Feet	Meters	3.28
.914	Yards	Meters	1.094
1.609	Miles	Kilometers	.621
VOLUME			
.473	Pints	Liters	2.11
.946	Quarts	Liters	1.06
3.785	Gallons	Liters	.264
.016	Cubic inches	Liters	61.02
16.39	Cubic inches	Cubic cms.	.061
28.3	Cubic feet	Liters	.0353
MASS (Weight)			
28.35	Ounces	Grams	.035
.4536	Pounds	Kilograms	2.20
—	**To obtain**	**From**	**Multiply by**

Multiply By	To Convert	To	
AREA			
.645	Square inches	Square cms.	.155
.836	Square yds.	Square meters	1.196
FORCE			
4.448	Pounds	Newtons	.225
.138	Ft./lbs.	Kilogram/meters	7.23
1.36	Ft./lbs.	Newton-meters	.737
.112	In./lbs.	Newton-meters	8.844
PRESSURE			
.068	Psi	Atmospheres	14.7
6.89	Psi	Kilopascals	.145
OTHER			
1.104	Horsepower (DIN)	Horsepower (SAE)	.9861
.746	Horsepower (SAE)	Kilowatts (KW)	1.34
1.60	Mph	Km/h	.625
.425	Mpg	Km/1	2.35
—	**To obtain**	**From**	**Multiply by**

Tap Drill Sizes

National Coarse or U.S.S.

Screw & Tap Size	Threads Per Inch	Use Drill Number
No. 5	.40	.39
No. 6	.32	.36
No. 8	.32	.29
No. 10	.24	.25
No. 12	.24	.17
1/4	.20	8
5/16	.18	F
3/8	.16	5/16
7/16	.14	U
1/2	.13	27/64
9/16	.12	31/64
5/8	.11	17/32
3/4	.10	21/32
7/8	. 9	49/64

National Coarse or U.S.S.

Screw & Tap Size	Threads Per Inch	Use Drill Number
1	8	7/8
1 1/8	7	63/64
1 1/4	7	1 7/64
1 1/2	6	1 11/32

National Fine or S.A.E.

Screw & Tap Size	Threads Per Inch	Use Drill Number
No. 5	.44	.37
No. 6	.40	.33
No. 8	.36	.29
No. 10	.32	.21

National Fine or S.A.E.

Screw & Tap Size	Threads Per Inch	Use Drill Number
No. 12	.28	.15
1/4	.28	3
6/16	.24	1
3/8	.24	Q
7/16	.20	W
1/2	.20	29/64
9/16	.18	33/64
5/8	.18	37/64
3/4	.16	11/16
7/8	.14	13/16
1 1/8	.12	1 3/64
1 1/4	.12	1 11/64
1 1/2	.12	1 27/64

Drill Sizes In Decimal Equivalents

Inch	Decimal	Wire	mm
1/64	.0156		.39
	.0157		.4
	.0160	78	
	.0165		.42
	.0173		.44
	.0177		.45
	.0180	77	
	.0181		.46
	.0189		.48
	.0197		.5
	.0200	76	
	.0210	75	
	.0217		.55
	.0225	74	
	.0236		.6
	.0240	73	
	.0250	72	
	.0256		.65
	.0260	71	
	.0276		.7
	.0280	70	
	.0292	69	
	.0295		.75
	.0310	68	
1/32	.0312		.79
	.0315		.8
	.0320	67	
	.0330	66	
	.0335		.85
	.0350	65	
	.0354		.9
	.0360	64	
	.0370	63	
	.0374		.95
	.0380	62	
	.0390	61	
	.0394		1.0
	.0400	60	
	.0410	59	
	.0413		1.05
	.0420	58	
	.0430	57	
	.0433		1.1
	.0453		1.15
3/64	.0465	56	
	.0469		1.19
	.0472		1.2
	.0492		1.25
	.0512		1.3
	.0520	55	
	.0531		1.35
	.0550	54	
	.0551		1.4
	.0571		1.45
	.0591		1.5
	.0595	53	
	.0610		1.55
1/16	.0625		1.59
	.0630		1.6
	.0635	52	
	.0650		1.65
	.0669		1.7
	.0670	51	
	.0689		1.75
	.0700	50	
	.0709		1.8
	.0728		1.85

Inch	Decimal	Wire	mm
	.0730	49	
	.0748		1.9
	.0760	48	
	.0768		1.95
5/64	.0781		1.98
	.0785	47	
	.0787		2.0
	.0807		2.05
	.0810	46	
	.0820	45	
	.0827		2.1
	.0846		2.15
	.0860	44	
	.0866		2.2
	.0886		2.25
	.0890	43	
	.0906		2.3
	.0925	42	
3/32	.0938		2.38
	.0945		2.4
	.0960	41	
	.0965		2.45
	.0980	40	
	.0981		2.5
	.0995	39	
	.1015	38	
	.1024		2.6
	.1040	37	
	.1063		2.7
	.1065	36	
	.1083		2.75
7/64	.1094		2.77
	.1100	35	
	.1102		2.8
	.1110	34	
	.1130	33	
	.1142		2.9
	.1160	32	
	.1181		3.0
	.1200	31	
	.1220		3.1
1/8	.1250		3.17
	.1260		3.2
	.1280		3.25
	.1285	30	
	.1299		3.3
	.1339		3.4
	.1360	29	
	.1378		3.5
	.1405	28	
9/64	.1406		3.57
	.1417		3.6
	.1440	27	
	.1457		3.7
	.1470	26	
	.1476		3.75
	.1495	25	
	.1496		3.8
	.1520	24	
	.1535		3.9
	.1540	23	
5/32	.1562		3.96
	.1570	22	
	.1575		4.0
	.1590	21	
	.1610	20	

Inch	Decimal	Wire & Letter	mm
	.1614		4.1
	.1654		4.2
	.1660	19	
	.1673		4.25
	.1693		4.3
	.1695	18	
11/64	.1719		4.36
	.1730	17	
	.1732		4.4
	.1770	16	
	.1772		4.5
	.1800	15	
	.1811		4.6
	.1820	14	
	.1850	13	
	.1850		4.7
	.1870		4.75
3/16	.1875		4.76
	.1890		4.8
	.1890	12	
	.1910	11	
	.1929		4.9
	.1935	10	
	.1960	9	
	.1969		5.0
	.1990	8	
	.2008		5.1
	.2010	7	
13/64	.2031		5.16
	.2040	6	
	.2047		5.2
	.2055	5	
	.2067		5.25
	.2087		5.3
	.2090	4	
	.2126		5.4
	.2130	3	
	.2165		5.5
7/32	.2188		5.55
	.2205		5.6
	.2210	2	
	.2244		5.7
	.2264		5.75
	.2280	1	
	.2283		5.8
	.2323		5.9
	.2340	A	
15/64	.2344		5.95
	.2362		6.0
	.2380	B	
	.2402		6.1
	.2420	C	
	.2441		6.2
	.2460	D	
	.2461		6.25
	.2480		6.3
1/4	.2500	E	6.35
	.2520		6.
	.2559		6.5
	.2570	F	
	.2598		6.6
	.2610	G	
	.2638		6.7
17/64	.2656		6.74
	.2657		6.75
	.2660	H	
	.2677		6.8

Inch	Decimal	Letter	mm
	.2717		6.9
	.2720	I	
	.2756		7.0
	.2770	J	
	.2795		7.1
	.2810	K	
9/32	.2812		7.14
	.2835		7.2
	.2854		7.25
	.2874		7.3
	.2900	L	
	.2913		7.4
	.2950	M	
	.2953		7.5
19/64	.2969		7.54
	.2992		7.6
	.3020	N	
	.3031		7.7
	.3051		7.75
	.3071		7.8
	.3110		7.9
5/16	.3125		7.93
	.3150		8.0
	.3160	O	
	.3189		8.1
	.3228		8.2
	.3230	P	
	.3248		8.25
	.3268		8.3
21/64	.3281		8.33
	.3307		8.4
	.3320	Q	
	.3346		8.5
	.3386		8.6
	.3390	R	
	.3425		8.7
11/32	.3438		8.73
	.3445		8.75
	.3465		8.8
	.3480	S	
	.3504		8.9
	.3543		9.0
	.3580	T	
	.3583		9.1
23/64	.3594		9.12
	.3622		9.2
	.3642		9.25
	.3661		9.3
	.3680	U	
	.3701		9.4
	.3740		9.5
3/8	.3750		9.52
	.3770	V	
	.3780		9.6
	.3819		9.7
	.3839		9.75
	.3858		9.8
	.3860	W	
	.3898		9.9
25/64	.3906		9.92
	.3937		10.0
	.3970	X	
	.4040	Y	
13/32	.4062		10.31
	.4130	Z	
	.4134		10.5
27/64	.4219		10.71

Inch	Decimal	mm
	.4331	11.0
7/16	.4375	11.11
	.4528	11.5
29/64	.4531	11.51
15/32	.4688	11.90
	.4724	12.0
31/64	.4844	12.30
	.4921	12.5
1/2	.5000	12.70
	.5118	13.0
33/64	.5156	13.09
17/32	.5312	13.49
	.5315	13.5
35/64	.5469	13.89
	.5512	14.0
9/16	.5625	14.28
	.5709	14.5
37/64	.5781	14.68
	.5906	15.0
19/32	.5938	15.08
39/64	.6094	15.47
	.6102	15.5
5/8	.6250	15.87
	.6299	16.0
41/64	.6406	16.27
	.6496	16.5
21/32	.6562	16.66
	.6693	17.0
43/64	.6719	17.06
11/16	.6875	17.46
	.6890	17.5
45/64	.7031	17.85
	.7087	18.0
23/32	.7188	18.25
	.7283	18.5
47/64	.7344	18.65
	.7480	19.0
3/4	.7500	19.05
49/64	.7656	19.44
	.7677	19.5
25/32	.7812	19.84
	.7874	20.0
51/64	.7969	20.24
	.8071	20.5
13/16	.8125	20.63
	.8268	21.0
53/64	.8281	21.03
27/32	.8438	21.43
	.8465	21.5
55/64	.8594	21.82
	.8661	22.0
7/8	.8750	22.22
	.8858	22.5
57/64	.8906	22.62
	.9055	23.0
29/32	.9062	23.01
59/64	.9219	23.41
	.9252	23.5
15/16	.9375	23.81
	.9449	24.0
61/64	.9531	24.2
	.9646	24.5
31/32	.9688	24.6
	.9843	25.0
63/64	.9844	25.0
1	1.0000	25.4

Index

Chilton's Repair & Tune-Up Guides

The Complete line covers domestic cars, imports, trucks, vans, RV's and 4-wheel drive vehicles.

RTUG Title	Part No.
AMC 1975-82	7199
Covers all U.S. and Canadian models	
Aspen/Volare 1976-80	6637
Covers all U.S. and Canadian models	
Audi 1970-73	5902
Covers all U.S. and Canadian models.	
Audi 4000/5000 1978-81	7028
Covers all U.S. and Canadian models including turbocharged and diesel engines	
Barracuda/Challenger 1965-72	5807
Covers all U.S. and Canadian models	
Blazer/Jimmy 1969-82	6931
Covers all U.S. and Canadian 2- and 4-wheel drive models, including diesel engines	
BMW 1970-82	6844
Covers U.S. and Canadian models	
Buick/Olds/Pontiac 1975-85	7308
Covers all U.S. and Canadian full size rear wheel drive models	
Cadillac 1967-84	7462
Covers all U.S. and Canadian rear wheel drive models	
Camaro 1967-81	6735
Covers all U.S. and Canadian models	
Camaro 1982-85	7317
Covers all U.S. and Canadian models	
Capri 1970-77	6695
Covers all U.S. and Canadian models	
Caravan/Voyager 1984-85	7482
Covers all U.S. and Canadian models	
Century/Regal 1975-85	7307
Covers all U.S. and Canadian rear wheel drive models, including turbocharged engines	
Champ/Arrow/Sapporo 1978-83	7041
Covers all U.S. and Canadian models	
Chevette/1000 1976-86	6836
Covers all U.S. and Canadian models	
Chevrolet 1968-85	7135
Covers all U.S. and Canadian models	
Chevrolet 1968-79 Spanish	7082
Chevrolet/GMC Pick-Ups 1970-82 Spanish	7468
Chevrolet/GMC Pick-Ups and Suburban 1970-86	6936
Covers all U.S. and Canadian 1/2, 3/4 and 1 ton models, including 4-wheel drive and diesel engines	
Chevrolet LUV 1972-81	6815
Covers all U.S. and Canadian models	
Chevrolet Mid-Size 1964-86	6840
Covers all U.S. and Canadian models of 1964-77 Chevelle, Malibu and Malibu SS; 1974-77 Laguna; 1978-85 Malibu; 1970-86 Monte Carlo; 1964-84 El Camino, including diesel engines	
Chevrolet Nova 1986	7658
Covers all U.S. and Canadian models	
Chevy/GMC Vans 1967-84	6930
Covers all U.S. and Canadian models of 1/2, 3/4, and 1 ton vans, cutaways, and motor home chassis, including diesel engines	
Chevy S-10 Blazer/GMC S-15 Jimmy 1982-85	7383
Covers all U.S. and Canadian models	
Chevy S-10/GMC S-15 Pick-Ups 1982-85	7310
Covers all U.S. and Canadian models	
Chevy II/Nova 1962-79	6841
Covers all U.S. and Canadian models	
Chrysler K- and E-Car 1981-85	7163
Covers all U.S. and Canadian front wheel drive models	
Colt/Challenger/Vista/Conquest 1971-85	7037
Covers all U.S. and Canadian models	
Corolla/Carina/Tercel/Starlet 1970-85	7036
Covers all U.S. and Canadian models	
Corona/Cressida/Crown/Mk.II/Camry/Van 1970-84	7044
Covers all U.S. and Canadian models	

RTUG Title	Part No.
Corvair 1960-69	6691
Covers all U.S. and Canadian models	
Corvette 1953-62	6576
Covers all U.S. and Canadian models	
Corvette 1963-84	6843
Covers all U.S. and Canadian models	
Cutlass 1970-85	6933
Covers all U.S. and Canadian models	
Dart/Demon 1968-76	6324
Covers all U.S. and Canadian models	
Datsun 1961-72	5790
Covers all U.S. and Canadian models of Nissan Patrol; 1500, 1600 and 2000 sports cars; Pick-Ups; 410, 411, 510, 1200 and 240Z	
Datsun 1973-80 Spanish	7083
Datsun/Nissan F-10, 310, Stanza, Pulsar 1977-86	7196
Covers all U.S. and Canadian models	
Datsun/Nissan Pick-Ups 1970-84	6816
Covers all U.S and Canadian models	
Datsun/Nissan Z & ZX 1970-86	6932
Covers all U.S. and Canadian models	
Datsun/Nissan 1200, 210, Sentra 1973-86	7197
Covers all U.S. and Canadian models	
Datsun/Nissan 200SX, 510, 610, 710, 810, Maxima 1973-84	7170
Covers all U.S. and Canadian models	
Dodge 1968-77	6554
Covers all U.S. and Canadian models	
Dodge Charger 1967-70	6486
Covers all U.S. and Canadian models	
Dodge/Plymouth Trucks 1967-84	7459
Covers all 1/2, 3/4, and 1 ton 2- and 4-wheel drive U.S. and Canadian models, including diesel engines	
Dodge/Plymouth Vans 1967-84	6934
Covers all 1/2, 3/4, and 1 ton U.S. and Canadian models of vans, cutaways and motor home chassis	
D-50/Arrow Pick-Up 1979-81	7032
Covers all U.S. and Canadian models	
Fairlane/Torino 1962-75	6320
Covers all U.S. and Canadian models	
Fairmont/Zephyr 1978-83	6965
Covers all U.S. and Canadian models	
Fiat 1969-81	7042
Covers all U.S. and Canadian models	
Fiesta 1978-80	6846
Covers all U.S. and Canadian models	
Firebird 1967-81	5996
Covers all U.S. and Canadian models	
Firebird 1982-85	7345
Covers all U.S. and Canadian models	
Ford 1968-79 Spanish	7084
Ford Bronco 1966-83	7140
Covers all U.S. and Canadian models	
Ford Bronco II 1984	7408
Covers all U.S. and Canadian models	
Ford Courier 1972-82	6983
Covers all U.S. and Canadian models	
Ford/Mercury Front Wheel Drive 1981-85	7055
Covers all U.S. and Canadian models Escort, EXP, Tempo, Lynx, LN-7 and Topaz	
Ford/Mercury/Lincoln 1968-85	6842
Covers all U.S. and Canadian models of FORD Country Sedan, Country Squire, Crown Victoria, Custom, Custom 500, Galaxie 500, LTD through 1982, Ranch Wagon, and XL; MERCURY Colony Park, Commuter, Marquis through 1982, Gran Marquis, Monterey and Park Lane; LINCOLN Continental and Towne Car	
Ford/Mercury/Lincoln Mid-Size 1971-85	6696
Covers all U.S. and Canadian models of FORD Elite, 1983-85 LTD, 1977-79 LTD II, Ranchero, Torino, Gran Torino, 1977-85 Thunderbird; MERCURY 1972-85 Cougar,	

continued on next page

RTUG Title	Part No.
1983-85 Marquis, Montego, 1980-85 XR-7; LINCOLN 1982-85 Continental, 1984-85 Mark VII, 1978-80 Versailles	
Ford Pick-Ups 1965-86	6913
Covers all 1/2, 3/4 and 1 ton, 2- and 4-wheel drive U.S. and Canadian pick-up, chassis cab and camper models, including diesel engines	
Ford Pick-Ups 1965-82 Spanish	7469
Ford Ranger 1983-84	7338
Covers all U.S. and Canadian models	
Ford Vans 1961-86	6849
Covers all U.S. and Canadian 1/2, 3/4 and 1 ton van and cutaway chassis models, including diesel engines	
GM A-Body 1982-85	7309
Covers all front wheel drive U.S. and Canadian models of BUICK Century, CHEVROLET Celebrity, OLDSMOBILE Cutlass Ciera and PONTIAC 6000	
GM C-Body 1985	7587
Covers all front wheel drive U.S. and Canadian models of BUICK Electra Park Avenue and Electra T-Type, CADILLAC Fleetwood and deVille, OLDSMOBILE 98 Regency and Regency Brougham	
GM J-Car 1982-85	7059
Covers all U.S. and Canadian models of BUICK Skyhawk, CHEVROLET Cavalier, CADILLAC Cimarron, OLDSMOBILE Firenza and PONTIAC 2000 and Sunbird	
GM N-Body 1985-86	7657
Covers all U.S. and Canadian models of front wheel drive BUICK Somerset and Skylark, OLDSMOBILE Calais, and PONTIAC Grand Am	
GM X-Body 1980-85	7049
Covers all U.S. and Canadian models of BUICK Skylark, CHEVROLET Citation, OLDSMOBILE Omega and PONTIAC Phoenix	
GM Subcompact 1971-80	6935
Covers all U.S. and Canadian models of BUICK Skyhawk (1975-80), CHEVROLET Vega and Monza, OLDSMOBILE Starfire, and PONTIAC Astre and 1975-80 Sunbird	
Granada/Monarch 1975-82	6937
Covers all U.S. and Canadian models	
Honda 1973-84	6980
Covers all U.S. and Canadian models	
International Scout 1967-73	5912
Covers all U.S. and Canadian models	
Jeep 1945-87	6817
Covers all U.S. and Canadian CJ-2A, CJ-3A, CJ-3B, CJ-5, CJ-6, CJ-7, Scrambler and Wrangler models	
Jeep Wagoneer, Commando, Cherokee, Truck 1957-86	6739
Covers all U.S. and Canadian models of Wagoneer, Cherokee, Grand Wagoneer, Jeepster, Jeepster Commando, J-100, J-200, J-300, J-10, J20, FC-150 and FC-170	
Laser/Daytona 1984-85	7563
Covers all U.S. and Canadian models	
Maverick/Comet 1970-77	6634
Covers all U.S. and Canadian models	
Mazda 1971-84	6981
Covers all U.S. and Canadian models of RX-2, RX-3, RX-4, 808, 1300, 1600, Cosmo, GLC and 626	
Mazda Pick-Ups 1972-86	7659
Covers all U.S. and Canadian models	
Mercedes-Benz 1959-70	6065
Covers all U.S. and Canadian models	
Mereceds-Benz 1968-73	5907
Covers all U.S. and Canadian models	

RTUG Title	Part No.
Mercedes-Benz 1974-84	6809
Covers all U.S. and Canadian models	
Mitsubishi, Cordia, Tredia, Starion, Galant 1983-85	7583
Covers all U.S. and Canadian models	
MG 1961-81	6780
Covers all U.S. and Canadian models	
Mustang/Capri/Merkur 1979-85	6963
Covers all U.S. and Canadian models	
Mustang/Cougar 1965-73	6542
Covers all U.S. and Canadian models	
Mustang II 1974-78	6812
Covers all U.S. and Canadian models	
Omni/Horizon/Rampage 1978-84	6845
Covers all U.S. and Canadian models of DODGE omni, Miser, 024, Charger 2.2; PLYMOUTH Horizon, Miser, TC3, TC3 Tourismo; Rampage	
Opel 1971-75	6575
Covers all U.S. and Canadian models	
Peugeot 1970-74	5982
Covers all U.S. and Canadian models	
Pinto/Bobcat 1971-80	7027
Covers all U.S. and Canadian models	
Plymouth 1968-76	6552
Covers all U.S. and Canadian models	
Pontiac Fiero 1984-85	7571
Covers all U.S. and Canadian models	
Pontiac Mid-Size 1974-83	7346
Covers all U.S. and Canadian models of Ventura, Grand Am, LeMans, Grand LeMans, GTO, Phoenix, and Grand Prix	
Porsche 924/928 1976-81	7048
Covers all U.S. and Canadian models	
Renault 1975-85	7165
Covers all U.S. and Canadian models	
Roadrunner/Satellite/Belvedere/GTX 1968-73	5821
Covers all U.S. and Canadian models	
RX-7 1979-81	7031
Covers all U.S. and Canadian models	
SAAB 99 1969-75	5988
Covers all U.S. and Canadian models	
SAAB 900 1979-85	7572
Covers all U.S. and Canadian models	
Snowmobiles 1976-80	6978
Covers Arctic Cat, John Deere, Kawasaki, Polaris, Ski-Doo and Yamaha	
Subaru 1970-84	6982
Covers all U.S. and Canadian models	
Tempest/GTO/LeMans 1968-73	5905
Covers all U.S. and Canadian models	
Toyota 1966-70	5795
Covers all U.S. and Canadian models of Corona, MkII, Corolla, Crown, Land Cruiser, Stout and Hi-Lux	
Toyota 1970-79 Spanish	7467
Toyota Celica/Supra 1971-85	7043
Covers all U.S. and Canadian models	
Toyota Trucks 1970-85	7035
Covers all U.S. and Canadian models of pick-ups, Land Cruiser and 4Runner	
Valiant/Duster 1968-76	6326
Covers all U.S. and Canadian models	
Volvo 1956-69	6529
Covers all U.S. and Canadian models	
Volvo 1970-83	7040
Covers all U.S. and Canadian models	
VW Front Wheel Drive 1974-85	6962
Covers all U.S. and Canadian models	
VW 1949-71	5796
Covers all U.S. and Canadian models	
VW 1970-79 Spanish	7081
VW 1970-81	6837
Covers all U.S. and Canadian Beetles, Karmann Ghia, Fastback, Squareback, Vans, 411 and 412	

Chilton's Repair & Tune-Up Guides are available at your local retailer or by mailing a check or money order for **$12.50** plus **$2.25** to cover postage and handling to:

Chilton Book Company
Dept. DM
Radnor, PA 19089

NOTE: When ordering be sure to include your name & address, book part No. & title.